A LIFE IN
LEADERSHIP

A LIFE IN LEADERSHIP

From D-Day to
Ground Zero

JOHN C. WHITEHEAD

BASIC
BOOKS

NEW
AMERICA
BOOKS

A New America Book, Published by Basic Books
A Member of the Perseus Books Group
New York

Published by Basic Books
A Member of the Perseus Books Group

Library of Congress Cataloging-in-Publication Data

Whitehead, John C., 1922-
  A life in leadership : from D-Day to Ground Zero / by John Whitehead.
    p. cm.
  ISBN 0-465-05054-9 (hardcover)
  1. Whitehead, John C., 1922– 2. Cabinet officers—United States—Biography. 3. United
States. Dept. of State—Officials and employees—Biography. 4. Investment bankers—New
York (State)—New York—Biography. 5. Goldman, Sachs & Co.—Biography. 6. Lower
Manhattan Development Corporation—Biography. 7. City planning—New York (State)—
New York. 8. Executives—United States—Biography. 9. Nonprofit organizations—United
States. I. Title.

E840.8.W48A3 2005
332.66'092—dc22

                                                                    2005005209

05 06 07   10 9 8 7 6 5 4 3 2

To Cindy
For your selfless loyalty and
your warm, caring way

CONTENTS

ACKNOWLEDGMENTS

—∞—

I had a lot of help in writing this book. The most important help came from John Sedgwick, an experienced writer of many books and magazine articles, who took my own account of my life and, after many probing conversations with me, reshaped it into the more compelling tale you hold in your hands. To him I am very grateful.

A Haverford College friend, Ted Rybeck, brought another capable writer to the task at an earlier stage of the development of the book. Andrew Szanton helped me think through my involvement with the many nonprofit organizations I have worked for over the years, and to condense my recollections into the coherent narrative which is the basis for that part of the book.

Ted Halstead, the inspired and energetic founder of the New America Foundation, has kindly provided me with steady encouragement in undertaking this memoir, and has been instrumental in seeing it through to publication. He also secured for me the services of the talented and gracious Sherle Schwenninger, an editor at New America, who edited the final draft, providing any number of useful suggestions that made the book sharper and clearer.

I am enormously indebted to my longtime assistant Denise Emmett. Since 1989, she has handled many of the details of my philanthropic efforts, art collecting, investments, and personal scheduling with a perfect balance of tact and dispatch. With this book, her contributions have been invaluable—deciphering the hen-scatchings of my lengthy first draft to type it into a computer, and then doing a lot of research and fact-checking, and, along the way, providing innumerable helpful editorial comments besides. I am also grateful to my other assistant, Ann Marie Kane, who has proved to be wonderfully adept at coping with the many tasks of a complicated office, and has been an invariably cheerful presence besides. A computer illiterate myself, I always marvel at the computer savvy of both these talented women in being able to keep track of the many drafts of this book, to retrieve them in seconds, and then to send them anywhere around the globe. What magic!

In reconstructing the story of my life, I have largely had to rely on my own memories. I never kept a diary or a scrapbook. The insightful questions of John Sedgwick and others have spurred me to recall details and further reminiscences that have done much to fill out this narrative. In many cases, my helpers and I have been able to check my facts against the historical record. Where there was no record, I have relied on the recollections of other friends and business associates to confirm, and occasionally to correct, my account. While I have done my best to make sure the book is accurate, I accept full responsibility for any errors.

1

GOVERNOR PATAKI ON THE LINE

———◦∾◦———

W HEN GOVERNOR PATAKI CALLED, I thought he was going to ask for
another contribution. I'm a loyal Republican, and I'd already donated
to his campaign for a third term. Still, I figured he was looking for something
more.

But his first word was "Congratulations," which troubled me. In my experience, when a politician calls to offer congratulations, it is not always good
news.

"Well, thanks a lot, governor," I told him. "But for what?"

"You've been selected to be chairman of the Lower Manhattan Development Corporation."

This was late November 2001, almost two months after the terrorist attack
on the World Trade Center. There had been a few articles about the governor's plans to rebuild the city, but I'd been so busy I hadn't paid much attention to them. I had to ask him what the Lower Manhattan Development
Corporation was.

Once he started to explain, I could see that chairing the LMDC would be
an immense undertaking. It was the commission that would decide what to
build on the near-sacred sixteen-acre site of Ground Zero. The area was
prime real estate, the center of Wall Street and Lower Manhattan, but for the
families of the victims of the disaster it was hallowed ground, like Gettysburg
or the Lexington Green. For many it was their only remaining tangible connection to loved ones who had simply vanished, leaving behind not so much

as a belt buckle or a wrist watch. I knew instinctively that, with all the competing interests involved in the rebuilding plans for the site, the LMDC would be facing some massive, complex, and extremely contentious issues, ones that would be made all the more difficult to resolve because of the powerful emotions stirred up by the tragedy. All of America and much of the world were looking to see how we'd respond.

Not until later did I learn that, in fact, the LMDC was even more. It would have responsibility for planning the redevelopment of *all of southern Manhattan*, from Canal Street down to Battery Park, and from the Hudson across to the East River. If the LMDC decided that the area needed an art museum or a movie theater or a supermarket (all of which it lacked), it could use the governor's power of eminent domain to seize the necessary property to create them. So this wasn't just about sixteen acres. It was about twenty square miles of some of the most valuable, most important, and most heavily populated real estate in the world. It would be by far the biggest redevelopment project in the history of the city, much bigger, more complex, and more expensive than anything that even Robert Moses, New York's legendary power broker, had ever attempted.

"I see this as a ten-year project, John," the governor went on, "and I've been thinking of a twelve-member board." He ticked off a few of the names, and all of them were very distinguished and experienced people, leaders in the city's life. I knew many of them, people like Tom Johnson, head of the Greenpoint Savings Bank, who'd lost a son in the disaster; Frank Zarb, the former head of Nasdaq; and Lew Eisenberg, a former Goldman Sachs partner and former chairman of the Port Authority of New York and New Jersey. It was a first-class group of people.

"And you want me to be the chairman?" I wanted to be sure I'd gotten that right. Many of the other proposed members seemed to be well qualified for the job. I knew from painful experience that it was one thing to be a board member and quite another to be the chairman of the board.

"Chairman. Yes, absolutely. Chairman. You're my only choice, John." And he gave me his reasons. "You're a longtime New Yorker." (I think he called me a "leading citizen.") You've had considerable business experience here, having worked for Goldman Sachs for thirty-seven years, eight of them as co-chairman. You've served in Washington as deputy secretary of state. You've been heavily involved in philanthropy in the city. You've chaired any number of nonprofit boards across the country. And you've made a lot of friends over the years. Friends that could be very useful in a job like this." His staff had prepared him well, for it was all true. From global leaders like Mikhail Gorbachev, Lech Walesa and Margaret Thatcher to New York celebrities like Tom Brokaw, Yogi Berra, Leslie Stahl and Diane Sawyer, I had made a lot of friends over the years from many walks of life. I'd even been a part owner of the New Jersey Devils hockey team, played the violin with the New Jersey Symphony, and joined in a mujahedin raid on a Russian fort in Afghanistan. I like to joke that in ten minutes of conversation with just about anyone, I can find a mutual friend we both know well.

"Look, John, I've talked to a lot of people about this over the last couple of weeks, and everybody says your name," Pataki assured me. "Mayor Giuliani and Mayor-elect Bloomberg are both very enthusiastic."

That was flattering, of course. I wasn't surprised about Bloomberg. I'd known Mike for thirty years, ever since he interviewed for a job at Goldman Sachs when he was fresh out of Harvard Business School. As he remembers it, we turned him down, which is possible because we rejected a lot of applicants. But my recollection is that he simply got a better offer at Salomon Brothers, which is why he ended up there instead. He later told me that this might have been just as well: if he'd come to Goldman Sachs he probably would never have left to start Bloomberg, and he would never have become the multibillionaire he is today.

Giuliani was a different story. Although I greatly admired his leadership after 9/11, I'd always been troubled by the way he treated a partner at Goldman Sachs who was charged with insider trading back in the eighties when Rudy was U.S. attorney for the Southern District of New York. Giuliani had him taken out of our building in handcuffs—after tipping off the newspapers, so that photographers were there to record the scene. This partner was a fine man, and we knew that he would never have done anything improper. Giuliani's people never found a single thing he'd done wrong. The charges were dropped the night before the trial was to start. Still, because of all the bad press, the partner felt he had to resign from Goldman Sachs and later on to plead guilty to a minor charge, his reputation shredded. I always thought that was the worst sort of political opportunism. All the same, I was glad to know Giuliani had approved my selection.

Finally, I managed to get a word in edgewise with the governor. I could tell that this job would be the most challenging assignment I'd ever taken on, and I practically pleaded with him: "But governor, you've told me this is a ten-year project. I'm almost eighty years old! I don't think you want me down there a decade from now in my wheelchair, pointing my cane at some build-ing and saying, 'I'll put this building here, not there.' I'm ready to retire. I'm too old to take on something like this."

As well-briefed as he obviously was, I think my age came as a surprise to him, but he insisted that my being eighty was a favorable thing. "Everybody will know you have no personal agenda. You won't be looking ahead to your next job."

I desperately wanted to turn him down right there, since I simply could not envision taking this on. But I knew that would be rude, so I asked him how long I had to think about it. At that point, it was 4 P.M. on a Tuesday. He said he'd called the press conference for Thursday at 2 P.M.! That left me a little less than forty-eight hours.

I said I'd let him know as soon as I could, and we hung up. Then a strange thing happened. Within an hour or so, half a dozen people called me. The first was David Rockefeller. A tremendous philanthropist and distinguished banker, David had been a friend since he established the New York City Part-nership back in the 1970s. He'd always been a mentor and role model for me, and I'd served for a time as a trustee of the Rockefeller Family Trust.

"I hear the governor has appointed you to be chairman of the Lower Man-hattan Development Corporation," David told me. I couldn't imagine how word had traveled so fast. "And I hope very much that you accept. You're just the person to do it." That was flattering, I have to say. We exchanged a few pleasantries, and then I hung up the phone. Seconds later it rang again. And then again. And again. Each time, some city leader or other was on the line. Bill McDonough, the president of the Federal Reserve Bank of New York, where I'd been chairman. Jerry Speyer, a leading real estate developer in the city. John Weinberg, my co-chairman when I was at Goldman Sachs, and sev-eral others. Each one had the same message.

It was obviously a well-orchestrated sales effort. I laughed at that, but I was impressed. I figured the governor must be a pretty capable guy if he'd set this campaign up so craftily.

The truth was, I did have a large stake in the rebuilding of New York. Not a financial one, but an emotional one. September 11 was an attack on my city. The Goldman Sachs headquarters that we'd built when I was co-chairman was located at 85 Broad Street, just a few blocks from the World Trade Center, and the Federal Reserve Bank of New York—where I'd been chairman some years later—with its wonderful fortress of a building, was even closer. I'd eaten at Windows on the World any number of times. I had many friends who worked in the Twin Towers. This was a blow struck right at my heart.

As it happened, on that fateful day I was in London attending a meeting of the Caux Roundtable, an international conference on business ethics, a subject that has always been a major concern of mine. It's named for the Swiss town where the group first met. There were about thirty of us in a big conference room at the Royal Garden Hotel Kensington, a modest hotel not far from Buckingham Palace. We were just finishing lunch when a staff member came in to say she was sorry to interrupt, but—

We turned on the BBC, and, over and over, we saw the awful sequences of the planes flying into the twin towers, and then the towers catching on fire and finally collapsing, these great quarter-mile-high buildings, just dropping straight down into the earth. It was absolutely horrendous, inconceivable. It seemed as though tens of thousands of people must have been killed. Sickened and distressed, I went back to my room to watch the TV by myself, and I stayed glued to it for the next eight hours straight until I forced myself to go outside to try to clear my mind. I was eager to get back home, but the next morning, my plane had been canceled. I felt like a sailor who's missed his ship and, watching from the dock, sees it going off to war without him.

With nothing else to do but watch more horrible TV from New York, I walked over to Buckingham Palace and arrived just in time to see the changing of the guard. I always loved those old British customs. Normally the band plays "God Save the Queen," but this time it played "The Star Spangled Banner." I was so moved, the tears just streamed down my face. I don't cry a lot, but I did that day. The British were loyal allies to us. They supported us, just as we've supported them.

On D-Day, as a twenty-two-year-old Navy ensign, I'd landed in the first wave in Normandy, sailing past the mouth of the Thames on the way from Portsmouth. I was in one of the landing boats that delivered our soldiers to Omaha beach. That was a terrifying experience, but so was this. It was so hard to tell what it meant. Were we at war? Would the White House be destroyed? Was the president safe? Terrorism had been a major topic while I was at the State Department during my stint in the Reagan administration. I was there for the *Achille Lauro* hijacking by terrorists, and the period when Qadhafi established a base for terrorists in Libya. But that was nothing compared to this. The thought of terrorists turning planes into bombs and flying them into skyscrapers was more than I could imagine. I tried to telephone to find out whether my family and friends were all right, but no calls were going through. I enlisted the Goldman Sachs office there in London to get me a flight out, but no planes could land in New York. It was all immensely frustrating.

Finally, I got on the first flight out on the fifteenth. As soon as the plane touched down at JFK and I disembarked, I checked to make sure that my nine children and stepchildren and all the friends I could find out about had survived the attack. Of the nearly three thousand people who died, the vast majority were in their thirties and forties, so I wasn't likely to know many of them. I did know Neil Levin, a former colleague at Goldman Sachs who was the executive director of the Port Authority, which had its office in the North Tower. Scott Johnson, whose father, Tom, was a man I knew well from the business world, had been killed. I was close to Howard Lutnick, the head of the brokerage firm Cantor Fitzgerald and a fellow Haverford graduate. His brother was one of the 658 Cantor employees to be killed, over three quarters of the workforce, a terrible tragedy.

But beyond the people I knew who had died, I was overwhelmed by the scale of the disaster. Shortly after I got back, I took the subway as far south as I could go, and I walked around the whole perimeter of Ground Zero. It took nearly a full hour. The fires were still burning, there was ash everywhere, the air had a hideous stench to it, and the sun was nearly blocked out by the smoke that hung over everything. I was shocked to see not just the extent of it, but how far down into the ground the destruction went in many places, as much as eight stories.

Still, I had no idea that I would ever get involved in the rebuilding effort. At that point, I'd been thinking only about retirement. My health is good. But I'm not going to live forever, and I was looking forward to a little relaxation after an extremely active life. I'd worked it all out: I was planning to spend a third of my time on philanthropy, a third with my children and grandchildren, and a third traveling. I've been married three times. The first two marriages ended in divorce, I'm sorry to say. And my third wife, the TV correspondent Nancy Dickerson, died several years ago. For years, I'd looked forward to doing more reading. I had great stacks of unread books set aside for when I had more time.

So I'd been trying to disengage from my various responsibilities. After coming back from my service in the Reagan administration as the deputy secretary of state, I'd joined a number of civic or nonprofit organizations, and had been chairman of more than ten of them at one point or another. They included the Federal Reserve Bank of New York, the Harvard Board of Overseers, the Brookings Institution, The Asia Society, the National Gallery of Art, the International Rescue Committee, the Mellon Foundation, the Boy Scouts in New York, and several others, probably too many. But by the time Governor Pataki called, I'd passed every one of them on to others. The slate was clean. For the third, and I thought final, time in my life, I was ready for retirement. Twice before I'd tried to retire and failed. Once when I left Goldman Sachs, and once when I left the State Department. Now I was faced with flunking retirement again.

I'd also retired as part-time chairman of a small investment firm called AEA Investors, although I still maintain an office there on Fifty-fifth Street. Several old friends were investors: David Rockefeller; my boss at the State Department, George Shultz; Henry Kissinger; and a large number of Fortune 500 CEOs such as Roger Smith of General Motors, Hank Greenberg of AIG, Reg Jones of General Electric, and many others, all friends from my Goldman Sachs days. It was exciting, and the business had gone very well, but I was happy finally to leave the investment world behind after more than half a century.

For all these reasons, I was dead set against accepting Pataki's offer. But in order to clarify my feelings, I did what I always do when I am facing a major decision. It's a process I learned from Bob Rubin, Clinton's treasury secretary, back when we were at Goldman Sachs together. I took out a yellow pad and drew a line down the middle. I put all the pros on one side of the line, and the cons on the other. It may seem simple, but it helps sort things out.

The sheet was filled with nearly all cons: my retirement plans, my age, the tremendous difficulty of the task. I'd never been a city planner, nor an architect, nor a parks commissioner, nor anything else that would prepare me to make what amounted to a vast design decision for the city. Nor did I have any particular political experience in state or city government, which would help a great deal in working with all the political figures involved, from the governors of New York and New Jersey down to the local political leaders in Lower Manhattan. My only expertise in electoral politics came from twelve years as chairman of the finance committee on the unpaid town council of tiny Essex Fells (population 3,600), the New Jersey suburb where I used to live. This was something else entirely.

And there were so many decisions we'd have to make! How much space should be accorded to a memorial to the victims of the disaster? And what sort of memorial would do justice to their memory? And who should design it? How to replace the vast quantity of office space of the Twin Towers—not to mention the other, smaller World Trade Center buildings that were also destroyed? And what about all the little retail shops that had been damaged in the disaster, their owners pushed to the brink of ruin? And all the ripped-up commuter lines, the cratered subway stations? It was not only a matter of repairing the physical and economic damage, but also of helping heal the trauma caused by this horrendous assault on our city and our nation. I could see that if we didn't get the rebuilding right, we would only open up new wounds, new divisions. There would be lots of controversy, lots of conflict, and I'm not very good at fights.

On the pro side, all I could think was that if my health and energy held up, I probably could do the job. As a board chairman, I'd always prided myself in my ability to bring about consensus, even on the most divisive issues such as bringing coeducation to Haverford, or deciding who deserved to become Goldman Sachs partners.

Still, when I saw the wide imbalance on the sheet in front of me, it was clear to me that I had to say no. And I had fully that intention when I picked up the phone to call Governor Pataki Thursday morning. I'd formulated the words in my mind: *I'm very grateful, but I'm sorry, I just can't accept.* But something happened when I actually picked up the receiver. As I held it in my hand, I looked around my office at all the photographs and memorabilia I have of my years in the war, in government, in business, in sports, and in the nonprofit world—years and years of service, many of them to a cause higher than myself. There were pictures of me with Reagan, with Gorbachev, of me as a young ensign in the Navy, of me as a young man just starting out at Goldman Sachs.

I set the receiver back down in its cradle. I took a deep breath, and I knew what I had to do.

I picked up the phone again and dialed the governor, and when he came on the line I told him I'd accept.

And that was it. Pataki told me he'd see me at the press conference. Then he put me on to an aide to go through some of the details.

It was done. The governor's problem—and with it the city's and even the nation's problem—had become my problem.

Why did I change my mind? I'd have to look back over a lifetime to say. But I guess the short of it is that I felt I had a duty. For me, duty is a rise to a call. If I think a job is important and I'm asked to do it, I really feel that I don't have any right to say no. When the fireman hears the bell go off, he's off to the fire. And I guess I heard the bell.

And so, that Thursday afternoon, I joined Governor George Pataki at City Hall for the press conference at which he announced that I would be chairing the new Lower Manhattan Development Corporation. There were maybe fifty press people in attendance, and the usual bright lights and cameras. Old hat for a governor, but something I hadn't faced since my Washington days.

Mayor Giuliani and Mayor-elect Bloomberg were also there, and they all spoke quite knowledgeably and confidently about what lay ahead. I said a few words, too, but unlike the politicians, I had little to say. I offered only a few platitudes about how honored I was, and how I was confident this would end in a great result, even though I had no idea at that point what it would be.

When the press conference was over, the politicians, each of them surrounded by a phalanx of underlings to fend off the press, returned to their government cars. They were jovial, even jaunty, relieved of a big responsibility. But I was just there by myself. And the press was all around me, firing questions as I tried to find a taxi for the ride back to my office. I shouted back a few answers, trying to make them as innocuous as possible without seeming completely vapid. Finally, I made it to a cab and was relieved to be able to shut out the din when I closed the door.

It was on the ride back uptown that it hit me. In front of just about every TV camera in New York City, I'd agreed to take on, as virtually my own personal responsibility, the monumental task of rebuilding Ground Zero. Maybe I knew a few of the board members. But I had no staff. No money. Not even an office.

That moment in the car was possibly the loneliest moment of my entire life.

2

A MISCHIEVOUS YOUTH

———

WHY DID I EVER SAY YES TO GOVERNOR PATAKI? I've wondered about that quite a bit, especially when the Lower Manhattan Development Corporation gets attacked by the press for supposedly wasting the government's money, or some troublemaker leaks something that's not true, or I have to work through another stack of papers after dinner when I'd rather be heading to bed.

Still, I have never regretted my decision to chair the LMDC board, difficult as it has sometimes been. I don't allow myself that luxury. Once I've made a decision, it's a waste of time to reconsider it. What's done is done. But I've rarely been forced to think as hard about my life as I was after I was called by Governor Pataki. It was a time of enormous introspection for me, a kind of summing up. At my age, I don't have much time left, and right then I had to decide what to do with that time. But every life has a certain trajectory, and my decision to join the LMDC has a lot to do with the way I have spent my life so far. I am not a contemplative person. I much prefer to do things—and to leave to others the job of ferreting out any meaning they might have. But ever since Pataki called, I've felt a need to take a look back, all the way back to the very beginning, to see why I am the man I am, and why I choose to do the things I do.

I was born on April 2, 1922, at about four in the morning. I know the time because my mother used to joke that she held me back for four hours so I'd avoid the embarrassment of being born on April Fool's Day. This epic event occurred in the General Hospital in Evanston, Illinois. My father was in training there for his first job as a telephone lineman for Western Electric. He learned to climb up telephone poles with cleats attached to his shoes and a big strap around him, and I thought that was the most marvelous thing.

Dad was a southerner, born in Rome, Georgia. His name was Eugene Cunningham Whitehead, the middle name—which I share—taken from his great-grandfather, a Civil War colonel who lost a leg at Shiloh. He was trim and dark-haired, and sported a slim mustache for a bit of flair. He always carried a slight southern accent, calling his mother "Momma" and a dollar a "dollah." He went to Georgia Military Academy, or GMA—which he must not have liked because he always referred to it as Gorillas, Monkeys, and Apes—and then to Georgia Tech, where he studied electrical engineering. Twenty-four when World War I broke out, he enlisted in the Army Air Corps (this was before the Air Force was its own branch of the military) and learned to pilot a small single-engine plane called a Flying Jenny. He never did get into the war in France, but he must have buzzed around the Northeast a good deal because when he was courting my mother he used to circle about the Bryn Mawr campus, outside Philadelphia, where she'd come from Illinois to study. He would land his plane on the athletic fields near where she played field hockey. I like to think he had a long white scarf streaming out behind the cockpit like some dashing barnstormer, but I doubt he did. Still, he must have greatly impressed my mother, Winifred—he always called her Freddie—because they were married shortly after she graduated. Oddly enough, once the war was over, neither one of them ever went up in a plane again. My father was a very cautious person. "Never push your luck too far," he used to say. It was a wonderful marriage. I never once heard them argue.

My mother was sweet and pretty, and she was the more ambitious one of the two, especially where her children were concerned. Perhaps because of attending Bryn Mawr, she'd had a broader education. Years later, whenever I was struggling over a passage from *Julius Caesar* in my high school Latin class, she'd look over my shoulder and read out the translation as if the lines had been written in English in the first place.

Our stay in Evanston was brief, and my father soon shifted to a junior management job at Western Electric's manufacturing plant in Kearny, a heavy industrial area near New Jersey's Meadowlands. He settled the family in nearby Montclair, then, as now, a town of about 40,000 people. At first, we had a second-floor apartment in a house on Oakwood Avenue, but when I was about eight or nine, my parents, my younger sister, Margaret, and I moved into a small house of our own on Summit Avenue, a few blocks from the center of town. Our house was set back from the street, with shrubbery in front, and it had a little backyard, and a separate garage.

My room was up on the third floor. It was under the eaves, so the walls went up at unusual angles. The piece of furniture I remember best was the chest, a kind of captain's sea chest that my father had made for me in his basement workshop. I placed that chest under the window that faced west. In the evening, it offered the best light for reading, and in the summertime, long after I was supposed to be in bed, I'd sit on that box, reading the adventure books I'd borrowed from the library. Tales of settling the West, fighting Indians, things like that. I would read for hours, until the sun set and the daylight finally ran out. It was there that I wrote my first (and last) novel, at age eleven. It was called "The $10,000 Jewelry Robbery," ran about 100 handwritten pages, and was eventually stashed in a shoe box from which it never emerged.

I was a tow-headed child, small for my age; for school, I often wore knickers with stockings or high-laced boots, which was the fashion for boys. I was a big collector. There were some giant oak trees behind that first apartment of ours, and each fall I raked up all the acorns, stored them in dozens of big "number ten" tin cans I dug out of the neighbors' trash, and then stashed my hoard in the garage for the winter. The acorns were all rotten and filled with worms by spring, of course, but that didn't keep me from collecting a whole new lifetime supply the next fall. I also collected Indian-head pennies, and I never allowed an incoming envelope to be thrown away without soaking off the stamp—even the standard three-cent first-class one—for my collection.

I also kept pigeons. Not the despised "common" pigeons you find everywhere in the city, but "racing" pigeons, the ones with a remarkable homing instinct that allowed them to fly back at top speed to their home coop from wherever they were, even if it was hundreds and hundreds of miles away.

When I was about ten, my backyard neighbor, Bill MacConnachie, gave me a couple of his pigeons to get me started. They weren't his best, but they were pretty good, and I was immediately hooked. With my father's help, I built a coop behind the garage. It was a sturdy little structure, with small cubicles for nests, a trough for feed, and water dishes. It had a door for me to go in and out, and a "trap" to allow the birds to go in but *not* out. Other neighborhood kids soon joined in with pigeons of their own. My next-door neighbor, Jimmy Walker—not to be mistaken for the New York mayor—was one, Junior Lindsley in the next house was another, and John Read up the street was a third. Together, we formed the Montclair Pigeon Association, a branch of the New Jersey Pigeon Association. Since none of us were even teenagers yet, we made up the group's youngest chapter by a wide margin.

To a racing pigeon, the homing part is instinctive, but the bird still has to be trained. As soon as a baby pigeon was able to fly, we'd start by taking him by bicycle a few hundred yards away from the coop, and then release him. It always went exactly the same way: the bird would fly up a hundred feet into the air, circle once to get his bearings, and then make a beeline for his coop. I found this astounding, and for years I'd ask people why—and how—a homing pigeon did this, but I always got the same answer: nobody knows. And I found that fact nearly as fascinating as the mysterious behavior. How could no one know?

Every few days, we would increase the distance by several miles, and the pigeon would always respond the same way. Fly way up into the air, circle, and zoom. I trained about fifteen pigeons over several years; inevitably, some were better racers than others. We'd place our best performers in carriers for one of our fathers to drive to Penn Station in Newark on a Friday evening after work for the big racing competitions of the New Jersey Pigeon Association. We'd add our carriers to the big jumble of all the others. A night train would take all the birds in their carriers to a station down the line. There, the stationmaster was instructed to release the birds all at once in the morning, make a note of the time, and return the empty carriers on the next train back.

First, we'd send the birds to race back from Trenton, then we tried Philadelphia, then it was on to Baltimore, and then Washington, and finally, with our very best birds, all the way to Wilmington, North Carolina, five hundred miles from Montclair. It was always a wonder to see my birds return to my coop, their stubby wings flapping mightily as they swooped down out of the southern sky and fluttered toward the coop in the back of our garage. The best of them could average up to forty miles an hour, and they'd go nonstop until they got home. A few of my birds never made it. A hawk might nab them, or they might go astray, or drop from exhaustion, or, we sometimes guessed, they might be diverted by a pigeon of the other sex. But it would be awful to wait and wait for a bird that never came home. I don't think any of us ever won a race. The pros, as we thought of them, from Newark always seemed to take all the ribbons. But, still, we were excited to be racing against adults.

Along with the coins, stamps, and racing pigeons, I did my best to collect a little money, too. I weeded the lawn for ten cents a bucket. When I was eight, I joined the boys choir of the local Episcopal church, largely because of the pay involved—$1.35 a month, plus a twenty-dollar gold piece at the end of the year if you had perfect attendance, which I nearly always did. And my father's mother down South, a former schoolteacher whom we called our "Dixie grandmother," used to give me a dollar for a good report card. I kept my money in a little metal safe in my room until my mother opened up a savings account for me, and I was given a passbook to record my holdings. I was impressed that, thanks to compound interest, my money could make more money all by itself.

I wasn't what you'd call a money grubber. While I appreciated getting paid to sing in the choir, I probably would have done it for free. I enjoyed wearing my black cassock and freshly starched cotta with a stiff collar and flowing black bow tie. And I loved the music, too. Eddie Bergamini had the best voice of all of us, and he usually sang the solo in his clear, bell-like soprano. But if there was a duet, I would sing the second part, although my voice wasn't anywhere near as good as Eddie's. Our choirmaster was the brother of the actor Fred MacMurray, who later played the father in *My Three Sons* on TV. Fred came to church himself one Sunday, dramatically increasing attendance.

The singing led to my taking up the violin. That came about in fifth grade, when my school allowed us all to pick a musical instrument to play. Because my name began with a W, I was among the last to choose and, by then, only violins were left. I would have much preferred to have a trumpet or a clarinet or a drum—any instrument I could play in a marching band, which I was very keen to do. There were no violins in bands. But I accepted my fate and I struggled through violin lessons and orchestra performances for nearly ten years until, in my senior year in high school, I was considered good enough to play in a concert with the New Jersey Symphony Orchestra. This was something that would never be allowed today and probably shouldn't have been allowed then. I sat in one of the very last chairs of the first-violin section, practically off the stage, and I was told not to play during the more demanding passages. But I did play the rest, and that was surely the peak of my violin career. I also played violin in Billy Moxley's Band, a high school friend's six-man jazz group that once had a two-week engagement providing live entertainment on the Hudson River Dayline boats that plied the Hudson between Manhattan's Forty-fifth Street and West Point. In later years, I've played in several pickup string quartets with some musical friends. One group was so amateurish we each played one of the four parts of some of the hymns in the Episcopal hymnal. These musical soirées always occurred in private, with not even spouses allowed to listen.

I found money interesting. I was good at numbers, and inclined to be hard-working, so money was a natural focus for some of my energy. But it certainly wasn't paramount, even after the Depression struck when I was seven.

I remember the week the stock market crashed that October in 1929. We were vacationing in the little fishing town of 'Sconset on Nantucket. It was remote enough that the city papers took several days to get there, so my father would listen to the radio every day to keep up with the news, and that's how he found out about the stock market collapse. The events of Black Tuesday, October 29, must have been a terrible shock. He had carefully invested his entire life savings in the market, with AT&T his biggest holding. It wasn't a huge amount of money, maybe $50,000, but it was a lot to him and quite a lot of money for the time—perhaps the equivalent to $500,000 today. I watched him take out a little book to calculate his losses, and I saw him get quite nervous, which was *very* unusual for him. We left a few days earlier than we planned to so he could get back to New York City and "see to his invest-ments," as he put it.

When Dad was working for Western Electric, he normally drove off to work in the family's gray Dodge every day at seven, and he came back every night at six. Before long, the Depression claimed his job, as it took so many others'—not that he ever said a thing about it to me—and he *still* drove off every morning at seven and came back every night at six. He eventually found work selling porch furniture on commission door-to-door. He had to make his quota every month, and we ended up taking a lot of the furniture ourselves. I always thought that ours was the best-furnished porch in Montclair.

We ate a lot of macaroni and cheese, and heaps of codfish cakes, which were actually a favorite meal of mine (and still are). Otherwise, I wasn't aware of any hardship. I didn't think of us as poor, probably because we were no worse off than anyone else I knew. Yet there were a couple of years when Mother did not take me to Bamberger's, Newark's biggest department store, for our annual back-to-school shopping trip. The message there was: "make do." People worry today when the unemployment rate goes up from 5 to 6 percent. They forget that in the Great Depression more than 20 percent of the workforce was unemployed. But I remember, and the memory has made me very cautious about borrowing, and reluctant to indulge myself with lux-uries. I've never borrowed money to buy anything since my first house; I'm afraid I might not be able to pay it back. I don't even like credit cards!

We were able to buy a new car in 1934, a Model A Ford, the successor to the better-known Model T. At $500, it was the cheapest new car on the mar-ket, but impressive all the same. It had a starter on it instead of a crank in the front, inflatable tires, bumpers, and fenders over the wheels, all of which were extremely innovative. I liked to sit in that car when my mother went shopping, so that I could hear people exclaim over the "new Ford." As a fam-ily, we listened on the radio to Amos 'n' Andy, Jack Armstrong, and, of course, Roosevelt's celebrated Fireside Chats. My parents were both Republicans, my father especially rock-ribbed, and they both disliked Roosevelt. So I won points for mocking him, with his Hahv'd accent, and the way he always started his talk with "My friends."

As I look back on my childhood, I can see the beginnings of many of the traits I still have. Just as now, I devoted myself to a wide variety of activities, and I tended to focus intensely on each one of them as it came along. And, of course, I am still a loyal Republican, although much more of a moderate one than many in the party. But there is one aspect of my early character that has, so far as I know, never resurfaced, and it will come as a surprise to those who think they know me.

I was a mischievous child, even a naughty one. One memorable time, I hurried home from second grade to flush my little sister's birthday goldfish down the toilet before she got back from kindergarten. On another occasion, when my mother parked me for the day at my imperious Aunt Nell's house, I crayoned all over her bedroom wallpaper when I was supposed to be taking my nap. In school, although I did get virtually straight A's in my academic subjects, my grades for conduct were often U's—for "unsatisfactory." I did particularly badly in categories like "Works well with others" and "Listens in class." In church, I used to launch paper airplanes from my seat in the choir when our minister, Reverend Trenbath, delivered his lengthy sermons. And I was even more abusive to his successor, Reverend Orrin Judd. He had an unfortunate fondness for the phrase "so to speak," and I, along with a few other scalawags in the choir, used to count the number of times he resorted to it during his sermon. One Sunday, when the number hit the all-time-high of ten, I started a round of soft clapping that spread through the choir. I received quite a "talking to" from the choirmaster for that.

Worst of all, I used to snitch cookies from the rear window of Marker's Bakery, across the street from the Episcopal church where I sang on Sundays. The bakery was famous for its cookies. They were baked late in the afternoon and then set out to cool on a tray just inside an open window. The smell of those fresh-baked cookies wafting through the air was just too tempting. Some friends and I would sneak around to the back of the store, the tallest one would hoist me—since I was the smallest—up onto his shoulders, and I would reach through the window, swipe the cookies off the cooling tray, and we would all run off, munching. We did this month after month until one evening a friend lifted me up to the window as usual—and there was a shrill and terrifying whistle, and two bright flashlights shined out at us. My friends dumped me on the ground and ran for it, so I was the only one left to face the music. I could see the flashlights were held by a pair of immense policemen! Caught red-handed! And, most shameful of all, I was on my way home from a Boy Scout meeting, so I was still wearing my revered khaki Boy Scout uniform. The two officers threw around words like "grand larceny" and "thirty days," which terrified me, just as I am sure they were supposed to. Finally, the policemen called my father and he drove around to the bakery to collect me. He looked very grim when he climbed out of our car.

When we got home, I was sent to my room, and Dad did what he sometimes did when I was caught in a severe transgression, as I too often was. He went out to the back yard and cut a switch—it was not particularly stiff, but it was snappy—from what my sister and I called the "switch bush." And then, with a slow and heavy tread, he climbed the steps to my bedroom. I dreaded that sound. And he came into my room, told me to drop my trousers and bend over, and then he would warm my bare backside with the switch, while I tried hard not to cry.

I think the bakery incident must have disturbed my mother. She was never the disciplinarian in the family—she left that to my father—but she was the conscience. She came into my bedroom one afternoon a few days later, sat down on the bed with me, and took my hand. "There's something in our family that you should know about," she began solemnly. "About a year after Dad and I were married, I gave birth to twins. Two boys." She took a breath; it seemed she was trying to hold back tears. "And they died at birth. It was a terrible tragedy for your father and me, and also for my father, since he was my doctor at the time." Her eyes were moist and red, and she had to stop a moment to dab at them with a handkerchief. Mother was rarely emotional, and I don't think I'd ever seen her cry before.

I was terribly shaken. Twins? Dead? Delivered by my grandfather? I had no idea about any of this. I learned later that my grandfather had, in fact, delivered me, but he'd died a few years after I was born, and I hadn't realized that he was actually my mother's doctor. In those days, a doctor did everything—set bones, wrote prescriptions, and delivered babies.

Mother went on, in an even voice that went straight into me. "About two years later, you were born, a very healthy, normal little boy. We were so grateful!" She looked at me. "Now, John, your father and I hope and pray every day that you will grow up to be a fine person and help us make up for our terrible loss."

I would have cried, but I knew it was wrong at my age to cry in front of my mother. It was nearly impossible to speak, but I managed to mumble, "Yes, Mother. I'll try." But her words, and the sight of her tears, went deep inside me. It's hard to believe that my life changed right then and there but, as I look back on it, I can see I was a very different boy afterward. I never got into any mischief again. Well, hardly ever. For the rest of my life, I did everything I could to make my mother proud of me. Joining the Navy; marrying a fine woman; starting a family; making my way up the ladder at Goldman Sachs. I'm only sorry that my mother didn't live to see me sworn in by President Reagan as deputy secretary of state. That would have been the fulfillment of a dream for her, I'm sure.

My mother never spoke of the dead twins again, and I didn't either. If they had a grave, I never saw it. Nor did I ever mention our conversation to my father or to my sister.

I now threw myself into Scouting activities. My father was Assistant Scoutmaster of Troop 19, which met on Monday evenings in the basement of St. James Church, the Episcopal church where I sang in the choir. For years, I had enviously watched him go off every week to troop meetings in his dashing scoutmaster's uniform, complete with a handsome set of leather puttees left over from his Army Air Corps days. I had to wait until I turned twelve to join the troop, and that seemed like forever. I'd learned all my knots, and I had the Scout Oath by heart. "On my honor, I will do my best to do my duty to God and my country, and to obey the Scout Laws; to help other people at all times; to keep myself physically strong, mentally awake and morally straight." Corny as they may sound, I still find that those words are a pretty good code to live by. I also knew all the Scout Laws, requiring Scouts to be "trustworthy, loyal, helpful, friendly, courteous, kind, obedient, cheerful, thrifty, brave, clean and reverent." I still aspire to be all those things, too.

I joined up practically on the day of my twelfth birthday. I became a Tenderfoot (the first level of Scouting) in a jiffy and was soon placed in the Flying Eagle Patrol. After two or three years I became a Patrol Leader, and an Eagle Scout two years after that. With each new merit badge, Scouting opened up some new world of activity and gave me a greater degree of self-confidence, as well. Not satisfied with the twenty-one merit badges required by the Eagle rank, I kept going and earned fifteen more.

But I did not achieve absolutely everything I set out to. In 1938, when I was sixteen, I was desperate to attend the Boy Scout World Jamboree that was being held in Washington, D.C. Each troop could send one delegate. To my chagrin, I discovered that someone else had been selected from my troop, but there would be a competition for a single at-large delegate from a number of local troops, and I was determined to win it. Each candidate was to submit a five-hundred-word essay on the topic, "Why I want to go to the Jamboree." Whoever wrote the best essay would be selected to be the delegate. How I struggled over my essay! I wrote and rewrote it, polishing every word, and submitted what I was sure would be the winner. But no, my essay placed second behind one written by a scout from Troop 1 in North Caldwell, and I didn't go to the Jamboree. There was no second prize. I took away a useful lesson in the inevitability of at least occasional disappointment, and the value of gracefully accepting defeat, and moving on. Still, I was gratified to discover, many years later, that the boy who beat me out was Richard Wilbur, who grew up to become a famous poet, the nation's poet laureate, and winner of a Pulitzer Prize.

There was a Boy Scout summer camp called Camp Glen Gray in Oakland, New Jersey, about twenty miles away from home. The first time I went, I became so homesick I almost didn't last the full two weeks I'd signed up for. It was my first time away from home. I hated the food; I couldn't swim; I couldn't sleep; I wasn't making any friends; and I was all-round miserable. Alarmed, my parents came to visit that first weekend and had a talk with the camp director, a man named Ernie McCoy. He'd been an All-American football player at Michigan and coached the high school team in Montclair. One of the Scouts at the camp, John McMullen, was a player of his, the only sophomore on the varsity. He was sixteen, an Eagle Scout, handsome and rugged, and all the boys idolized him. He had a tent all to himself, right at the center of the camp. After speaking to my parents, McCoy said that, if I could commit to finishing out the two-week session, he'd arrange for me to bunk in with John McMullen. That sounded very good to me. During breakfast the next morning, I sat out on the little porch in front of McMullen's tent while the other campers passed by whispering about that skinny little guy in John McMullen's tent. And just from the newly respectful way everyone looked at me, I could tell I suddenly belonged. My homesickness disappeared in a hurry. I ended up staying in that camp not just for two weeks, but for eight. And I continued to spend my summers there at the camp all through high school, moving from camper to counselor and finally to assistant camp director, until I went off to college. As I look back, those early leadership lessons were invaluable.

Scouting has remained a central part of my life ever since, and John McMullen has become one of my best friends. Years later when I was at Goldman Sachs, we joined up to buy the New Jersey Devils. That was a thrilling experience, especially when the team first won the Stanley Cup, and one that I will get into later. And, like so many of the other developments in my life, it all came about through a quirk of fate, in this case because of a bout of homesickness at Scout camp when I was twelve years old.

3

Haverford College via the Great White Way

※

THE MOMENT I SAW HAVERFORD, I knew it was the college for me. A friend of my parents' named Alan Hastings was a Haverford grad, and one bright spring day during my junior year at Montclair High, he took me down to see the campus. Haverford is just outside Philadelphia, about a hundred miles from home, and it was the most beautiful college I'd ever seen, not that I'd seen very many. It had a cluster of handsome, stone buildings spread out over two hundred acres of what could have been a botanical garden. There were flowers everywhere, and the whole place could not have been more attractive to me.

Haverford was small though, just four hundred students then (and only eleven hundred now). My high school class *alone* had four hundred students. But I'd always felt somewhat anonymous in my four rather uneventful years at Montclair High, and I wanted to go to a small college where I might have the chance of distinguishing myself. I wasn't put off by the fact that Haverford was then all-male. Most good colleges were then, and nearby Bryn Mawr could provide dates for Saturday night. But I wasn't especially interested in girls at that point. The closest I'd come to going steady was to take Montclair High's unofficial beauty queen, Carolyn Brown, to the movies twice—before her father scared me off by telling me in no uncertain terms that I was not to walk her home again through Anderson Park, a notorious necking spot. I also liked the idea that Haverford was for the serious student. At Haverford, they liked to say that if you weren't a serious student, you should go to Princeton.

But I was sure I had blown my interview with Arch MacIntosh, Haverford's director of admissions. I spent the whole time talking to him about Toga Day, when all of the members of the high school Latin Club dressed up like ancient Romans for a Roman banquet. Afterward, I was afraid that sounded childish. But my grades and College Board scores were decent, and I was overjoyed when I received my letter of admission a few months later. I was also relieved, since I hadn't applied anywhere else.

I was concerned about how to pay the tuition. Haverford cost $900 a year, which was an enormous sum for a family like ours in 1939. My father had been rehired by Western Electric, but I doubted his entire annual salary was much more than $3,000 or $4,000 (not that I'd ever bring up something like that with him), and I didn't feel right about presenting him with such a large bill. But I couldn't think how I'd ever come up with that much money myself.

That summer, I had already earned $200 for eight weeks as assistant director at the Boy Scouts' Camp Glen Gray, and another $200 running a canoe trip down the Delaware River with my friend Tom Connell. But, with little more than a month left before college was to start, that still left me $500 short. I scoured the few help-wanted ads I could find in the Sunday newspapers, and noticed an item in the *New York Times* offering a chance to "EARN $100 A WEEK OR MORE!" at the 1939 World's Fair in Flushing Meadow, Queens. It sounded like very good money to me, and the next morning I took the first train from Montclair and headed for the fairgrounds near what's now La Guardia Airport to check into the job opportunities.

The fairgrounds seemed to stretch out forever in every direction. At its center was a seven-hundred-foot spire and mammoth orb that covered nearly a city block, with streets radiating outward from it with names such as Rainbow Avenue and the Court of Commerce, and rousing, streamlined visions of the future from corporations like General Motors and AT&T rising up all around. This has since become standard World's Fair material, but it was exciting at the time—just the thing the country needed to pull itself out of the Depression.

But I ignored that part of the fairground completely, and struck out for what was called the Great White Way, which lay just beyond. That was a vast, glittering, and fairly seedy Coney Island of a place, with Ferris wheels, carnival acts, magicians, card sharks, two-headed calves, fat ladies, and freaks of all sorts. To a boy like me from Montclair, it offered all the forbidden allure of the big city.

The best-paying jobs were at the concession stands, where individual operators sold everything from shots in a shooting gallery and a chance to dunk a fat man into a vat of water to other enticements that I thought I probably shouldn't investigate. It happened that the man who had the concession guessing customers' weights had quit the day before. Weight guessing sounded to me like a fairly glamorous way to make some easy money. I didn't think my parents would like it much, but I was thrilled by the prospect of telling my old friends on Summit Avenue that I held such a job.

Happily, that interview went more smoothly than the one at Haverford. The concession manager thought that, at seventeen, I might be a little young, but I talked him into giving me a shot, and I started right in.

The deal was that each customer would pay a quarter for the privilege of having me guess his weight. Then I'd sit him down in a big chair that was connected to a scale that rose up maybe fifty feet into the air behind him. The more he weighed, the higher the needle would go—all the way up to five hundred pounds at the very top (which, mercifully, no one ever did reach). If I guessed right—within two pounds either way was what the small print said—I kept the quarter and that was it. If I was wrong, I still kept the quarter, but I had to give the customer back a stuffed animal, which cost me twenty cents. So I'd come out ahead in either case, but obviously I'd make my tuition money more quickly if I guessed the weight correctly. The concessions manager gave me a microphone to wear around my neck. He plugged it into a loudspeaker, and told me I was all set.

"But what do I say?" I asked him.

"Whatever you want, kid. It's your show. Whatever'll pack 'em in."

I'm a pretty shy person, and I was a very timid barker, and, at first, hardly anyone paid any attention to me. But I wanted those quarters, so I started using some of the better lines I heard from the other pitchmen around me, and I developed a bit of a patter that got more daring as time went on. "Ladies and gentlemen, step right up, and try your luck against the AMAZING GUESSTOMATOR. Easy for you, a challenge for me. Ladies and gentlemen, let me try to GUESS your WEIGHT. For just twenty-five cents, you'll get a chance to win this handsome teddy bear . . ." And so on like that. Perhaps this was my impish side coming out from under the Eagle Scout facade, but I had fun with it, and pretty soon I had a good line of customers waiting to sit in the big chair and prove my guesses wrong. That helped my confidence, and, who knows, maybe a little of that chutzpah stuck with me.

I got to be pretty good at guessing weights, too. The trick is to ignore people's faces and concentrate on their waistlines, since that's where the pounds are. After a while, I caught on to the fact that some people were stuffing their pockets with stones to throw me off. I accused one heavily endowed young lady of loading up her bra, but she indignantly peeled back a bit of her shirt to show me that it was indeed all her. That brightened my cheeks a little. Eventually, I got so good at guessing that I had to lose deliberately sometimes to keep customers lining up.

I kept that job for the rest of the summer, hard as it was on my feet and on my vocal chords. I had to do most of my talking in the mornings, when the crowds tended to be thin. They thickened up nicely in the evenings and contestants settled themselves into my chair one after another without much urging from me. At my best, I could get a customer in and out of the chair in sixty seconds, leaving me with a shiny quarter in my palm. My brain spun with the financial numbers—twenty-five cents a minute meant one dollar every four minutes, which meant ten dollars every forty minutes, which meant I was getting rich at a wonderful clip. A lot faster than the days when I'd had to fill an entire bushel basket with weeds just to earn a dime.

Thrilled by the money, I kept at my post twelve hours a day, six days a week for the next six weeks. To save time, I scarcely returned home, and every night but Saturday I bedded down at a cheap motel nearby and, to cut expenses, just about lived on twenty-cent hot dogs and nickel Cokes. By the time the summer was up, I had my $500.

I was proud of myself, but I knew enough to be careful just how I told Dad that I'd made the tuition fee on my own. He'd worked hard to provide for the family through a very difficult time, and I didn't want him to feel badly that he hadn't come up with the money himself. So I simply told him that I'd had such fun doing the fairgrounds job that I'd made more money than I'd expected, and it looked like I could cover the whole bill for my tuition. He was surprised, and I think he was impressed. I'm sure it made both my parents feel a bit better about that carnival job.

Haverford proved to be everything I hoped for. If anything, it seemed to take academics a little *too* seriously for me. As a public school boy, I was a bit behind the prep-schoolers in most subjects. I pulled down a 79 average that first semester, which put me below average—a spot I never liked to be in. That got me going, and, by the time I graduated, I'd made Phi Beta Kappa.

For a while I thought of majoring in chemistry—I was so impressed with the elaborate chemical reactions I observed in the lab of my chemistry professor, Bill Cadbury. But I ended up in economics, which seemed more my line. I'd always been fascinated by money.

Actually, I sometimes think my real major was extracurricular activities. I did a bit of everything. I sang in the glee club—now that my boyish soprano had settled down into a baritone. I played JV baseball and basketball. I was a high-jumper on the track team; in fact, one year I was the *best* high-jumper on the track team (although my highest jump was only a little over six feet at a time when the national record was nearly eight). I was director of intramural athletics. I ran the international relations club. I was president of the student council. And, perhaps because of all this activity, I was elected permanent president of my class in my senior year. After sixty-two years in the position, I figure I am now the longest-serving, democratically elected official in history.

I got especially interested in student government. Haverford was famous for its honor code, which required every student to pledge adherence to certain community standards regarding cheating, plagiarism, and the like, and any violations were handled by the student council. Some of the cases were very petty by today's standards. Smoking, for example, was a violation of the code—but only if it occurred outdoors, oddly enough. Healthy lungs weren't the issue; the problem was that discarded cigarette butts would defile the campus. As reminders, little sand-filled red cans were placed outside every door to collect the cigarette ends. The student council handled any violations of this peculiar smoking code.

We were also obliged to enforce the "women's rule," which banned women from the dorms after 11 P.M. These cases could get delicate, and students inevitably claimed—almost never truthfully—that the girl in question was their sister, and surely such sanctions didn't apply to *her*.

A few cases were simply laughable, like the one involving a student everyone called "Senator" Stiles because of his reputation for being able to talk his way out of anything. Or *almost* anything: the Senator was caught climbing back over a partition in the office of a chemistry professor after upping his grades in the grade book. He simply erased his old ones and wrote in new ones. No amount of eloquence could retrieve that particular situation. He was expelled.

A more difficult case involved a student named John Bush. No relation to "W" (or his father), he was the son of Vannevar Bush, the first head of the Atomic Energy Commission and a world-renowned scientist. That case taught me a few things about how life works beyond the reach of the Haverford honor code. The code forbade drinking on campus or having liquor in your room, but a righteous—and nosy—janitor had discovered a bottle of liquor in Bush's dorm room and turned him in. This was during Christmas vacation and, since the infraction was fairly minor, the council decided to let Bush off with a ten-day suspension; and several of the days were deemed to have already been served during vacation. Still, Bush's father was deeply unhappy about it when he found out. Worse for us, Vannevar Bush turned out to be a friend of Haverford's president, Felix Morley—a man who had previously been the editor of the *Washington Post*—and he asked Morley to intervene to remove this blot on his son's record. Sensitive to such pressure, Morley appealed to us on the council to reconsider. That made for some tense days, but we held our ground, and the sentence stood.

Founded by Quakers way back in 1833, Haverford was still entirely committed to the Quaker ideals of pacifism, community-togetherness, and the value of every individual. That squeaky-clean reputation may have put off some outsiders, but I found these principles quite inspiring and, maybe as a continuation of the four-square Eagle Scout side of me, I still try to live by many of them.

At Haverford, about one student in ten was from a Quaker family, and a fairly large number of faculty members were practicing Quakers as well. Regardless of personal faith, all students were required to attend Fifth Day Meeting every Thursday. At Meeting, there was no minister to do all the talking. Anyone could speak if the spirit moved him and, though I rarely spoke myself, I was often impressed by the expressions of faith from the students around me. I was too committed as an Episcopalian from my upbringing to consider converting, but I was especially impressed with the Quaker belief in an "inner light" in each of us, one that will guide us through difficult times if we only pay attention to it. And Quakers do mean *each* of us, regardless of race or class or religious belief. I discovered ample evidence of that inner light in the sensitive, caring observations of my schoolmates and the faculty members in Meeting.

Some of my Quaker classmates were extremely devout. One of them, Arnold Satterthwait, took the denomination's pacifism so seriously that, after the United States entered World War II, he refused to register for the draft in our senior year as the law required. I admired him for taking such a principled stand, but most Quakers thought there was an important difference between merely registering for the draft and actually serving in the army. In any case, Arnie was arrested for his refusal, and he was tried in a Philadelphia court. To show our support, I and a few other classmates attended the trial, but to no avail. Arnie was sentenced to a year and a day in a Philadelphia prison. It distressed me to think of him languishing in his cell while we finished up our college careers and went on to serve our country, but it also showed me once again how very deep Quaker beliefs can sometimes go.

As an undergraduate, I wasn't entirely the straight-arrow. I spent a fair amount of time at the local bar called the 10th Entry. I'd developed a taste for beer in the company of none other than Reverend Orrin Judd, the minister at my old Episcopal church. (He was the one who loved the phrase "so to speak.") He used to invite the leaders of the Young People's Fellowship over to his house and, perhaps to show that he was still one of the boys, served us beer, which I came to rather like. So I imbibed occasionally at 10th Entry. I used to play darts there, too, and once won the tavern's Saturday night dart tournament.

And I had some success on the romantic front, as well. As a sophomore, I invited a charming girl named Connie Dey to the junior prom, but that relationship never progressed. For my last two years, I went out with a lovely Bryn Mawr redhead named Rusty Hendrickson, whom I'd met when she was a freshman and I a junior. By the time I was to graduate, the war was looming, discouraging any long-term planning, so we decided to go our separate ways.

When my roommate Tris Coffin learned of the breakup, he asked me if I'd mind if he took Rusty out. I said no, of course not, and he invited her out on a date. Six months later they were married. Rusty dropped out of Bryn Mawr. Tris entered the Army as a private, and she followed him to Army bases all over the country. Now, after three marriages of my own, I'm a little jealous but also very pleased that they're still happily married sixty years later.

Despite my weight-guessing success, I still needed funds to cover my college expenses, so I enrolled in the work scholarship program for all four of my college years. I filled the acid bottles in the chemistry labs, an activity that left me with two small acid-burn scars that I still bear on my right thumb. I worked in the college library. And I annually updated the *Encyclopaedia Britannica* entries of one economics professor, and corrected exams for another, a task that caused me some unease, and kept quite secret, since I ended up grading the work of many of my friends.

But the real money maker for me was setting up the pins in local bowling alleys, a project I undertook with my classmate Jack Moon. Automation has long since eliminated the need for human pin setters, but back then the work was all done by hand. A "pin boy" would have a seat just past the pins on the far end of the lane. Whenever a bowling ball came crashing through, he'd have to lift his legs to keep from getting hit by the ball or the pins. He'd then retrieve the ball, send it back down a chute, and replace all the pins on little pegs that rose up from under the floor once he stepped on a lever. It was arduous work, and not a little hazardous with all the heavy lumber flying about, but the money was decent—although nothing compared to the lucre I received from weight guessing. A pin boy got ten cents a "string," twenty cents if he "worked double" by handling two adjoining alleys at once. I made a dollar most nights, plus tips.

It had all started one evening when Jack Moon, who had been working the alley at the nearby Ardmore YMCA, asked me to fill in for him. I didn't mind doing it, and we ended up pretty much sharing the job. Next year he and I came up with a better idea. We assembled a pool of pin boys from the college, and offered their services to a commercial alley in town. We charged fifteen cents a game, but guaranteed the proprietor a steady supply of pin setters. Jack and I pocketed the extra five cents for our ingenuity. That went well, so we recruited more students to work some of the other alleys in town. Then, the next year, we signed up the lanes at the Merion Cricket Club and, with our near monopoly were able to charge all the lane owners twenty cents a game for the services of our pin boys. This time, Jack and I split the extra money with our labor force. It was a useful economics lesson for us about the strength of monopolies, the value of unions, and the relatively easy life of managers. By senior year, Jack and I scarcely had to lift a finger as the money flooded in.

My senior year, I lived in a large double suite with five other guys. We called our rooms the "joie de vivre" suite, and we weren't being entirely ironic. That was my life at Haverford—a complete joy. So many of my friends from those years—an all-American soccer player named Morrie Evans; the football captain, Beef Meader; Bob MacCrate, who went on to the law firm Sullivan & Cromwell; my roommate Av Mason; Ho Hunter, Mather Lippincott, Paul Cope, Tris Coffin, and so many others—have been friends for life. My Haverford years are the source of some of my happiest memories.

They were good times, but part of the satisfaction for me came from developing into the person I wanted to be, someone who was more serious and more conscientious than the boy I'd been back in Montclair. This was certainly true in regard to my studies, but it was also true in about every activity I undertook. Commitment was always the key ingredient. And that commitment stemmed, I think, from the realization that I had a strong competitive drive. If I was up for the student council, or class president, I really wanted to win. This posed a dilemma for me, since at that time—unlike today—no one actively campaigned for such a position. That wasn't done, especially at a

Quaker school like Haverford. It was unconscionable even to vote for your-self. So there was nothing I could do directly to advance my cause. All I could do was work to become a person who was deemed worthy of holding such a position of responsibility. I would, in short, need to be admired and respected by my peers. (Would that all politics operated on this principle today!) And how was that to be achieved? Happily, by doing many of the things that ap-pealed to me anyway—like accepting my responsibilities, being industrious and useful, and trying always to do the right thing. I feel a little ashamed to admit that I didn't consider such virtue to be solely an end in itself. I wanted—indeed, needed—to be recognized for it.

I sometimes wonder why. Was it somehow to make up for my fairly hum-ble origins as just another one of the boys on Summit Avenue? Was it to prove myself to the preppies from Lawrenceville, Andover, and other such places? To redeem my parents' terrible loss of those twins? Or was it simply that I was endowed with a larger-than-average ego? I don't know. All I know is that I wanted to win the respect of my peers, to be viewed as an achiever, someone to admire. If one person was to end up on top—whether it was a class elec-tion, a dart tournament, or a high-jump competition—I wanted to be that person. And it was immensely gratifying to me that I often *did* become that person.

In those days, everyone in the graduating class voted for the student they most admired. It was the highest honor one's peers could bestow. The recip-ient received a large, carved-ebony spoon, and so he was called the Spoon Man, a title that did not, in my opinion, reflect its great significance. (It has since passed from the scene at Haverford.) I was elected Spoon Man my sen-ior year. Of all the awards I have ever received, that is the one I'm most proud of. To be voted by my ninety-nine classmates as the one who has made the most valuable contributions to the college over the four years that we were all there—well, it was an honor that made me flush with pride when I heard my name announced on graduation day.

Before I left Haverford, Arch MacIntosh, the dean of admissions who'd ad-mitted me, offered me a job as his assistant director of admissions, with the idea of my succeeding him when he retired five years later. I loved Haverford, and I couldn't think what else I'd do with an economics degree, and I told him that by all means I'd be happy to accept. He knew I had to go into the Navy first, though, and then, when the war was over, I'd be back.

By the time that came, though, I'd changed my mind and decided to pursue a business career instead. I had to face up to the terrible task of telling Mac that I wouldn't be taking the admissions job after all. I went down to see him, figuring that I'd better tell him in person. When I showed up, though, he thought I was finally reporting for work. He'd been counting on me, and he was disappointed to learn of my new plans.

To his credit, Mac finally came around, but he wouldn't let me entirely off the hook.

"All right," he said gruffly. "Go into business if you want to. But I'll only forgive you if you can come back and donate a million dollars to Haverford."

A million dollars was an unimaginable sum, especially to a Haverfordian whose only job had been in the Navy. But, sure enough, a couple of decades later I did indeed return to Haverford, and I presented Mac, now in his retirement, with that million-dollar check to the school we both loved.

In my gratitude to Haverford for all it did for me, I followed that donation with many more and at one point I was the largest donor to Haverford in the history of the college. However much I ended up giving back financially to Haverford, I still think I came out way ahead in the deal.

4

OFF TO WAR

—⁓—

I WAS WORKING AT THE CHECK-OUT DESK at the Haverford College library when word came in over the radio that Pearl Harbor had been attacked. It was almost exactly two o'clock on Sunday, December 7, 1941. The library started to buzz with the news.

I had been so busy with my student activities, I hadn't paid much attention to the risk of war. Europe seemed very far away from suburban Philadelphia, and the Far East, of course, even farther. I looked over the newspapers as often as I could, but Haverford was pretty isolated, and I'd had little time for world affairs. Indeed, we'd all been living in a beautiful ivory tower, far away from reality. I'd never been abroad; I'd never even left the Northeast. But the moment I heard the news about Pearl Harbor, I knew that the scope of my life would change dramatically. I was no longer just a student in a small college in Pennsylvania, but a citizen of a wider, far more dangerous world. Whatever plans I might have had to continue on in school, start a job, enter graduate school, or get married and have children (not that I had any thought about that yet)—well, I could forget about them. The war would transform the role in the world of all Americans, creating new opportunities and serious responsibilities for all the country's citizens. It was not just a short "time-out," as so many of my friends assumed it would be, but a sharp and permanent transformation for the country, and of our lives.

It's hard to exaggerate the terrifying drama of that time. In a matter of hours, almost half the United States Navy was either sunk or in flames. With that one blow, the Japanese took control of the whole Pacific. They were free to attack the West Coast if they wanted, and many people feared they would do just that. Off the other coast, Hitler's submarines roamed the Atlantic. U-boats were seen patrolling off New Jersey. For all we knew, the Nazis might storm the beaches on the East Coast at any moment. Today, not far from my summer house by the ocean in Little Compton, Rhode Island, there are remnants of gun turrets built to protect Newport Harbor against precisely that eventuality. It may seem silly now, but it was very real then. Most of Europe had been overrun. London was being bombed nightly. It was possible that England might fall, leaving the United States standing alone in defense of the free world.

Recognizing that this was history in the making, three of my classmates and I cooked up a plan to drive down to Washington in an old rattletrap that two of them shared. I wanted to be there to hear the President declare war before a historic joint session of Congress the next morning. It was in some ways a foolish quest. There were hardly any seats available in the Capitol gallery, and they were not likely to give them to the likes of the four of us. Sure enough, even though we arrived at the crack of dawn, we didn't get inside, so we stood with a crowd of other curiosity seekers near the Capitol steps huddled in our heavy winter overcoats against the chill of that bitter December morning. Loudspeakers had been set up outside to broadcast the President's speech, the one in which he referred to "the day of infamy." It was an electrifying moment, and I was swept up in a wave of patriotic fervor.

As frightening and unprecedented as the war was, I had no doubt that America would prevail. And I had no reservations about being part of it. Aside from a few Quaker pacifists, I didn't know anyone who was unwilling to serve. If ever there was a just war, this was it. When the Selective Service sent me my notice to register for the draft, I filled out the forms without the slightest hesitation. My only hope was that I could find a military program that would give me time to finish up my graduation requirements before going off to war. I was very happy to discover a Navy Supply Corps plan that would let me graduate and then be commissioned as an ensign in the Navy. The plan involved participating in a ninety-day program at the Harvard Business School, which had been transformed into a kind of Navy training school, to learn naval accounting before I shipped out.

I much preferred the Navy to the Army. I couldn't picture myself in the infantry, living in the mud and going face to face with the enemy. In the Navy, I'd be operating at what I imagined would be a safer distance from the Germans and Japanese, even if that safety was an illusion. And it didn't bother me that I'd never been on any water craft larger than the canoe we used on our Scout camping trips, or out to sea except to swim from the beach. The Navy was it for me.

My only problem was making the weight. To qualify for the program, I had to weigh at least 132 pounds, and I scarcely broke 125 when I was wet. The weigh-in was on a Monday, as I recall, and all weekend I ate bunches of bananas—supposedly the best way to gain weight quickly—and drank gallons of water. I was sure I was going to burst, but I still required a sympathetic physician to pass as a genuine 132-pounder. (Having struggled practically ever since to stay below 180, I find this fact more than a little ironic.)

Haverford added an extra semester that summer to accelerate the completion of the coursework we needed to graduate, and I finished up along with the rest of my class in January of 1943. The date for my being called up was set for June, so I filled my time serving as assistant to the president of Haverford, Felix Morley—the very man whose authority I had questioned during the John Bush episode of my student council days. Morley didn't hold that against me, though (nor I, him.) My job was to help the college accommodate itself to the war effort, not an easy thing for a pacifist Quaker school. It was eerie to have so few students and faculty on campus, all the rest having been mobilized for the war. The situation was so dire that I was pressed into service, teaching an introductory economics class at Bryn Mawr for students who were scarcely younger than I. Indeed, one of them was a girl I'd dated. Sensitive to Haverford's pacifist attitudes, the Army had agreed to use the campus only to train weather officers, a program that was about as far removed from actual warfare as anyone could think of. Still, it was disturbing to have the would-be meteorologists marching about Walton Field in military formation, with wooden replica rifles over their shoulders. I'll never forget seeing the aging former Haverford president, the Quaker leader William Wister Comfort—"Uncle Billy" to loyal Haverfordians like me—watching them while he leaned on his cane. He looked very sad, and it made me sad to see him.

The quiet, idyllic life ended abruptly when I was called to active duty that June. Such are the ways of the Navy that, while I waited for the next Harvard Business School class to start, I was made commanding officer of the Brooklyn Navy Yard's Twentieth Street Pier. Who knows why. It was the first of many occasions—both in the Navy and out—when I would find myself in way over my head.

When I took my first look around at the Twentieth Street Pier, I didn't have any idea what was going on, or how it worked, or anything. Plus, this was a very tough part of Brooklyn, a place full of grizzled longshoremen who didn't necessarily appreciate college boys like me. So I was out of my element entirely. And it all looked like total chaos! Vehicles going every which way. Cargo seemingly dumped at random. Every kind of thing being unloaded there at the pier, from spare machine parts to crates of California oranges. Only gradually did I begin to see the method to this madness. All the freight came in by truck from various Navy suppliers to be stored by the longshoremen in different warehouses, and from there it was loaded onto boats and barges of every description—all of them bearing Navy insignia and painted battleship gray. Longshoremen had not come up in any of my economics classes, and this was over a decade before the movie *On the Waterfront* came out. But as a young Republican I was instinctively leery of such brass-knuckle unions.

But then I met Larry. He was a former longshoreman who now worked for the Navy as a civilian employee in charge of the pier. He was tall, lanky, frequently unshaven, and probably about forty-five, which made him over twice my age. Until I arrived, he'd been in charge of the place for years. To him I must have been about as green as they come. My uniform was fresh out of the box, and I was such a lightweight, he could have tossed me into the ocean if he'd wanted to. But he was a good sort. He recognized that this was a naval operation, so it wasn't unreasonable to have a naval officer in charge. And I sensed that, far from my union stereotype, he and the men working there were deeply patriotic and very proud to do their bit for the war effort.

Shortly after I arrived, Larry put a desk for me beside his own in his little office. And he was properly deferential, but not excessively so. He called me

Mr. Whitehead. I called him Larry. And he took me around the pier every day answering my many questions about what I was seeing. Once I got the hang of it, I went about on my own on a motor scooter, and I would check to make sure that nobody was accepting a bribe for a special parking place or anything like that, and that all the goods that came onto the pier were properly accounted for.

Since I respond to healthy competition myself, I tried to get a little friendly rivalry going between our pier and the other ones along the waterfront in order to induce a kind of pier pride. And that seemed to pay off. Whenever a higher-up came to inspect our operation, the men would do their best to show it off to its best advantage. I was always thinking up different ways to improve efficiency, and I came up with what I thought was an ingenious system of using pallets so that the freight would stack better in the warehouses. I sent my plan to the commanding officer of the entire Navy Yard, a man well up the ladder from me. I never heard anything back. No doubt commanding officers have a cylindrical file for such helpful suggestions. Still, things turned out well for me at the Twentieth Street Pier. By the time I left three months later, the pier won an award as the most efficient pier in all of South Brooklyn. I framed the certificate and hung it on the wall over Larry's desk. He wasn't one to say much about something like that, but I think he was pleased.

One of the highlights of those months on the pier for me was the opportunity to play on a Navy Yard softball team coached by Larry French, a former pitcher for the Brooklyn Dodgers. I was a passionate fan of their archrival, the New York Giants (and I still follow the team even though it's now in San Francisco), and I knew all about Larry. As a pitcher, he had a respectable lifetime ERA of 3.44, but a career batting average of only .021. It's amazing to me now that I kept track of such things. I played second base for the team — I was one of the few left-handed second basemen in all of baseball — and one day during fielding practice, Larry cracked a line drive between first and second, and I reached up to grab it with my bare hand — and broke my little finger. None of my teammates were sympathetic. They could not believe that my finger had been broken by a ball off the bat of a weak hitter like *Larry French*.

The ninety-day Harvard Business School portion of my naval training was a complete bore. It was basically a course in How to Fill Out Navy Forms, with the same teacher droning on and on eight hours a day for six weeks. It took tremendous willpower to keep from laying my head down on my desk and falling asleep.

Finally, the tedium ended and we all received our naval assignments. Some of us would be sent to various U.S. naval bases around the world; others, like me, were given sea duty. I was to report immediately to the U.S.S. *Thomas Jefferson*, then located in Oran, Algeria. I was to be the ship's disbursing officer and assistant supply officer, which meant that I'd handle all the cash and keep track of the flow of provisions and materiel on the ship.

Oran, I soon discovered, was a major port inside the straits of Gibraltar, in Algeria, about a hundred miles east of Morocco. To get there, my orders were to take a train to Staten Island and board a troop transport ship for the passage overseas. This would be my first introduction to the rigors and hazards of war. The troop transport carried three thousand soldiers, all of them bedding down below decks in densely packed bunks that were stacked five tiers high. There were so many men, we had to come to the deck in shifts to get a breath of fresh air because there wasn't room for everyone at one time.

It was October 1943, probably the height of the Nazis' domination of the Atlantic. Because their submarines could be anywhere, all ships attempting to cross the Atlantic traveled in convoys, escorted by Navy cruisers, destroyers, and other vessels. Ours was a closely packed square of fifty ships—a vast flotilla—in roughly seven rows of seven ships across. A convoy could only travel as fast as the slowest ship, and that left all of us moving at just eight knots. It took twenty-one days to make the entire passage.

The transatlantic passage was like the war itself—long stretches of nearly unendurable boredom interrupted by an occasional burst of terror that was made all the worse for the seeming calm that preceded it. To pass the time, men played endless rounds of dice games down in the hold, putting up hundreds of dollars at a throw. They were laying out money as if there was no tomorrow.

For too many of the men, there wouldn't be. Of the fifty ships that started out in our convoy, seven disappeared. Just disappeared. They were there when the sun went down, when all the ships were blacked out to conceal themselves from Nazi submarines. But they were gone when the sun came up in the morning. No announcement was ever made, but we could count. I asked around, and no one ever knew exactly what had happened. Presumably, they were torpedoed during the night and had either been sunk or been so damaged they had to be left behind. We didn't have any extra destroyer escorts to protect them. The abandoned ships were freighters, mostly, with maybe a dozen men each. No troop ships as far as I knew, which was a mercy.

Finally, we reached the Straits of Gibraltar. From there, some ships went on north up the Spanish coast to England; others, south to Casablanca and beyond. Ours passed through the straits to North Africa and plied the waters along the coast to Oran.

Oran was a port city that had been transformed by the war into a bustling staging area for supplies to be shipped across to Italy to support our troops fighting in the mountains. From a distance, Oran looked a bit like Florida to me, a state I knew mostly from posters. It had beautiful, long, sandy beaches, with palm trees rising up behind and swaying in the wind. Once I disembarked, I discovered that Oran was also hot and dry, and very poor. Houses were little more than shacks, and there were beggars everywhere. In this Muslim country, the women all wore veils and the men all had beards.

My orders, of course, were to join up with the U.S.S. *Thomas Jefferson*, which I did straightaway. I didn't have much trouble spotting it. It was a former luxury liner, its once-shining hull and bright trimming now dulled to a naval gray. The *T.J.*, as I learned to call her, before the war had sailed between California and Hawaii under the name of another far less distinguished president, James Garfield, for the American President Lines. Now, in Navy-speak, it was an APA, an auxiliary personnel assault vessel, capable of carrying two thousand Army and Marine troops for onshore invasions. On the deck, where rows of deck chairs had once been set out for tourists taking the sun en route to their Hawaiian vacations, there now stood about twenty LCVPs (for "landing craft, vehicle, personnel") — small, flat-bottomed, steel landing craft that were also called Higgins boats, after their ingenious American inventor in Louisiana. They were thirty-six feet in length, with a ramp in front, and designed to do one thing only: ferry troops ashore. They could

have carried a jeep or a small truck but I never saw them used for that. The
T.J. had already been battle-tested, having participated in the Allied landings
in Casablanca; Sicily; Salerno, near Naples; and Anzio, just south of Rome.
The T.J. would be my home for the next two years.

"Permission to come aboard, sir?" I called out very properly to the watch officer on the quarterdeck.

"Granted, ensign."

And I was on board. Hastily converted to wartime use, the T.J. still had
more than a few trappings from its previous life as a luxury liner. I found my
way down the ladders—as Navy men call stairs—to my stateroom, which was
small, but nicely fitted out with hardwood and brass. I shared it with a tough
twenty-five-year Navy veteran, Lieutenant Ed Carmody, who served as the
ship's engineering officer. We had bunk beds, and I, as the junior officer, was
given the less desirable upper bunk. For a homey touch, I put a picture of
Anne Burnett on the shelf beside my bed. She was the Bryn Mawr girl I
started to go with after Rusty Hendrickson; in fact, she'd been one of Rusty's
friends. I liked to think of her as my girlfriend, but she really wasn't. I'd written her a few letters from Brooklyn, but she'd never responded. Still, I liked
to think she might be waiting for me.

I was scarcely settled in before the ship's massive engines started to throb
and we were out into the Mediterranean again, bound for Naples with our
first load of troops and supplies to reinforce the men fighting in the mountains. That crossing was relatively uneventful, as were the others across the
Mediterranean that succeeded it. And I settled into a rather comfortable life
aboard ship. We ate our meals in the officers' wardroom at small tables for
four, set with heavy white tablecloths and napkins. The dishes were served by
stewards' mates, all of them black, wearing spotless, perfectly creased white
uniforms and white gloves. The wardroom was presided over by Commander
Ernest Kiefer, the ship's executive officer. He was a mustang (meaning an officer who'd come up through the ranks of the enlisted men), and he had the
naval equivalent of street smarts, but as a young college grad I was startled by
his lack of education. He used to regale us with tales of his Navy days, stories

that would invariably end, "Them were the halicorn days, boys. Them were the halicorn days." I think he meant "halcyon."

I had misgivings about the disparities in the treatment of the men on board. I didn't think it was fair that I got to eat so splendidly while the enlisted men who might be about to give their lives for their country were lining up for their food in the cafeteria-style mess hall. However, this was the Navy way and there wasn't anything I could do about it.

In addition to my other duties, I was in charge of the "Sixth Division," which included about a dozen storekeepers, cooks, and bakers, and some twenty-five black steward's mates. These men had been in the Navy longer than I, and most of them were older, many significantly so. This posed a real challenge of leadership. I'd known a few blacks before. Montclair High had been about a third black, but most of the "coloreds"—as we called them then—ended up in vocational courses such as typing and bookkeeping. In those days, shameful as it seems now, blacks routinely sat in the balcony of the movie theater, and all the whites down below on the main floor. And there were other inequities that you now associate only with the Deep South, but were much in evidence in Montclair. Blacks routinely sat in the back of the city buses, they usually drank out of black-only fountains, and they were expected to use black-only public toilets as well.

At the time, this seemed normal, and I was too young to think any differently. But in the Navy, possibly inspired by my nascent Quaker ideals, I began to think it unjust that blacks' contributions on the ship were limited to service as stewards' mates, waiting on white officers. And they lived in separate and inferior quarters in the most airless part of the hold. I wanted to do what I could to improve the situation. I worked closely with Chief Steward Young, a handsome black man who'd been in the Navy a full thirty years, and together we gave the blacks' living quarters a full inspection. The conditions were deplorable. Paint was peeling, the heat was stifling, the pipes leaked, and the shower heads were so clogged they produced just a dribble of lukewarm water. I immediately had the walls repainted, brought in some fans, fixed the plumbing, and installed new shower heads. That improved morale considerably.

I did make the mistake, though, of becoming too chummy with the men. On one occasion, I accompanied a few of the guys to a bar when we went on shore leave. That embarrassed us all, and seemed to undercut my authority. That taught me an important lesson in leadership: you need to maintain some distance between yourself and any group you're leading. If anything, too much friendliness hampers good, orderly, disciplined relations. Helpful actions count for far more. Those fans, for instance, improved my standing with the men far more than my sharing a drink with them.

My principal job on board the *T.J.* was to be the ship's disbursing officer (or purser) handing out the $1 million cash that the ship carried in its safe and for which I was personally responsible. To me that was an immense sum, and I learned to be very precise in keeping the books, always checking and rechecking my accounts. Since the largest denomination we had on board was a twenty, it also made for quite a stack of bills in the ship's safe, and I would dole out the men's pay mostly in fives and tens for them to spend on shore leave. Later, when I returned to New York City for a resupply of cash from the Federal Reserve Bank in lower Manhattan, I was outfitted with a special money bag manacled to my wrist, and I was driven about by Jeep. Anyone who tried to steal the bag would have had to saw my arm off.

In Oran, my fellow officers had leased a villa a few miles down the beach from the port to use when they were at liberty. It was a beautiful spot overlooking the Mediterranean, with a delicious sea breeze. The officers had acquired a prodigious supply of liquor, which we all freely drank while we sunned ourselves on the beach, swam, played endless games of backgammon, and told the usual lies that men everywhere, once they are far from home, tell each other to improve their standing. Mine, as I recall, seemed to involve an exaggerated accounting of my personal wealth, which, at the time, was less than one thousand dollars. Most of the others related sexual exploits. But I was always shy about such things. Them were my halicorn days.

5

THE RUN TO DOG RED BEACH

AFTER TWO MORE TRIPS FERRYING TROOPS to Naples, the *Thomas Jefferson* was ordered to Scotland. As usual in the Navy, no explanation was offered. But it was clear to all of us that we were preparing for the invasion of Europe that everyone knew was imminent.

It was January of '44 when we arrived at the wide inlet known as the Firth of Clyde, due west of Glasgow, and directly across from a little village called Greenock. Like all of Scotland in winter, the shore offered near-constant drizzle from slate-colored clouds and the kind of cold that penetrates as many layers of clothing as you can wear. At night, all of Britain went dark to throw off the German bombers, who were determined to break the Brits' spirit. Scotland was rarely a target, though. The Nazis reserved most of their firepower for their attempt to pound the English into submission. They failed, of course.

Our captain, a career naval officer named P. P. Welch, was a godlike figure on the ship. He didn't mingle with us mortals, nor did he waste many words on us. He dined alone in his cabin up on the bridge and often retreated there. But he controlled our fates as much as anyone by deciding what jobs to give us.

He was also the one to award us our liberty. When we dropped anchor in the Firth, he decreed that we'd be free to go ashore on a "one night on, one night off" basis. After all the dreary days at sea, that offered some appealing possibilities.

In one of those "small-world" coincidences, my table mate in the officers' wardroom hailed from none other than my native Montclair. Al MacIntyre was a lively red-headed fellow who was, by my standards, extremely worldly. We hadn't actually known each other in Montclair, and he'd gone on to Princeton. But we still had a lot in common, and we immediately fell in with each other. It was his job to scan the night skies through binoculars for incoming enemy warplanes, and then to identify the various types of bombers and fighters as friend or foe. His "battle station" was on the signal bridge, an open deck above the main bridge. I was assigned to be Al's assistant up there—not that he really needed one—and I quickly became pretty good at identifying the different silhouettes and markings myself. In truth, it wasn't very hard. If you can tell a Ford from a Chrysler, you can certainly learn to distinguish a Messerschmitt from a Spitfire. In the weeks leading up to the invasion, we had occasion to identify "friend or foe" only once, and that was when a Focke Wulf 190 came thundering down from the north while we were still lying at anchor. There were other APAs in the harbor, and we all fired furiously at the plane with the few anti-aircraft guns we had. Fortunately, we succeeded in bringing it down, smoke pouring from its engines just like in the movies, and then it plunged into the sea. We considered it our first kill and, following custom, painted a small German flag on the *T.J.*'s smokestack as a kind of trophy—although the other APAs deserved their share of the credit.

Al and I were assigned to alternating days of shore leave, and on my very first liberty, I considered myself extremely lucky to meet a charming Scottish lass named Nanette MacGregor at a newsstand in Greenock, where she worked behind the counter. She was very attractive, with her black hair and bright eyes, not to mention a very appealing figure. Nanette was just seventeen, and I a full twenty-two, but we fell into conversation there in the store and, to my delight, she invited me home for dinner that evening with her family.

The MacGregors had a small house, with a smoldering peat fire—an extremely inviting scene to someone who'd been out at sea for months. And they became a kind of surrogate family for me. I'd become a little homesick by this point. I depended on the regular letters from my mother, which usually included a brief P.S. from my dad. Mom was by far my most faithful correspondent. (We'd even worked out a code by which—in complete violation of military regulations—I could indicate my location through the initial letters of the first word in my opening sentences. "Oh, boy, do I ever miss you. Remembering home drives me crazy! Any chance you could send me some of your famous brownies? Never have I wanted them more." That would be my clue I was in Oran. The censors never caught on, and I sincerely hope the Germans didn't, either.)

I loved all of Nanette's family: her chatty parents and her two scrappy younger brothers. And of course I was quite taken by the green-eyed Nanette herself. It seemed that every other night I'd be hurrying off to dinner at the MacGregors, laden with oranges, raspberries, chocolates, and other hard-to-come-by delicacies that I'd purloined from the ship's larder. Mrs. MacGregor would happily add them to the meal she'd cooked up. After dinner, Nanette and I would go for a stroll or just sit together by the fire. We used to tell each other our plans for our lives. She dreamed of being a schoolteacher; I told her about returning to Haverford to work in admissions, which was still my dream at that point. I was beginning to think that my plans might include her.

After a while, I shyly confided to Al a few details of my nights in Greenock. In return, he regaled me with increasingly ribald tales of *his* nights on shore. Apparently, he'd met a Scottish girl, too. And his girl was absolutely insatiable. Al seemed extremely experienced in this area. But then, he was a *Princeton* man, with no aspirations to be a Quaker. Even so, he'd never seen anything like this girl. She wore him out! They spent their entire time in bed at some cheap hotel. He told me he was losing weight because they never got around to dinner.

One morning, Al was in a foul mood when he arrived in the wardroom for breakfast, and I asked him what was wrong. "That goddamn Nanette got so smashed last night, she passed out. I had to leave her in the hotel in order to get back to the ship on time."

An uneasy feeling came over me. "Wait—who?" I sputtered. "Who did you say?" In all of his stories, Al had never mentioned his girl's name before.

"Nanette."

My heart plunged. "*Nanette?*"

I thought I'd mentioned my own friend's name to him, but, if I had, it obviously had never registered.

"Yeah, Nanette. Why?"

I was nearly panicking now. This couldn't be. "Not Nanette *MacGregor*," I practically shouted.

"Yes, that's right." He seemed completely unconcerned. "Nanette MacGregor. Why—you know her?"

"*Know* her!" I exclaimed. "*She's the girl I've been seeing for weeks now!*"

Under the circumstances, his unconcern was almost maddening. He offered a few details about "his" Nanette MacGregor—details I could scarcely bear to hear. It was all too clear we were both speaking of the very same girl.

Al found this merely an amusing coincidence, but in all my life, I don't think I'd ever been quite so shocked. I'd been completely hoodwinked! Not only was Nanette not at all the nice, innocent girl I'd taken her to be, but she'd been two-timing me with my best friend! I felt doubly betrayed. And that wonderful home-away-from-home with her family, all the fruits and sweets I'd lavished on them, the wonderful meals we'd shared . . . It was all too painful to contemplate. I was absolutely sick with disappointment.

It was my turn for shore leave that night, and with a heavy heart I took the train into Glasgow. I couldn't bring myself to see Nanette that night, or ever again. And—at least as far as I know—Al never saw her again either.

Gradually, more ships began to gather in Loch Long there by the Firth of Clyde. It was clear that the date of the long-awaited invasion of Europe was fast approaching. It also became apparent that we might not be landing on a gently-inclining beach, either. For we received orders to "rent or otherwise acquire" twelve twenty-four-foot extension ladders from the Glasgow Fire Department. Clearly, a perilous ascent up some steep cliff was in the offing.

The ladders proved to be a tall order, pun not intended. When I dutifully went around to ask the Glasgow fire chief about giving me any "extra" ladders, he did not respond warmly. It took the intervention of the British Foreign Office to get him to see the light, but in due course, we stowed our bounty on the *T.J.* Later we were told to transfer the ladders to another ship.

Finally, toward the end of May, just when the gloomy Scottish weather was finally beginning to admit some heartening sunshine, we got our orders to proceed with all the other ships to Portsmouth on the south coast of England.

Just before we left, I received a call from the captain to see him in his cabin on the bridge. I felt as though I'd been summoned to appear before the Almighty. Captain Welch and I had never exchanged a single word the whole eight months I'd been aboard. He was sitting at his desk when I arrived, and gestured for me to take a seat in the chair beside him. I wasn't quite ready for such familiarity with such a god, and would much rather have stayed stiffly at attention. But I did as I was told.

The captain was not one for small talk. "I want to assign you to some extra duty," he declared.

"Yes, sir." I knew my naval manners.

"One of my boat officers has become ill. He'll have to leave the ship, and I'd like you to replace him for the next few weeks."

"Yes, sir."

"I've been watching you from the bridge, ensign," he added. "I've seen you driving the LCVP to and from the dock. You handle it pretty well." It was true: I'd been tooling around in one of the Higgins boats to gather supplies at the Navy base, or to swap goods with one of the other ships in the harbor. Even with the wind and the tide, I found that driving an LCVP wasn't particularly difficult—not much harder than driving a car. Plus, the ocean is a lot wider than the road, and offered many fewer obstacles. Still, I felt I'd received a compliment from God Himself.

"See to it, then," the captain concluded.

"Yes, sir."

And that was it. I would be in charge of one of the landing craft during the invasion of Normandy. It was an honor, but also a terrible risk, and a heavy responsibility. It would be my job to deliver twenty-five soldiers from the *T.J.* right onto the French shore. Danger had lurked about before, chiefly in the form of those Nazi submarines in the Atlantic, but this would be a risk of another order. I wouldn't be standing on the signal deck watching for Nazi warplanes nine miles offshore. Ferrying soldiers to the beach, there was sure to be furious enemy fire—machine guns, artillery, mortars, not to mention mines and sea barriers. Everything the Nazis could possibly throw at us. The seas could get rough, there might be severe weather, and darkness all around me. I doubted that Eisenhower would order such an assault in broad daylight. The thought of maneuvering an LCVP amid hundreds if not thousands of other craft in such conditions was daunting. Plus, I'd have only two weeks to practice. It wasn't until later that I discovered that I would be in charge of not just my own boat, but of a group of five boats that would be heading to shore together in the first wave of assault troops.

But I knew I couldn't say no and, in truth, I didn't want to. If the captain was asking me to, I would do it, damn the consequences. Yes, sir.

We sailed down the west coast of England and around Cornwall to Portsmouth, about seventy-five miles southwest of London. The ship was immediately put "under seal," meaning that without a special pass, no one could come on or off as we prepared for our part in Operation Overlord, as the massive, historic assault on Normandy was code-named. I pored over maps and did my best to memorize landmarks of the shoreline from reconnaissance photographs and even a few postcards that naval intelligence had collected. It was crucial that I be able to identify our assigned landing spot. With so many boats hitting the beach, each LCVP had to stick exactly to its target, or everyone would get in everyone else's way, and the whole invasion could be fouled up. Our landing site was a fifty-yard stretch of shoreline the operation planners dubbed Dog Red Beach near the little French town of Vierville. It fell near the middle of the sector called Omaha Beach, which in turn fell roughly in the middle of the entire assault. So I would definitely be in the thick of things. It wasn't clear how prepared the Germans would be for us. The high command spent a lot of time contemplating ways to throw them off with feints as far north as Norway, where the Germans had an array of fuel depots to protect, and Calais, which fell along the route to the Ruhr Valley, a key manufacturing center for the German arsenal. But we knew the Germans were well dug in all along the Normandy coast across from England, and we also knew that they recognized that if the Allies succeeded in gaining a foothold in Europe, the game might soon be up.

I spent a lot of time on the deck, too, going over every inch of an LCVP. It was a kind of floating boxcar, really—rectangular, with head-high walls, and, for a bow, an iron ramp that could be dropped down to let the soldiers storm out. I didn't want any surprises out there in the surf. I'd be delivering soldiers from the Army's 157th Infantry Battalion of the Twenty-ninth Infantry Division, under the ultimate command of General Omar Bradley. They had been training for this moment for nearly two years, and some of them would, for a few hours, be depending on me.

By June, Portsmouth harbor was jam-packed with ships, as was about every port city on the south coast of England. We tied up at the pier to make it easier to load the troops on board. On June 1, the Army troops came up the gangway, one by one. They were very disciplined, and very quiet. No one could be sure he would ever see England again.

Now—when to go? A storm whipped up, raising winds and bringing down a strong rain, but word came down on June 4 that we would leave that night. We cast off at about 8 P.M. and, in storm-tossed seas, set forth across the Channel for France. But after we had gone halfway across we were ordered to turn back because the weather was too fierce. That was brutal. To get all steeled for this furious assault, and then to just let it go . . .

The rain was still coming down the next morning, but the seas were somewhat calmer than before, and that afternoon, twenty-four hours after our first attempt, we again received orders to go, and this time it was the real thing.

As before, we left at about eight. The slower ships went first, and the fastest ones brought up the rear, so that we would all arrive at the landing area at roughly the same time. The *T.J.*, being neither particularly fast nor particularly slow, went in the middle. The skies were still dark, rain lashed the slickened deck, and the *T.J.* rolled as the seas surged all about. Fortunately, there was no sign of any enemy submarines, nor were there any air attacks. Despite the size of our armada, the Germans seemed to have no idea we were coming. We all tried to grab whatever sleep we could. Shortly after midnight we reached our destination nine miles off the French coast and dropped anchor, and were all roused for a big breakfast of eggs and bacon.

At two o'clock, deck crews began lowering the LCVPs over the side by crane, and the troops started to climb down wide nets to get aboard. The men had practiced this any number of times but, as Eisenhower always said, "In wartime, plans are only good until the moment you try to execute them." We hit our first snag right away. The flat-bottomed Higgins boats were pitching about so much in the choppy water that it was nearly impossible for the soldiers to get into them off the nets, especially now that they were all loaded down like mountaineers under a massive amount of gear. Not just rifles, but parts of Bangalore torpedoes, flame-throwers, a change of clothes, artillery parts, radio equipment, tarps, food, fresh water, even a carton of cigarettes, which were considered indispensable in those days. One poor soul slipped off the net, splashed into the water and sank like a stone. I will never forget the sight of him simply disappearing into the depths of the sea. But there was nothing anyone could do. We all just turned away shaking our heads.

This plan obviously wasn't working, so Captain Welch ordered a change in tactics: "Have the men board all remaining boats while the boats are still on the deck, and use the cranes to lower them fully loaded into the water."

We'd never practiced this method before. My LCVP was one of the first to try it, and I climbed in with the other men and did my best to hold on. There were no seats, of course. We merely stood there as if crammed into a jam-packed subway car and tried to keep upright as the crane lifted us off the deck. But, as it was swung over the side, the boat got snagged on the ship's rail, threatening to tip us all out sideways into the open water. That was very nearly the end, and we shouted in panic at the crane operators, but fortunately a heavy wave came along to roll the *T.J.* back the other way, freeing the boat from the snag, and we were lowered safely to the sea.

There were five LCVPs in our little group, each one with about twenty men jammed together like vertical sardines. I took up my position just behind the coxswain who would do the actual driving. As commander of the boat and sole navigator, I'd bend down to yell in his ear to work out which way to go. In my role as the leader for all five boats, I had a walkie-talkie to communicate with the other coxswains. But I had to really shout to be heard over the din of the engines and the sloshing sea. Once we were all well clear of the ship, I had all the boats circle about, like a cat chasing its tail, to make sure we were all together before we advanced toward the beach once more. We re-peated this procedure every mile or so—circling, then advancing, only to cir-cle again, all in accordance with the op-plan. Altogether, it took about four hours to cover the nine miles to the beach.

They were the worst hours of our lives. It was just about pitch-black and stormy, and the rain was coming down in sheets, drenching us. Worst of all, the boats were being tossed about by the waves, making all of us violently sea-sick. We'd all had that big breakfast to get us through what would surely be a long day, and hardly anyone could hold it down. Packed in like that, with the LCVP's high walls, we couldn't vomit over the side, either, and the wind would send the stuff everywhere. It was horrible. Pretty soon the cry went up, "For Chrissake, do it in your helmet!"

Around four, the dawn slowly broke in the east and a very pale light spread across the sea, and we could begin to see that we were in the midst of a vast armada, probably the greatest array of sea power ever gathered. There was every kind of boat: several destroyers, dozens of APAs like the *T.J.*, the smaller LCIs, which carried only infantry, the medium-sized LCMs, the tank-carry-ing LCTs, and many other ships from other countries, all in vast numbers.

Soon we began to hear the deep booms of the sixteen-inch shells from the monster battleships farther out to sea, which were shelling the beach to clear a path for the infantry. And, barely visible through the clouds, we could oc-casionally see the fat B-52s pushing through the sky overhead to drop para-troopers from the 82nd and 101st Airborne Divisions—truly courageous men—where they would land farther inland and secure key bridges and towns before the invasion troops arrived. It looked as though everything was going precisely as planned.

Appearances, however, were deceptive. Around 5 A.M., we were close enough to shore that I could begin to pick out our designated landmarks—some small beach houses, a spit of land, a slight rise to the bluff above the shore—and orient myself pretty well. In front of us we could see the faster, sleeker British boats trying desperately to stay afloat in the choppy water. As we watched, three of them flipped over and sank, drowning all the men. Later, I heard from one of my shipmates, Lieutenant Bill Steele, that he'd seen a British navigator go by in a different kind of boat around this time. He was standing up, and he called out to us in a very jaunty British accent, "I say, fellows, which way is it to Pointe de Hoc?" That was one of the landmarks. It was the toughest beach of all; we'd turned over our ladders to the ships unloading there. Bill yelled out to him that it was up to our right, just to the north of our own landing site. "Very good!" he cried out, and then went on by with a little wave of his hand. That was the last Steele had seen of him; I doubt he lived another hour.

The shore bombardment had by now begun in earnest, raising a furious din, like a Fourth of July celebration multiplied by a thousand, with each piece of fireworks seemingly exploding right in your face. It went on for a good half hour. Air Force bombers rained down bombs on the Nazi fortifications, the nearly impregnable concrete "pillboxes" from which the Germans could spray the beach with machine-gun fire and launch mortar shells. And Navy cruisers and destroyers were blasting away from behind us. It didn't seem as though the Nazi defenses could possibly withstand it.

By 6 A.M. we'd circled up at about eight hundred yards from shore, before our final run to the beach. All five of the boats in my little squadron had stayed together and were ready to go. The light had brightened enough that I could actually see the hands on my wristwatch, and I could communicate with the other boats by hand signals. At about twenty past, I waved them in with a hard chop of my arm. Go!

We roared ahead until about a hundred yards from shore, when a long string of heavy metal bars called Element C's, or "Czechs," for the country where they were made, angled up menacingly toward us out of the water. We'd been warned to look out for them. Early reconnaissance that morning by a group of courageous Navy SEALS from the *T.J.* —led by yet another townsman of mine, Bill Seidler—had not discovered them.

Our orders were to crash straight through to the beach, but I gave the signal to hold up, and it's lucky I did. For the Element C would almost certainly have hung us up, capsizing us all in the surf and creating a log jam of incoming boats.

I had all the LCVPs in my group make a sharp left and run parallel to the beach in search of an opening. We finally found one about a hundred yards down, and we turned toward the beach again. This brought us well to the south of where we were supposed to be, but there was nothing to do about it. Actually, it proved to be a lucky break, for German mortar shells soon blasted the shoreline at the spot where we were supposed to have landed.

When our LCVP finally beached in a foot or two of water, the impact was supposed to jar loose the landing ramps, releasing the soldiers. That worked for the other four boats, but the bolt holding up our ramp jammed, penning all the men in. I scrambled to the bow, found the pair of hammers that had been placed up there for just such an eventuality and, along with the bowman, started whaling away at the stuck bolt. We finally got it to drop the ramp and our soldiers lunged forth. Everyone managed to make it safely out of the boat, but a few of the men were hit with shrapnel from exploding mortar fire as they struggled through the knee-high water to get to the beach. Others made it to the shore, only to be hit as they crossed the beach. (If you've seen *Saving Private Ryan*, you know what it was like. The director, Steven Spielberg, relied on the memories of one of the sailors from the *T.J.* to reconstruct the scene. In the movie, one LCVP bears the marking "PA 30," as the boats from the *T.J.* were marked.)

Of all the attack forces, the troops at Omaha Beach took the worst of the enemy fire that day, and half the soldiers who landed from the *T.J.* were killed or wounded in the assault. It was a horrible sight, completely unreal. But I had to concentrate on just doing my job, and it was critical that we get all our boats out of the way of the next wave of LCVPs, which was due to land just a minute and a half behind us. They'd seen us veer left to avoid the Element C's, and were right on our tails. The bowman and I raised the front ramp again, and secured the bolts. Then we backed out, turned around, and speeded back to the *T.J.* I remember waving hello to the soldiers in the incoming boats as if we were on board a pair of launches on a pleasure cruise. How odd that such gestures of civility should persist even amid such horror.

Back at the *T.J.*, it was as if we had returned to the civilized world. I went down to my quarters for a piping hot shower. Then I settled myself into my customary table in the wardroom for a second breakfast, which was served, as usual, off white tablecloths by those stewards' mates. After the terrors of Dog Red Beach, it felt more than a little strange to be dining as if I were at the Ritz, and the war for the liberation of Europe, just an occasional quiet boom from a distant shore. I couldn't help but think of the men we'd landed, those that were still alive. Our job was nearly over, but theirs had just begun.

After breakfast I returned to my LCVP for a second and final run of the day to the beach. The seas were calmer now, and we were able to get the boats into the water and the soldiers into the boats according to the original plan. The second run went relatively smoothly, and we arrived slightly ahead of schedule. The German defenses of the beach had been broken by now, and the drop-off was considerably less perilous. Happily, the ramp worked well this time. An Army lieutenant needed some extra time to get ashore with a large machine gun. He had plenty of help, which left me a moment to myself. I stepped down the ramp into the shockingly cold water and splashed up onto the shore for a look around.

Dog Red Beach was virtually secure. The bodies of the many dead had been carried up onto a slight rise on the beach below the bluff, and medics had taken the wounded up there as well. The heavy rain had cleared off; it was barely drizzling now. What had been that morning a pell-mell dash to the dunes beyond the beach had turned now into a more methodical unloading of equipment and supplies, almost as if Omaha Beach had become just another staging area.

It wasn't entirely orderly, but it was far removed from the utter chaos it had been just hours earlier. Despite the many rough moments, the unexpected obstacles, and the frenzied German counterfire, the mission had achieved its objective, and we had indeed gained a foothold on the continent of Europe. We were beginning to push the Nazis back.

I felt thankful that I had survived the worst part. I took a few deep breaths and suddenly felt elated, proud to have played a part in what was maybe the biggest battle in history. At that moment, soaked to the skin, seasick, dead tired, cold, still scared, I would not have wanted to be anywhere else.

6

ALL HANDS ON DECK!

———

TWO MONTHS LATER, ON AUGUST 15, another European invasion was planned, this one in southern France, near Marseilles, and the *Thomas Jefferson* was ordered back to Oran to prepare. That invasion is little remembered today, and it proved to be an anticlimax after D-Day, since the Axis offered no resistance whatsoever. The beaches were empty when the landing troops arrived, and there were no gun emplacements lurking inland. Still, Eisenhower left nothing to chance, and we prepared for the landing as if our troops would have to fight their way ashore once again. The *T.J.* transported French troops this time. And they showed a certain Gallic flair, however unsoldierly, as each infantryman carried several bottles of wine in his knapsack for the assault.

Still, I thought it was sad that the French had not exerted themselves to be more involved in the emancipation of their own country. Not a single French soldier had landed at Normandy. The conventional argument is that it might have overtaxed the command structure to include another ally along with the American, British, and Canadian forces, but still, it seems surprising to me that the French largely left to others the job of reclaiming their native soil. It was somehow all too typical that the French troops were still off in the South of France when the Allied troops marched in to liberate Paris.

While the French troops continued inland, the *T.J.* docked once more in Naples, where we'd been several times in my earlier Mediterranean duty. This time we came under attack from a lone Italian plane. The anti-aircraft guns of the various APAs moored with us knocked it out of the sky and we, for our part, added a small Italian flag to our smokestack, bringing our kill total to two.

With no more invasions planned for Europe, the *Thomas Jefferson* was shifted to the Pacific theater of the war. We left Oran and passed through the straits of Gibraltar one last time to make our way west. At first, life at sea seemed a pleasant respite from all the rigors of war, but it turned painfully boring soon enough. With a crew of five hundred and fifty officers, there simply was not enough work to go around. There were seven doctors on board in anticipation of the *T.J.*'s possibly becoming a hospital ship, and they busied themselves performing optional circumcisions; the ship's two dentists provided cosmetic dentistry, mostly capping teeth. The enlisted men engaged in some furious dice and card games and, in the wardroom above, the officers battled on the backgammon board.

As for me, I continued on as the disbursing officer. After Normandy, I had been promoted to the rank of lieutenant junior grade, but this had nothing to do with any military accomplishments on my part. Virtually everyone in my cohort of inductees received a similar promotion after that period of service. And it had no effect on my naval duties. To keep my mind occupied, I must have read every book in the ship's library. The officers rotated nighttime watch duty—four hours on and eight hours off—and, starved for conversation, we engaged in endless discussions of which hours were best.

I performed my watch from the communications office up on the bridge with another young officer, Ed Kellogg. He was prone to seasickness and a waste basket always needed to be kept handy. We two had been given the job of decoding incoming messages. A constant stream of them came through to the shortwave radio operator, all of them encrypted in an endless series of capital letters—AXFZPGQRBTS . . . Primitive computers applied the day's code-breaking key, and Ed and I plucked out the communications that were meant for our ship. The messages covered everything from broad fleet movements to congratulations from President Roosevelt to notice of individual promotions. The volume of information pouring forth from that radio made me realize the immense importance of communications in the maintenance of large organizations in wartime—or any other time, for that matter.

On our way home, we stopped in Bermuda to drop off our absentee ballots for the presidential election in November. President Roosevelt was running for a fourth term against a relative unknown, Senator Robert Taft, who'd been a staunch isolationist in the years before Pearl Harbor. I had turned twenty-two in April 1944, and this was my first chance to vote; I was not about to throw over our commander in chief for an isolationist, so I cast my ballot for Roosevelt. (In the next presidential election, I reverted to my familial Republicanism.)

After Bermuda, we berthed temporarily in the Norfolk Navy Yard in Virginia to have a more powerful gun installed on deck. We'd managed to fend off those two warplanes that swooped down on us in Europe, but in the main we'd faced little hostile fire there. In the Pacific, we were likely to come under attack not only from Japanese destroyers and submarines, but also from the kamikaze pilots who were beginning to terrorize the American ships in the region. Even after the upgrade, however, we still had little firepower: a single 5-inch gun on the fantail, four relatively feeble Bofer twin 40s, and maybe twenty 50-caliber machine guns, whose firepower wouldn't put a dent in a Japanese warship and would down a kamikaze only if the plane's fuel line were struck or we managed to kill the pilot himself.

Thus rearmed, we sailed south and west again, this time headed for the Solomon Islands of the South Pacific. We rounded Florida, crossed the Caribbean, and then passed through the Panama Canal. That was impressive: A series of water-filled locks could lift a vast ship like the *T.J.* up nearly a hundred feet to cross that mile-wide strip of land. Besides being a marvelous piece of engineering, it was (and is) also a critical element of geopolitics as it provided a shortcut between the Atlantic and the Pacific, sparing American ships a thousand-mile trip around South America. We would have been greatly hampered in the Battle of the Pacific without it. (That's why, much later, I did not approve of President Carter's handing over control of such a key passageway to the Panamanians.)

After Panama, our last view of land before the long haul to the Pacific islands came in the Galapagos Islands. To many, the Galapagos might be famous for Darwin's visit on the H.M.S. *Beagle* in the nineteenth century. But, in a rare utterance, our esteemed Captain Welch came over the PA system to give the Navy perspective. "We are now passing the Galapagos Islands," he declared as we stared out at the broad, low expanse of land off our starboard bow. "Famous for their turtles and for their beautiful women." I knew about the enormous Galapagos turtles; I wish I'd had a chance to confirm the part about the women.

After that, we saw the sea, as the Irving Berlin song goes, and nothing *but* the sea for days on end. It was utterly boring. At night I amused myself by staring at the phosphorescent spray that spumed up off the bow as the ship broke through the waves. Otherwise, I tried to stay busy deciphering messages and, in the evening, scanning the skies for any enemy planes. But there was little incoming news, and the skies were empty until we reached the naval base of Noumea, in New Caledonia. Beyond us to the east, the Solomon Islands on the easternmost fringe of the sprawling Indonesian archipelago had finally been secured after some furious fighting. The Japanese had been even more fiercely determined to hold their ground than the Germans, and they were more deeply dug in, besides. The Allies would advance west island by island if necessary, until they could undertake the final assault on the island of Japan itself.

It didn't help our confidence to have a new commander come on board in Noumea, to replace our beloved Captain Welch. The new man was Captain Joe Barbaro. He'd graduated from the U.S. Naval Academy but, even at that point late in the war, he'd had no previous experience at sea at all. His naval assignments to date had been entirely on land: naval attaché at a variety of embassies in Latin America, alternating with duty as a Spanish instructor at the Naval Academy. Why he had been selected to take over the *T.J.*, no one could imagine.

Worse, he tried to make up for his inexperience with a hollow bravado. Practically as soon as he came aboard, he insisted on personally "taking the con"—controls—to direct the ship's coxswain at the helm in a docking exercise. It was all too apparent that Captain Barbaro had never docked a ship before, not even a dinghy, because he failed to understand which way to turn the wheel when reversing. He had the poor coxswain completely confused, and before long he had the ship going in circles as we all rolled our eyes. Not a good start. We were convinced he posed a greater danger to us than the Japanese did.

Having moved on from my temporary duties as a small-boat officer, I watched the brutal assaults on Iwo Jima and Okinawa from the relative safety of the *T.J.*'s signal deck several miles offshore. At Iwo Jima, we transported a portion of the Fourth Marine Division, and at Okinawa, a portion of the First. The men in both of these units were remarkably battle-hardened—grim-faced veterans who knew too well what they were in for.

It was a frightening time for everyone. I'd had much more confidence going against the Germans than I did against the Japanese. It seemed to me that two of the most powerful nations on earth were locked in a death grip as they grappled for control of a pair of tiny islands halfway between Tokyo and the Mariana Islands. Both were of great strategic significance, though. Iwo Jima might have been a scant eight miles across, but it possessed an airfield that the Allies desperately needed as a base for the fighter planes that would be escorting B-29 bombers on any raids they hoped to make on Tokyo. The Marine Corps commander in the Pacific, General Holland M. ("Howling Mad") Smith, called the fight for Iwo Jima the most savage and costly battle in the history of the Marine Corps, and I believe it.

For us, there was a lot to contend with from the air. As the Allies closed in on the mother country, hundreds of Japanese pilots were willing to sacrifice themselves by trying to fly bomb-laden planes onto the decks of the invading fleet. They'd come in at sunset, very low in the sky so that their planes would disappear into the blaze of the setting sun while we were busy unloading supplies. Most of the time, the destroyers and destroyer escorts could knock the kamikaze planes down before they got too close. Occasionally, though, a few would get through, and of all the threats I faced during my two years of service in World War II, this was the most frightening.

For all of us, fear was our constant companion. Sometimes it was close by, sometimes it was further away, but it was always there somewhere. Aboard a ship in wartime, there were so many perils: the torpedoes of enemy submarines, fierce storms, a collision with another ship, bombs, kamikazes. Obviously, the fear peaked during invasions, when we drew near the enemy.

There would be an outbreak of anxious letters home, a sleepless tossing-about of bunkmates, a flare-up of tempers. I found I was able to put aside most of my fears by staying busy. The work distracted me during the day, and fatigue helped me sleep at night. So I didn't suffer too much from an awareness of the basic, low-level risk that hung about our lives.

Sudden full-scale attacks were another story. One night, I was sound asleep in my bunk when I was awakened by the bosun's shrill whistle, and then heard the call from the quartermaster echoing from loudspeakers throughout the ship: "General quarters! General quarters! All hands on deck! All hands on deck!" That got my pulse up, and I scrambled out of bed, pulled on my clothes, grabbed my lifejacket and helmet, and clambered up the five ladders to my station on the signal deck on the bridge at the very top of the ship. As I climbed, I could hear the bursts of machine-gun's fire and the deafening boom of artillery shells. I'd never heard such a din aboard ship before. It sounded like every gun on our ship, every gun in our whole fleet, was desperately blazing away, filling the night with explosions.

What was happening? What were they shooting at? Kamikazes? Were they attacking us?

I reached the iron hatch at the top of the very last ladder, all that stood between me and the dangers on deck. And I stopped there, my hand on the hatch's cold handle. For a moment, I could not make myself push that hatch open.

I was wondering: Did I really need to go out there, to expose myself to the possibility of being hit by a kamikaze slamming into the deck? Could my presence there on the bridge really improve the situation? After all, I would be there only as a backup, ready to man a phone from the bridge to a gunner if someone got hurt. I'd simply be an extra. If I didn't show, I wouldn't be missed. And why risk dying for that?

All these questions ran quickly through my mind as I squatted there, my hand on the hatch door. Where did my duty lie? Was it to perform my mission—or to keep myself alive? To return home, start a career, raise a family, live my life?

Put like that, the answer was clear. I pushed the hatch open and climbed on through.

All I could see was tracer bullets zipping everywhere, and hundreds of flares bursting overhead. At least fifty of our ships were there lying at anchor, and all were putting up a barrage of defensive fire to fend off the kamikazes that were bearing down on us just as I'd feared.

I stepped out onto the signal bridge. Judging by the anti-aircraft fire that was blasting away from our own ship, I could sense that at least one of the kamikazes was getting close. Sure enough, with a roar, one of the planes came down towards us at a steep angle and then roared by over my head, barely clearing the bridge where I stood and then slamming into the ocean no more than fifty feet from us. That felt almost personal.

A dozen more kamikazes hit the sea farther off. But two struck a pair of smaller LSTs, causing them to explode into flames, and another APA was hit, with less damage.

Finally, the guns went silent again, and the attack was over. I unclenched the railing I'd gripped for the onslaught. All my muscles were so tight they hurt. I'd done my duty, but I sure was glad it was over.

In the morning, we added a small Japanese flag to our smokestack. Soon, we added another, but this was one we weren't proud of. By an awful mistake, we brought down an American fighter that came in low towards us. It had approached so fast, and come in head-on, that we couldn't identify it. To be safe, our gunners fired on it. We tried to assure ourselves that the plane had already been crippled by enemy gunfire, or it wouldn't have come so close. But no one could be certain of that.

As soon as we finished unloading troops at Okinawa, we were ordered back to Pearl Harbor. No reason was given, but orders were orders. Clearly, there wasn't much more to do in the waters off Japan. With Okinawa about to be under our control, we'd taken all the islands we needed before we closed in on Japan itself. They couldn't spare us an escort, so we took off on our own.

The trip to Pearl Harbor was a little too exciting. A few days out into the open sea, we ran into a great, swirling corkscrew of wind—a typhoon—that twisted the ship about for a couple of days. We had to stay belowdecks to keep from being swept overboard by the gale, but fortunately, little damage was done.

Shortly afterward, we found ourselves in a mess of our own making when the *T.J.* ended up smack in the path of a vast assemblage of American warships, fifty altogether. It was the famous Task Force Fifty-eight, the best fighting ships in the American Navy, which roamed the Pacific at very high speeds searching for stray Japanese targets. We were heading east all by ourselves. They were heading west, fifty-strong. We were receiving radio messages, first encoded, but then in urgent English, to *get out of the way*. These we were ignoring, for Captain Barbaro had once again taken the con. What a horror. He had simply frozen when he realized the situation. Unable to get out of the way, he had absolutely no idea what to do next. Saying with a voice of resignation, "Shea, take over," he finally handed the wheel over to a nervous young ensign named Paul Shea and, his heels clicking, removed himself from the bridge. With a few simple orders, Shea maneuvered our APA out of harm's way while the noble captain remained alone in his cabin, the door shut behind him.

I spent most of my time decoding incoming messages, and so I was the first one on board to learn that Lieutenant Whitehead—after Okinawa I had received another promotion—would be released to shore duty upon our arrival at Pearl Harbor.

When I finally descended the gangway at Honolulu and the young ensign relieving me came aboard, I was immensely relieved to have come through the war alive and unharmed. I also felt a great weight of sorrow to have concluded the most meaningful work I'd ever done up to that point—in fact, expected ever to do. And there was sadness to think of all the fine men lost in the tragic struggle. But I was enormously proud to have served my country in its time of need, to have done my duty, and to have contributed, albeit in a very small way, to the final victory that was, then, just a few months away.

From Honolulu, the Navy transported me to Portland, Oregon, and then flew me back to New York on a United Airlines DC-3, one of those fat propeller planes that were, in fact, the fastest of the commercial aircraft. This was the first time I'd ever flown. It took twenty-one hours, and we made five stops to refuel along the way, but we made it.

Ever since those two years, I have felt an instant loyalty to any man who served in either theater of that war—a bond of understanding and of shared pride. Haverford had done a lot to develop my confidence in my abilities, but the war gave me something more profound—a strong sense of patriotism. How good it felt to have been part of a great joint effort to fight for the things that we believed in. When Tom Brokaw many years later declared us to be the Greatest Generation, I had to agree with him.

7

A Pair of Big Decisions

—◦◦◦—

I wasn't out of the Navy yet, but I was out of the war. For my final year of military service, I was sent to the Harvard Business School to teach the same course for supply officers that I had taken two years before. I'd dubbed it "How to Fill Out Navy Forms," and that was still the subject matter, alas. Few topics could have been duller. Even though World War II officially ended that September when the Japanese surrendered aboard the U.S.S. *Missouri*, the Navy still needed more supply officers to restock the fleet after all the losses suffered during the war, and to replace those of us who were being released from duty.

The Navy had taken over the Business School for the war effort, and it still maintained programs at the school after V-J—Victory in Japan—Day. To make room for all the classes for naval personnel, the Navy had erected several temporary buildings on the Business School campus, across the Charles River from Cambridge, in Allston. They weren't much to look at, but at least they were new. I was one of six staff assigned to teach part of the program. Like the other teachers, I had exactly a hundred students. In my classroom, the students' desks ran ten across and ten deep—a perfect square, rather like the convoy that had escorted me across the Atlantic to the *T.J.* As with that other convoy, the pace was excruciating, the whole experience seemingly designed for maximum boredom. But at least there was no threat of torpedoes.

The course went six hours a day, five days a week, for two months with just me up there for the students to listen to and stare at. At this point, I bore two

impressive stripes on the shoulders of my uniform as a senior-grade lieutenant, and I had two bright rows of battle ribbons and four battle stars on my
chest for the times I had been under fire.

That may have added a bit to my authority, but I sensed early that I needed
to be tough if I was going to keep control of the class. The least bit of whispering in the back rows, and I'd send the offenders out into the hallway. But
I tried to provide at least some entertainment. I told the class some of my sea
stories and the occasional off-color tale. I regaled them with the story of my
romance with Nanette MacGregor. That was a big hit, although I did worry
that I may have come off as the sap in that little tragicomedy. Maybe this was
my hammy, carnival-barker self rising to the fore. But teaching is a performing art, and a teacher has to be more than a bit of an actor to be successful.

Still, my essential job was to get the material out of the textbooks and into
the heads of these hundred young men, and I was determined to find the best
possible way to do that. I could tell that formal lecturing wouldn't cut it. That
induced little beyond sleep in my naval charges, just as such lectures had in
me back when I'd had to sit through them. So I tried a version of the Socratic
method: Instead of my doling out information from the textbook to them, I
got them to tell it to me.

I'd fire questions at the class. "So, with what office do you file form seven-
teen-B?" I'd ask, then pause dramatically before turning to my first victim.
"Mr. Jones?" If Mr. Jones stumbled, I'd move right on to Mr. Smith, hoping
that Mr. Jones's humiliation would spur him on to a better effort next time.

I moved out from behind the podium, too, to roam up and down the aisles.
That raised the class's attention level in a hurry. Students craned their necks
to see where the next question was coming from, and a hundred pairs of eyes
followed me as I roved about the room. Later, I discovered that this was the
way most of the genuine B-school professors operated. It had just made common sense to me.

Once again, I used my own innate competitiveness to try to engage theirs.
What else is there to do, I always figured, but try to be the best? I was bent on
having my students' marks on the Navy's standard final exams be the highest
of all the six classes', and I took satisfaction in finding out that, with the exception of the first cycle, they were.

That teaching experience was instructive for me as well. I discovered that you don't really know the material until you try to help someone else understand it. The process helps you summarize, clarify, and organize your own thoughts. Even now, when people ask me for career advice, I sometimes tell them to take on a teaching job for a little while. It really helps develop your thinking.

I also received important advice from one of the Business School professors I came to know, Sterling Livingston, a terrific teacher who, unlike most of the other professors, did lucrative work outside the school as a corporate consultant in exotic places like New York City. I met him in the business school faculty club's plush dining room overlooking the Charles, where I was allowed entrance as a temporary professor. Most of the faculty regarded me as a "mere" naval officer and gave me a wide berth, but a few professors struck up conversations with me. Livingston was one of them, and one day at lunch, he asked me whether I'd thought about my career plans.

I told him of my commitment to return to Haverford.

He furled his eyebrows. "Do you really think you'd be happy in academe?"

That set me back. At that point, I'd been counting on returning. "Why do you ask?"

"It's just that teaching can be very frustrating, you know." He sighed. "Even the best teacher can affect the world only indirectly—through the students he's able to inspire." He looked at me out of the corner of his eyes. "And you can't expect too many of *them*." He sighed again, obviously disgruntled. "No, if I had it to do all over again, I would never have gotten into this."

That shocked me. I regarded Professor Livingston as about the best that Harvard had to offer. And if he didn't enjoy the academic setting, how could I? That got me to raise my sights a little higher—and to seriously reconsider the commitment I'd made to Arch MacIntosh. Maybe Haverford wouldn't be enough for me after all.

The more I thought about it, the more I knew he was right. And that's when I went down to see Mac and tell him I was sorry, but I'd changed my mind.

When my year of teaching was over and I was discharged from the Navy, I followed another piece of Professor Livingston's advice and applied to the Business School as a full-time student. Since I had virtually been a professor there the previous year, I expected that admission would be a formality. But Harvard's was the country's premier business school, by an even larger margin than it is today, and any number of bright young men wanted to jump-start a business career with the Harvard imprimatur. I took it as an honor when I received notice that I had indeed been accepted for the following fall.

Still, it was a comedown in at least one way. I had to move from my rather august faculty quarters into a dingy and crowded student dorm. And I also lost my privileges at the faculty club as I shifted from being a crown prince on campus to being just another serf.

Those two years at the business school were tough academically, though. My classmates weren't just smart. They were also some of the most ambitious and hard-working people I'd ever met. Many of them had, like me, come out of the military, and they were eager to make up for lost time by barreling out of Harvard Business School with straight A's. While everybody else worked hard on their cases—teaching at the B-school was done by studying specific concrete business situations, or cases—I was a bit lackadaisical, at least at first. I felt things would be easier for me, having been a member of the faculty. If so, my old friend Professor Livingston cleared that up in a hurry. I took his first-year Business Policy class, and he gave me a "low pass" (only one notch above "fail") on my first paper. I felt terribly ashamed, and that motivated me.

Still, I had my troubles. It wasn't that the curriculum was difficult, it was that the approach to it was so new. At Haverford, studying and doing well were largely a matter of absorbing the material from the textbook and from lectures, and then reproducing it on tests and exams. But Harvard Business School was much more free-wheeling. The case-study method—still used— required a kind of adaptive thinking that required much more creativity than the rote learning of college. Each business problem had to be considered afresh and on its own unique terms. XYZ Corporation is losing market share to ABC Corporation on its key product line, and its overall costs are rising. What would you do? Fortunately, I was able to call upon some of the real-time analytical skills that I'd had to develop in the Navy. Once I buckled down, I did well, and ended up graduating with distinction, which put me in the top tenth of my class. I was not an elite Baker Scholar, I'm sorry to say; for that distinction I would have had to finish in the top five percent.

By then, I'd also started to date. I'd seen a bit of Connie Dey on shore leave from the Navy, but that never developed into anything serious. And I'd had several dates with a stylish Bryn Mawr grad named Kate Rand, who went on to become a longtime editor of *Vogue*. She was a marvelous young woman, and I'd been a little sorry I never followed up on that. And just months before I left Haverford, I'd met a lovely southern girl named Anne Burnett, whose father was a judge in Louisville. Her picture graced my bureau on the *T.J.*, and I dreamed of postwar romance. We were both poor correspondents, though, and without telling me, she went off and married a man named von Ass. (The last word was correctly pronounced Ahs," but I ignored that little fact when I reported the name to friends.)

And then I met Sandy. Properly, she was Helene Shannon, but her father was named Alexander and somewhere along the line people started to call her Sandy. She was a senior at Wellesley when I met her on a blind date. In fact, it was my first real date since Nanette. I'd been introduced to Sandy by another Harvard Navy instructor who was going with another Wellesley girl. Sandy was smart, energetic, popular, and good-looking, and I was immediately captivated. Like me, she was an economics major, and I admired the practicality of that. By then, I'd become a fairly impatient person, eager to get a wide variety of things done quickly and well. And she was like that, too.

I also liked her parents—shades of Nanette. Sandy's mother was a good cook, and I delighted in going to their house in Newton, just down the road from Cambridge, for a home-cooked meal with the Shannons. Since I didn't have a car, her mother would drive me back to school afterwards. Sandy's father was a telegrapher for Western Union, and he handled the Red Sox games, cabling the sportswriters' accounts back to their papers. Even though I was a committed Giants fan, I found that watching baseball games for a living seemed to be a very glamorous job.

We were married in June after I had completed my first semester at the Business School and Sandy had graduated from Wellesley. The wedding ceremony was at Trinity Church, the glorious Episcopal edifice in Boston's Copley Square, with several hundred people in attendance. We took the train down to New York afterwards and spent the first night of our marriage at the Waldorf, and then honeymooned for a week at Skytop Lodge, a beautiful resort hotel in the Poconos. We found a small third-floor apartment in a big old Victorian house in Newton Centre, not far from Sandy's parents' house, and I returned for the summer semester of the accelerated business degree program. Sandy put her economics degree directly to use in a job as a dividend clerk at John Hancock Mutual Life Insurance Company downtown. Along with generous help from the GI bill, Sandy kept us afloat financially while I got my M.B.A.

As I began my final semester the following fall, I started to think about careers now that Haverford was out of the picture. In business school, I'd concentrated mostly on finance and accounting, largely because those were the areas I'd handled in the Navy. I thought I'd ultimately end up in the treasurer's office of a manufacturing company like DuPont or General Electric. That might sound stodgy, but I thought it would be secure, and security was a prime consideration for a child of the Depression. I didn't expect to land such a plum position right away, and I imagined that a little Wall Street experience would help. At the time, investment banking had almost none of the glitz that it has today. It was a small, little-known, and rather genteel segment of a financial industry that was almost completely dominated by a handful of old-line, privately-owned firms. I didn't think I'd stick in it very long.

Goldman Sachs was the only Wall Street firm that came up that year to interview HBS graduates for a position in the company. It had hired one graduate the year before, but only one. I didn't rate my chances of being selected this year as very high, but I figured it was worth a shot. Along with about twenty others, I signed up for an interview. I honestly don't know why Goldman picked me as one of only four to bring down to New York for a day of interviews. Was it my grades? My Navy career? Such were the secretive ways of Goldman Sachs that no one ever told me. And I was extremely apprehensive when I took the train down to New York. After meeting with the two partners in charge of investment banking at the firm, I sat down with the top brass, a rather imposing group of older men who seemed very worldly to a business neophyte like me. For much of the afternoon, they peppered me with questions that often left me tongue-tied. But I must have handled myself adequately because a few days later, I received word that I had been accepted for employment at Goldman Sachs & Co.

As it turned out, I was the one person added to the firm's investment banking division that year. In later years, they sometimes added over a hundred at a time.

By this time, I had also received an offer from a flamboyant New York lawyer named David Milton, who'd been married for a time to David Rockefeller's sister Abby. They'd divorced a few years before, but Milton retained some of that Rockefeller luster. Well established as a lawyer and financier, he was trying to build a kind of holding company for a variety of corporations he planned to acquire. Milton asked me to be his personal assistant, an enticing opportunity for a twenty-five-year-old, as he must have known. Unsure what to do, I turned for advice to a man named Grant Keene who'd worked for both Milton and Goldman Sachs. He told me it would be safer to go with Goldman Sachs, and I did. This proved to be a wise choice, because nothing much came of Milton's dream of becoming a corporate titan.

Goldman Sachs paid me a starting salary of $3,600. Not a month, or a week, as later graduates would come to expect, but a year. A few Business School classmates pulled in better pay, but $3,600 was a fantastic sum to me. Sandy and I closed up our Newton apartment, and she said a tearful goodbye to her parents, whom I would miss also. We moved to a smaller apartment in the tiny New Jersey town of Great Notch, not far from Montclair. Sandy would be moving into the realm of *my* parents now. Fortunately, she got on well with them, especially with my mother, who was quick to welcome a daughter-in-law into the family. My sister had long since left home. A graduate of Hood College in Maryland, she'd gone to work as a scientific researcher for the William R. Warner Company in New Jersey. It later became part of Warner-Lambert.

Though small, the apartment was brand-new, one of the many residences that were sprouting up all over the country to house returning servicemen. The rent was steep, though. At $135 a month, it was nearly half my salary. Sandy secured a job with the head of the chamber of commerce in nearby Montclair. But it would still require some careful budgeting to cover such a sum. Together, we started in on a new life.

8

A Desk in the Squash Court

‒‒‒‒‒‒

WHEN I JOINED GOLDMAN SACHS in October, 1947, the firm was located at 30 Pine Street, just off Wall Street, in a tall, narrow, twenty-one-story building that was squeezed between a much higher office tower and a tavern. "Goldman, Sachs & Co." was printed in large gold letters at the entrance, but the firm didn't actually own the building; it rented only eight floors, four on the bottom, and four at the top.

The ground floor looked like a regular bank, with teller windows and a line of customers, but no cash was being dispensed, only receipts for the commercial paper that was the firm's principal stock in trade. One flight up was the trading floor, dealing in bonds mostly. The floor above that was for "operations," where a bevy of accountants and clerks kept track of all the transactions. The partners' plush, mahogany-paneled offices were way up on the seventeenth floor, a hushed, rather majestic place that I found intimidating. The twentieth floor was for the investment banking staff, whose ranks I would be joining. The very top floor had been a solarium in the heady days of the twenties, but had since been converted to a private dining room for the partners and their guests.

That first day, I was taken up to the twentieth floor and delivered to my desk. It was in the firm's former squash court. The squash markings had long since been removed, but the original purpose of the space was all too apparent. It was a bare cube, as high as it was wide, which wasn't very. And I would not be alone in it. When I arrived, there were already six other men working away at metal desks along the walls. A seventh desk had been squeezed in for me. The other six gentlemen weren't terribly happy to see me, but we got along reasonably well once I was settled in.

The room was ventilated only by a tiny porthole very high up one wall; it was opened and shut by a long pole with a hook at one end. Without any heating vents (that we could find, anyway) and certainly no air conditioning, the place had its Dickensian aspects—nippy in the winter and broiling in the summer. All the same, we were expected to keep our suit jackets on year-round. Woolen ones, actually, since that was the fashion. That was the Goldman Sachs way.

I complied for most of that first year, but when I started to roast in mid-summer, I bought myself a light-weight cotton seersucker suit that I thought very handsome. The next morning I felt quite snappy as I passed through the Goldman Sachs entrance's revolving door, and then boarded the elevator. Before the doors could close, though, Walter Sachs entered just behind me. The grandson of the cofounder, he was one of the great eminences at the firm. Short, stocky, with a distinguished white beard, he inspired a certain awe, if not dread, and I started to feel awkward as he surveyed me.

"Young man, do you work at Goldman Sachs?" he asked me in a withering tone.

"Yes sir, I do," I proudly replied.

He scowled. "In that case, I would suggest that you go home right now and change out of your pajamas."

Utterly crestfallen, I exited the elevator and meekly did as I was told.

Looking back at it, I probably should have said something in return. Nothing impertinent, but simply factual like "But it's hot as blazes up there, sir." After all, I'd seen something of the world by then. I'd had men under my own command, taught at the Harvard Business School. But I was grateful for a paying job, let alone one at such a distinguished firm as Goldman Sachs. So I was inclined to be humble.

Nevertheless, the sting of being so upbraided stayed with me. An entire year passed before I could bear to bring my lovely seersucker suit out of the closet again, and that was only to wear around town on my days off. I never did wear it again to the offices of Goldman Sachs.

The truth was, there was an unusually broad gap in the ages of the employees of the firm, and that was bound to lead to some collisions in manners. Because of the Depression and the war, Goldman Sachs had hired virtually no one for nearly twenty years, leaving a gap between the overlords of the firm and their underlings. Though this led to occasional misunderstandings over small matters like my seersucker suit, it also provided an opening for a young man like myself trying to make his way up the firm. Indeed, almost everyone hired out of business school for the first few years after the war became a partner in due course, in part because there was little competition.

Although at that point, Goldman Sachs had been in business for nearly eighty years, it was still a small place, with control concentrated in the hands of just five partners. When I retired thirty-seven years later, there were about eighty, and now there are over two hundred fifty. It was essentially a family firm, just as it had always been, and one whose atmosphere and attitudes still reflected its Old World origins. There were oil portraits of all the early partners there on the partners' floor. The company's founder, Marcus Goldman, had a prominent place on the wall. In his white beard, with a book in his left hand, he looked like a prosperous sage. But that was only later in his life, of course, long after he'd founded the firm.

Marcus Goldman was born and grew up in Bavaria, the son of a cattle dealer, and taught school there before emigrating to Philadelphia in 1848. A peddler first, and then a shopkeeper, he was married with five children when he moved to New York City in 1864 and rented an office right there at 30 Pine, as it happened. The firm soon moved, only to return later, to a new building at the same address. The first time around, however, his office was in the basement, by the coal chute. He dealt in promissory notes—IOUs, which we'd call accounts receivables today—that the city's diamond merchants and leather merchants had received from their more reliable customers in those long-ago days before credit cards. He'd buy the notes from businesses, stuff the notes inside his hat—literally—and then sell them, hopefully the same day, to the big banks on Wall Street. Those first IOUs of Goldman's were the precursor to the commercial paper that was Goldman Sachs's major line of business when I arrived. Commercial paper essentially consists of the promissory notes that large corporations issue to finance their short-term financial needs. For them, it is an alternative to bank borrowings and often has a lower interest rate. Corporations sell their notes for cash to commercial-paper dealers such as Goldman Sachs, who in turn sell them to investors who find these short-term, high-quality notes attractive investments.

Marcus Goldman did well, soon handling as much as $5 million of these promissory notes in a year, but his was still a tiny shop compared to some of the other German-Jewish banking houses of the day. Goldman's firm grew as his family did. His daughter married Sam Sachs, the son of a pair of Bavarian immigrants Marcus knew. Industrious and precocious, Sam had kept the books in a small importing house starting at age fifteen to put his two brothers through college. His father-in-law was impressed and, in 1882, Marcus Goldman invited Sam Sachs to be his partner, making the firm M. Goldman and Sachs. Sachs's portrait was on the partners' wall, too. Silver-haired, he sports a Van Dyke beard, and there is a nice shine in his eyes that suggests enlightenment.

The duo was productive. By 1880, Goldman had been doing $30 million a year in commercial paper. By 1894, M. Goldman and Sachs had more than doubled that, to $64 million. Marcus Goldman's son Harry joined the firm that year, and the company took the name it still bears: Goldman, Sachs & Co.

The two brothers-in-law carried the firm into the twentieth century, but they could scarcely have been more different. Sam Sachs was very proper, never removing his coat even on the summer's hottest days. (Probably it was from Sam that his grandson Walter developed his ideas about dress!) Harry Goldman worked in his shirtsleeves. Where Harry was daring, quick to seize opportunities, Sam was cautious, preferring to build the firm's reputation slowly, client by client, deal by deal. They made a good pair.

In building up Goldman Sachs, the two of them also helped build the investment banking business into the industry we know today. For many people, the term "investment banking" is something of a mystery, although it has a distinguished ring to it. What do investment bankers do? Essentially, they serve as the middlemen between two sets of clients. The first is made up of corporations and, sometimes, government bodies that need to raise money to finance their growing organizations. They are called "issuers" and they sell stocks or bonds (or their commercial paper notes) to investment bankers. The second set of clients is made up of a variety of investors, ranging from large institutions like pension funds down to private individuals, who are interested in purchasing these issues. The investment banker evaluates each issue and negotiates a price that is fair to both issuer and investor.

Investment bankers have always played a key role in allocating the nation's savings into the commercial enterprises that have the best chance of prospering. But the turn of the century was a particularly good time to be in the business, for it was a terrific period of our nation's growth. The nation was no longer the bumptious, gangly youngster of the late nineteenth century; it was becoming the global colossus of the twentieth. As the economy expanded, so did Goldman Sachs, adding offices in Chicago, Boston, Philadelphia, and St. Louis.

For all its impact, however, the investment banking business was still heavily dependent on personal relationships. Goldman Sachs caught a big break when, early in this period, Sam Sachs's sister Emelia married a cousin of Julius Rosenwald. A few years later, Rosenwald joined up with a former railroad ticket agent named Richard Sears who had the idea of selling wristwatches by mail order. That alliance became Sears Roebuck, the biggest mail-order house of its era. In 1897, Goldman Sachs purchased $60,000 of Sears's commercial paper, an impressive sum when Sears Roebuck's net worth was only $237,000. It was an important moment in the history of Goldman Sachs; I have a copy of the hand-written Sears balance sheet that records the transaction hanging on the wall in my house.

That deal proved to be good for all parties, and nearly a decade later, Rosenwald returned to Goldman Sachs for $5 million to build a large mail-order plant in Chicago. By then, Goldman had underwritten the first initial public offering—or IPO, as we now say—for United Cigar Manufacturers. Henry Goldman proposed a public offering to raise the money for Sears. Because of the size of the deal, Goldman Sachs felt obliged to team up with Lehman Brothers, and together they took Sears Roebuck public, offering $10 million in preferred and common stock (the separate classes reflecting slightly different entitlements for the owner).

Aside from the size of the deal, the important element in this transaction was the new way the company was valued. In earlier offerings, the companies were considered to be worth no more than the sum of their physical parts — their plants, equipment, real estate, and the other components making up its so-called book value. Harry Goldman recognized that the value of a firm was, in fact, some multiple of its annual earnings. This often yielded a much higher figure, which, in his view, more accurately reflected a company's true value: its price-to-earnings ratio. Today, this is still the key element in appraising a corporation's value. The Sears deal was so successful, it led to Goldman Sachs's underwriting a stock sale for F. W. Woolworth. Then came underwriting deals for Underwood Typewriters, Continental Can, Studebaker, and about a dozen other prominent companies. Virtually all of these were done jointly with Lehman Brothers, but the relationship between the two firms became increasingly distrustful, as each side thought it should receive the bigger share of the profits, and they finally agreed to abandon their joint relationship in 1936.

By then, Harry and Sam had broken up, too. The First World War separated them. Harry remained loyal to his German roots, while Sam sided with the British. This was painful on a personal level, but the split also had serious implications for the firm. Kleinwort's, the London financial firm that Harry Goldman had linked up with to internationalize the firm, didn't like to see Harry doing business with their German enemy. By 1917, the tensions were so high that Harry decided to withdraw from the firm. He would be the last of the Goldman family ever to work at Goldman Sachs.

To replace him, Sam Sachs turned to a man who had been a Harvard friend of his son Arthur, Waddill Catchings. With an impressive shock of white hair and abundant charm, Catchings was tremendously attractive and charismatic. A former partner for Sullivan & Cromwell and a writer on economics, he had written a best-seller called *The Road to Plenty*, which sums up his highly optimistic investment philosophy. In the euphoria of the postwar years, his sunny disposition mirrored the country's, for this was the Roaring Twenties, when the business of America was business, and nearly everyone thought that the law of gravity had been repealed where stocks were concerned.

In December of 1928, Catchings persuaded Goldman Sachs to establish and sell to the public a kind of mutual fund called the Goldman Sachs Trading Corporation. It was an investment company designed to buy controlling interests in other companies on a highly leveraged basis. Offered to the public at $100 each, by February, the shares traded at $222 and the price continued to rise through the summer. It was such a success that Catchings that spring started a companion company, the Shenandoah Corporation, and then created a behemoth called Blue Ridge Corporation to own most of Shenandoah. All of it, of course, was run by Goldman Sachs, and a substantial percentage of the shares was owned by the firm as well. Early 1929 was not, unfortunately, a good time to launch such speculative ventures. At their height, shares in the Goldman Sachs Trading Corporation reached $326. Then came Black Tuesday, October 29, 1929, and the price started to tumble, ultimately falling to just $1.75. The firm's losses were heavy, and lawsuits flew. Bad as it was for the company's finances, it was far worse for Goldman Sachs's hard-earned reputation.

Catchings was soon forced out, but it took years before Goldman Sachs was able to escape its painful associations with the Great Crash. The Depression, of course, was followed by World War II, and both were bad for the firm. I once calculated that from the crash of 1929 through the end of the war in 1946, the sum total of Goldman Sachs's profits was zero.

In the aftermath of the Catchings disaster, the firm turned to one of its own, Sidney Weinberg, to rebuild its business. The partners could have hardly chosen a less likely personage, or made a more inspired selection. Weinberg was then the firm's leading "producer," as we said, the man who was responsible for maintaining the relationships with most of the firm's corporate clients. He was still very much the reigning presence at the firm when I arrived in October of 1947. Of all the remarkable men I have ever known, from presidents on down, the most remarkable of them all was Sidney Weinberg.

I never called him Sidney to his face, of course. To a young man like me, he was Mr. Weinberg, his name spoken with great respect. But Sidney is the name that fits him far better. He was a little man, just five foot four, with legs so short his feet barely touched the floor when he sat in his office chair. He'd grown up poor in Brooklyn, the third of eleven children; his father was a wholesale liquor distributor. Sidney never lost that Brooklyn accent, largely because he never wanted to. A Brooklyn boy was what he was. Pearl Street to him was "Poil Street," just as a girl was a "goil."

Always enterprising, Sidney sold newspapers at the Manhattan-Brooklyn ferry terminal at age ten. By thirteen, he was a summer runner for a brokerage house. At sixteen, there was a banking crisis, and Sidney realized there was money to be made just waiting in line outside the Trust Company of America, which was rumored to be on the verge of insolvency. He'd rise early to be at the front of the line, and then sell his spot for $5 to an anxious depositor eager to reach the teller's window soon after the bank opened at ten, and before it ran out of cash and closed the window again.

He dropped out of school that year, ending his formal education at the eighth grade of P.S. 13 in Brooklyn. Years later, when he received an honorary degree from Harvard, he put it in the same frame as an honorary P.S. 13 certificate he'd received from the New York Board of Education. When he pointed the two of them out to me, the Harvard degree clearly inspired pride, but the certificate from P.S. 13 caused him to mist up a little.

Once the banking crisis was over, Sidney needed regular work, and he went to the tallest building, 43 Exchange Place, figuring somebody there would have a job for him. That skyscraper soared twenty-five stories, and Sidney rode the elevator all the way to the top and then stopped in at every floor on the way down to ask about employment. He had to try twenty-three floors before he came to the Goldman Sachs office there, where the chief clerk hired him as an assistant porter.

That was the beginning of his sixty-two-year career at the firm. The first job was menial work, cleaning the firm's cuspidors and brushing the partners' silk hats, but it was something. From there, he rose to become the office boy, filling the partners' inkwells. It wasn't until he was given the task of delivering a flagpole to the home of Sam Sachs's son Paul that Sidney caught a break. Paul Sachs, an erudite man who later left Goldman Sachs to join the faculty of the Harvard University Art History Department, must have been impressed by Sidney, because he handed him $25 to take a finance course at New York

University. He also had Sidney promoted to the mailroom. After Sidney offered copious suggestions on how to make the place more efficient, he was
put in charge.

This was still not the most stimulating work and, out of boredom, Sidney
started to indulge what would be a lifelong penchant for practical jokes.
He'd place thumbtacks on the chairs of his fellow clerks and be overjoyed
to see them spring up, yelping. His best gag, though, was to place an announcement in the paper that the now-elderly Sam Sachs was putting together a female chorus for a new Broadway musical, and all applicants
should come around to Sachs's office for an interview. A stream of comely
young women came around, which provided a great deal of hilarity around
the office.

Sidney joined the Navy in World War I, serving as a cook. He rejoined
Goldman Sachs afterward, but this time as a salesman of commercial paper.
He married and had a pair of sons, both of whom would eventually join the
firm. (One of them was John Weinberg, who would serve with me as co-
chairman.) By dint of hard work, a remarkable talent for friendship, and terrific business instincts, he rose up through the ranks to make partner in 1927.

I think it's a fine testament to Goldman Sachs's ability to identify talent
that it ultimately turned to an uneducated Brooklyn boy like Sidney to head
the firm in 1930 after Catchings's ignoble departure. Sidney proved so central to the firm that he was able to negotiate for himself a third of all of Goldman Sachs's profits by the time I came along—but of course that was
immaterial, since there were no profits.

Still, he had positioned Goldman Sachs to take full advantage of the business upswing he knew would come along eventually. The ultimate insider,
he was friends with everybody of importance—everybody!—from politicians
to showgirls. During the Second World War, President Roosevelt asked him
to join the War Production Board as vice chairman, which put him in contact with many of the chairmen of the country's largest corporations, including General Electric, Procter & Gamble, and Ford. The War Production
Board's task was to convert a peacetime economy to one tooled to win the
war. In his efforts to shift the American economy over to military production,
Sidney would jawbone these men into doing their patriotic duty by cranking

out, say, tanks instead of cars, and Sidney could be very persuasive. I wouldn't be surprised if he had a hand in the development of the Higgins boat I commanded at Normandy, since he was involved in a little bit of everything. Considering that the war was largely won by the speed and efficiency with which the needed economic conversion took place, I'm sure he contributed more to the Allied victory than many generals.

Many of those company chairmen became Sidney's friends for life and, after the war, quite a few of his new corporate friends asked him to join their boards. Sidney was only too happy to agree. To him, board membership was no honorific; he took his duties very seriously. By one accounting, he attended two hundred and fifty board meetings in a typical year, and he often asked the key questions that most board members were too polite to inquire about. Sidney would go right at them in his Brooklyn accent, often beginning his questions by saying, "Well, I'm just a Brooklyn boy from Public School Thirteen, but. . . ." Gradually, the other directors started to rely on Sidney to size up the tough issues, figuring that if something was okay with Sidney, it was okay with them. "Check it with Sidney" became something of a corporate watchword.

There was one time when even Sidney missed out on a key fact, though. Like so many other corporate heads, Donald Coster, president of a pharmaceutical company named McKesson & Robbins, asked Sidney to join his board, which he did. Unbeknownst to Sidney, however, Coster was a con man who, in his original incarnation as Philip Musica, had founded a company called A. Musica & Sons, which somehow had run afoul of U.S. Customs Service regulations. Worse, while Sidney was on the McKesson & Robbins board, it turned out that Coster had inflated the company's books by creating $21 million worth of nonexistent corporations. Once Coster's fraudulence was discovered, the board met to oust him. During the meeting, however, word came to the board that Coster had committed suicide. There was a period of stunned silence before Sidney piped up: "Well, come on, gentlemen, let's fire him for his sins anyway."

That was a moment of levity, but Sidney took the matter very seriously. To their credit, Sidney and his fellow board members offered up $600,000 of their own money to help restore the company's financial condition.

Sidney was always immensely loyal to the companies that he served, and bought their products religiously. For years, he applied only McKesson & Robbins hair tonic to his scalp. Any light bulb illuminating his house in Scarsdale had to be made by General Electric. And, after he joined the Ford board, any car in which he would be driven about had to be built by Ford.

In a famous story, Sidney once went on a sailing trip with several Boston businessmen on a yacht belonging to Paul Cabot, the Proper Bostonian investor who served with Sidney on the National Dairy Board. As a matter of principle, the only instant coffee Sidney drank was Kraft's Maxwell House — yet, horror of horrors, Paul Cabot had only Folger's on board. Cabot promptly put in to port for a jar of the good stuff. When the Maxwell House supply was depleted while they were still out at sea, however, Cabot surreptitiously replaced it with the illicit Folger's. Sidney never caught on, and continued to help himself to cup after cup, all the while exclaiming, "Why, this is the best coffee I ever had!"

Despite Sidney's efforts, Goldman Sachs still wasn't a major player in the small world of investment banking when I arrived in 1947. Morgan Stanley was the preeminent firm, the one with the best-known name and the most impressive client list. But there were others: Lehman Brothers was also a force, and so were First Boston; Kuhn Loeb; and Dillon Reed. Many of them were, like Goldman Sachs, basically still family firms, and they were all privately held.

To many people, Goldman Sachs was thought to be predominantly Jewish, but I never sensed that anyone ever minded my being an Episcopalian. Still, it had been founded by German Jews, as had many of its competitors, and Weinberg was Jewish, as were, of course, the two Sachs partners. Morgan Stanley, by contrast, was very much a Waspy, white-shoe sort of firm and, while there was little overt anti-Semitism, there was certainly an awareness of the cultural differences within the industry. A few years later, in fact, I was sitting in Sidney Weinberg's office when Perry Hall, the senior partner at Morgan Stanley, called Sidney up. The two were friends, even though their firms were bitter competitors. Everyone was friends with Sidney. Hall was calling to tell Sidney that he had "wonderful news!"

"Oh, what's that?" Sidney replied, taking his ever-present cigar out of his mouth.

"We've just made our first Jewish partner at Morgan Stanley."

Sidney didn't miss a beat. "Oh, Perry, that's nothing. We've had them all along."

That new partner, by the way, was Louis Bernard, a first-rate banker and a fine, public-spirited fellow who much later served on the Getty Foundation board with me.

Because the country was still recovering from the Depression and the war, there weren't many public offerings to be done in the years after I arrived. For us, commercial paper was our core business and it provided potential entrée into the delivery of other products and services to clients. When a company needed money to grow, it could take out a loan from a bank just as a private individual does. But because corporations are better credit risks than most individuals, they can turn to the commercial-paper market, selling their notes to investors through a commercial-paper dealer like Goldman Sachs. One advantage to corporate clients was an interest rate that was lower than the bank's best, or "prime," rate. With the gradual postwar revival of the economy, the commercial-paper market was expanding all the time, and Goldman Sachs did a lot of that business. In those years, and for many years afterward, Goldman Sachs was Wall Street's largest dealer in commercial paper.

I wasn't involved in that, though. I was involved in the only other significant revenue source that Goldman Sachs had from its corporate clients, and that was the bond-bidding syndicates, which were developed to handle especially large bond issues, spreading the extra risk around a number of firms. There were two of these syndicates, headed, respectively, by two of the country's largest investment banks: Halsey Stuart in Chicago headed up one group, and Morgan Stanley led the other—the one in which Goldman Sachs was a participant. Later I would start to wonder why Morgan Stanley always got to be top dog in the syndicate. But when I was starting out, I took it as a fact that it simply was.

In those years, the public-utility industry was the one that had the most immediate need for capital. Now that the servicemen were back, Americans were using more water, gas, electricity, and telephones, and the public companies which provided those services had to expand to meet demand. Because of the large size of the bond issues they were considering, they turned to the two syndicates to bid for each issue. Regulators required that the bond issues of these public utilities be put up for competitive bidding. The question was: What should each syndicate bid for the bonds of these companies? Although Morgan Stanley took the lead in the bidding of our group, there were often as many as a hundred investment banks involved altogether, and all of them, at least nominally, had a say in what interest rate to offer. If, for instance, Consolidated Edison wanted to float a $100 million bond issue, would our syndicate charge 4.23 percent or 4.24? This was the sort of thing we pondered for days on end. It may seem like a small difference, but it was critical to the institutional investors that would buy the bonds from us, to our own profit margin—and, most important, to whether we would win or lose the bidding.

I was very much the junior person on the buying team; all I did was brief the senior banking staff member, who briefed Walter Sachs, who, in turn, represented the firm at the big syndicate meetings. So I was a long way from the action. But I scrutinized the numbers on each company, comparing, in this case, Consolidated Edison's financial situation with that of other similar-sized public utilities that had issued bonds recently. We based our analysis on the financial figures (assets, net earnings, and the like) that came out of the company's prospectus, plus other sources like Moody's manual—a big red book of statistics on all the utility companies. It was very dull work.

I never did attend those big meetings of the syndicate, so I don't know what went on. Walter Sachs alone represented Goldman Sachs. In all probability, Morgan Stanley gave its opinion and that was it, so my painstaking effort may very well have gone for naught. I do know that the meetings were invariably brief. Both bids were due at a specified time. Usually, the two would be extremely close in price, since all the firms were performing virtually the same analysis on the same figures, and we won about half the time. On a $100 million offering, Goldman Sachs might gross about $50,000 if the Morgan Stanley Syndicate won. Not a bad day's work, I suppose, but then again, we'd get nothing if we lost.

I had become something of a numbers man by now, what with my years in the Navy as a disbursing officer and my MBA. Even though I found the syndicate work extraordinarily tedious, I always gave it my best. I've always been a team player and, by now, I'd become a fierce partisan of Goldman Sachs. I liked being part of such a storied institution that still held so much promise.

It was in February 1948, only a few months after I'd joined Goldman Sachs, that I woke up one morning and read the big front-page newspaper story that the Justice Department had brought suit against nineteen leading firms of the investment banking industry, charging that they had entered into a secret, non-compete agreement in violation of the antitrust laws. The suit was called *United States vs. Morgan Stanley, et al.*

"Et al." Who, I wondered, was included among the et al.? I hastily turned to the jump page and saw that, sure enough, along with eighteen others, including Kuhn Loeb, Dillon Reed, and Lehman Brothers, there was Goldman Sachs. It was practically at the bottom of the list, but it was there. Almost everyone else in the office was in deep distress over these charges that had been brought against us and our industry. To them, I suspect, this augured a return to the dark years after the Crash, when Goldman Sachs's reputation sank with the stock market. But to me, this was good news. I thought it would have been a terrible embarrassment for the firm if Goldman Sachs had *not* been included in such a highly publicized list of Wall Street's leading firms.

As it was, Goldman Sachs had only barely made the list. At this point, it had only 1.4 percent of the underwriting market; Morgan Stanley, by contrast, had 16 percent. And even that might have been overstating the matter, as a 1950 list of the top seventeen underwriters did not include Goldman Sachs at all. Given my Boy Scout ideals, you might wonder why I could have been so enthusiastic about my firm's being named in an antitrust suit. The answer is that I was convinced that the suit had no merit whatsoever. After all, the syndicates that the government was so concerned about were competing against each other on price. To me, it wasn't a matter of ethics; it was a matter of getting Goldman Sachs on the map.

Still, it proved to be a long, drawn-out case, one that cost the firm three quarters of a million dollars in legal fees to defend. In the end, the presiding judge of the U.S. Court of Appeals, Harold Medina, ruled against the government, decreeing that there was, in fact, plenty of healthy competition among the firms. He even cited Goldman Sachs's disagreement with Lehman Brothers as an example of proper competitive behavior. Now, fifty years later, competition has forced out of business all but three of the original nineteen firms targeted by the Justice Department—only Morgan Stanley, Lehman Brothers, and Goldman Sachs remain independent firms.

9

SIDNEY

—⁓—

ALTHOUGH I'D FEARED my work on the bond-buying team might be overlooked, I had somehow attracted the attention of Sidney Weinberg himself. To this day, I don't know exactly how. I'm sure I came across as bright and ambitious, but nearly everyone at Goldman Sachs was that. The exalted Harvard Business School degree probably made some difference, since it was a rarity at the firm in those days. Sidney was friends with the dean of the Business School, and held it in some awe. But Sidney had a complicated attitude toward academic credentials, since he had so few. He used to snap up Phi Beta Kappa keys from pawn shops and hand them out to well-pedigreed business executives who'd failed to impress him. "Here, bright boy," he'd say, "maybe one of these would help." He said this in a cheery, teasing fashion, but there was a put-down in there, too.

So my HBS degree helped to some extent, but I'm convinced that what made me stand out in Sidney's mind was that I knew how to use a slide rule. To Sidney, that was an extremely new-fangled piece of high-tech equipment, and he was always amazed when I pulled it out, slid the middle piece out a certain distance and read off the answer to just about any calculation. He'd be meeting with some important CEO, and Sidney would tell him, "I think you ought to sell stock, not bonds. If you went with bonds, they'd represent more than half your capitalization." And then I'd pull out my little slide rule and whisper to him, "Exactly fifty-six percent." And Sidney would say, "Fifty-six percent, as a matter of fact, and that's too damn much."

After a session like that, Sidney would pull me into his office and close the door behind us and then usher me to him as if he were going to tell me some deep secret. He would go to his desk, and open up the little center drawer. And he would pull out a giant slide rule that one of his corporate friends had given him as a joke. He'd hold up this huge device and, with a nod, bring me closer. "C'mere," he'd say. "Show me how to use this damn thing."

I'd take the slide rule from him and do my best to demonstrate how it worked. "See this bottom scale?" I'd tell him. "It goes from one to ten." And then I'd carefully show him how, by sliding out the middle piece, it could yield the product of two times two. "There it is—four. See? Two times two equals four."

"Get outta here," he'd tell me with a playful slap of the hand against my shoulder. "I already know what two times two are. That's the damnedest stupidest thing." And then he'd throw the slide rule back into the drawer, and it would remain there for several months until he got curious about it again, and we'd repeat the same procedure. He never did grasp it.

Still, he started to call me on the phone. Or rather, his secretary would. "Mr. Whitehead?" she'd ask. "I have Mr. Weinberg on the line." And then Sidney would come on with some little question. Gradually, he started calling me so often that it became a nuisance for him to keep having to explain the background of whatever topic he was calling about. He asked me to move into his office so I could stay up to speed. I wasn't sure this was such a good move for me. I was working on a variety of other matters, and I didn't want to be just his assistant. Of course, if I had to be anyone's assistant, it would be best to be Sidney Weinberg's. But I've always been leery of associating myself too closely with any one person. For one thing, I like to be my *own* person. But also, it's risky: If the person starts to fall out of favor, I would too. I couldn't imagine that ever happening to Sidney, but you can never be certain. Besides, what would happen to me when he finally retired? But it was clear he wanted me to join him, so I said okay, and he had a small table added to his office, across the room from his desk.

It proved to be an awkward arrangement, however. There were some telephone conversations that he didn't want me to overhear. So he'd start to whisper into the receiver. And then the other person would have trouble hearing, and Sidney would have to repeat himself, louder, obviously to his annoyance. And when corporate clients came into his office, they never knew whether to include me in the conversation. If they did, I'd sense that Sidney was growing irked because he always was curiously possessive of his business connections. That's one quality I've noticed about the many powerful people I've known: They are often surprisingly insecure—afraid that someone is going to take away their position at any moment. But if Sidney's intimates didn't include me, they felt uncomfortable having a third party listen in. So after a few months, I moved out of his office, and I think we were both relieved.

Still, we remained very close, and Sidney Weinberg became virtually an ideal role model for me. He believed that investment banking, at least at Goldman Sachs, was, and had to be, a matter of personal relationships—of friendships, really. Human capital of this sort was the coin of the realm. And, to Sidney, a friendship had to be a relationship where each side benefits. If not right away, eventually. For Sidney, it was a matter of close listening, of understanding, and of genuinely caring about whatever problems or issues his corporate friend might have. And I've tried to observe this philosophy in all my dealings since. It's not *all* that counts, but it's one of the things that *always* counts.

Sidney's own connections started to pay off even more handsomely a few years after I joined the firm. One of the big breakthroughs came when Goldman Sachs became involved in the Ford Motor Company's first public offering in 1956. As usual in those years, Sidney deserves nearly all the credit for that. But I played a small role in getting him to see the value of such a relationship. Even for a private company, Ford had always been remarkably secretive about the nature and extent of its business, and no one outside the company knew exactly how big Ford was. But in the course of my general research work a few years before, I'd learned that any company that did business in the Commonwealth of Massachusetts had to file an annual balance sheet with that state, and Ford was one such company. Curious, I took the train up to Boston and personally went through the public records in the government files, and I found Ford's statement for 1952. It was just one page, but it showed a company with a net worth in the billions, which made it the largest privately held company in the United States, and probably in the world.

When I brought a copy back to Sidney, he was impressed with the balance sheet and, I think, with my ability to get it, although he was never particularly lavish with praise. But he could see that it would certainly be worthwhile for Goldman Sachs to get a little closer to the Ford Motor Company. If the *U.S. vs. Morgan Stanley et al.* antitrust suit had helped get us established, there could be no greater triumph for Goldman Sachs than to manage the first public offering of the largest family-owned company in the world. It would solidify Sidney's reputation as the man to see in the investment world and, because I had become so closely associated with him, it might help my career a bit as well.

Sidney's relationship with Henry Ford II, as with so many other chief executives, had come about through his work with the War Production Board. After the war, Henry started turning to Sidney for advice, as so many chief executives did in those days. Sidney was in his mid-fifties then, and approaching the peak of his influence. Then in his thirties, Henry II had found himself in complete charge of the company, then the second largest car manufacturer in the world, after the deaths of his grandfather—the protean company founder, Henry Ford I—and, shortly afterwards, of his father, Edsel. Yet Henry knew almost nothing about business. He was fresh out of the Navy and had to oversee the complicated transformation of the company from producing military vehicles to the passenger cars that Americans were now desperate to buy.

Sidney started making regular trips to see the Fords at the family headquarters in Dearborn and, in due course, he brought me along to assist him at the meetings. They were held at the sumptuous home of Henry's mother, Mrs. Ernest Kanzler, who had remarried after Edsel's death. Mrs. Kanzler was not at all the retiring widow I'd been expecting, but a very formidable woman with strong opinions, and her four children—besides Henry, there were Benson, Bill, and Josephine—were hardly shrinking violets, either. The five of them were the family heirs to the company. It always amused me that Josephine had married an unrelated Ford, so she was Josephine Ford Ford.

The family was in a terrible bind, though, and it really needed the sort of help that Sidney was so good at providing. Largely in order to avoid steep inheritance taxes, Henry Ford I, unbeknownst to just about everyone—including his family—had left almost ninety-five percent of the Ford stock tax-free to a charitable foundation he created, the Ford Foundation. He left only five percent to the family. The family was completely blind-sided by this move, since Henry had never spoken particularly enthusiastically about charitable ventures before. (For that matter, it would have been a shock for Mr. Ford to see what the foundation went on to do with his money. Whereas he had always been a staunch pull-yourself-up-by-your-own-bootstraps conservative, the independent Ford Foundation later became known as one of the most politically liberal foundations in the land.) The family was not only blind-sided but also very distressed to find that they owned only five percent of the shares.

The family did retain full control of the company, however, since the stock the family now owned had one hundred percent of the voting rights. The foundation's Ford stock came with no voting rights at all. That was the problem. The foundation didn't care about control, but it was desperate for cash to build a staff, rent office space, make grants, and engage in the other activities of a charitable foundation. But its stock had no vote, and it was not in the interest of the family to vote to pay dividends. So the foundation wanted Ford to go public and, in the process, convert the dividend-less Ford stock into a dividend-payer. This would, at the very least, generate income for the foundation on its Ford stock and, over time, would allow the foundation to diversify its portfolio into other dividend-producing stocks. But it was powerless to make that happen since the New York Stock Exchange regulations required the stock of its listed companies to have voting rights, and the family was extremely reluctant to cede control of the family company to its ninety-five-percent owner. It was fairly obvious that the company had to be recapitalized to convert at least some of its stock and that, in return for giving up its exclusive voting rights, the family had to receive an economic interest larger than five percent. It was a situation that cried out for investment banking skills.

As it happened, the chairman of the foundation's board was, to no one's surprise, a good friend of Sidney's. This was Charles E. ("Electric Charlie") Wilson, the chairman of General Electric—not to be confused with the Charles E. ("Engine Charlie") Wilson, who was chairman of General Motors. Sidney had been Electric Charlie's number two man at the War Production Board. Their friendship established the trust necessary to work through many thorny issues.

Sidney and I ended up working on the Ford deal for the better part of two years. It was an immensely intricate matter anyway and, since it was very nearly the first major postwar public offering of any type, we had to be very careful writing the prospectus, as the SEC had not yet fully formulated the rules that issuing companies needed to follow. A lot of lawyers contributed their talents, and I had to check and recheck all the facts to make sure they were accurate.

Another complicating factor was the need to maintain strict secrecy. During the last summer before the offering, Henry went to Paris for vacation and stayed in the Plaza Athenée hotel. It was my job to keep him posted on each day's developments. We developed a code for our cables involving, for some reason, women's names, as if this were a novel by Louisa May Alcott. "Public offering" was "Mabel," "Sidney Weinberg" was "Edith," "Henry Ford" was "Alice," the "Ford Motor Company" was "Agnes," and so on. So a typical message might read, "Edith thinks Agnes should hold Mabel off until September if Alice agrees." Using this particular code, we were tempted to throw in a few salacious *double entendres* and we did indeed succumb occasionally, cabling things like "Alice eager for consummation with Mabel" and the like. Henry enjoyed the wordplay, but Sidney would never dream of kidding around with such serious business.

Actually, Sidney was the one who very nearly ruined everything back at the earliest stages of negotiations when he accidentally left an envelope containing Ford's ultra-confidential, eyes-only financial statements at a newsstand in the Detroit airport. He'd stopped to buy a paper, set down the envelope, and then absent-mindedly taken only the newspaper with him. It would have been calamitous if those documents had gotten into the wrong hands. The business press would have had a field day with the scoop that Ford was considering going public. When Sidney realized what he had done, he went into a panic. He was in a company car on the way to Dearborn, and he had the driver turn right around and race back to the airport, where he dashed to the newsstand and was immensely relieved to find the envelope still there.

During the negotiations over the offering, I committed a faux pas myself that took me a while to live down. It was the silly sort of goof that, while meaningless in itself, colleagues are inclined to rib you about indefinitely. We were flying back to New York in one of Ford's tiny company planes after a meeting with the family in Dearborn. As usual, Henry and Sidney sat in the two front seats and I squeezed in behind them into a tiny single seat that, in fact, doubled as the toilet. As we came in for the landing, I overheard Henry tell Sidney he was going to ask the pilot to call ahead to order a car to take the two of them back into the city. Sidney had an apartment at the Sherry-Netherlands, at Fifty-ninth and Fifth, and Henry always favored the Regency, at Sixty-first and Park.

Ever-helpful, I piped up to offer to drive them myself. "It's no trouble at all," I assured Henry. "I've parked my car right by the terminal, and I'll be passing through the city on my way home to New Jersey."

That sounded fine with Henry and Sidney. It wasn't until we were on the tarmac and I was leading the two men to my car that I remembered with a pang that I was driving a *Chevrolet*. Given Sidney's brand loyalties, this was crime enough. But I knew that Henry would rather die than be caught riding in anything but a Ford.

I kept silent, desperately hoping that my passengers would be so preoccupied with their business plans that they wouldn't notice anything so slight as the fact that my car bore a General Motors insignia. No such luck. Henry was the first to notice. "My *God*, John," he exclaimed as we drew near the offending vehicle. "You're not going to make me ride in *that*."

I prayed that Sidney would intercede on my behalf, but no. Instead, he joined in: "Jesus, Whitehead, I've gotta find me a guy who knows the difference between a Ford car and somebody else's." He was both joking and not, which was often Sidney's way of making a point, especially at the end of a long and tiring day.

The two of them continued to give me the business all the way into Manhattan. Once we arrived, Henry made me stop and let him out around the corner from his hotel, where he could disembark from such an embarrassing car without fear of being noticed. "What if there are photographers there?" he asked me. Jokingly, I think.

Sidney kept razzing me as we continued on to the Sherry-Netherlands. I had to laugh when I finally had him out of the car, but sure enough, it did win me notice back at Dearborn. I ceased being that "young fellow from Goldman Sachs that Sidney always brings with him," and I started being "the guy who drove Henry Ford in a Chevy." I didn't really mind. I figure you need to be known for something! For years, Henry ribbed me about that little incident every time he saw me.

In the end, the company was recapitalized. The family's equity interest was increased from five percent to sixteen and a half percent in return for giving up their exclusive voting rights to the foundation. When the foundation sold shares to the public, those shares had voting rights and could be listed on the New York Stock Exchange, but the family's voting rights could never be reduced below thirty percent. Everybody benefited, and everyone was happy with the solution. Now, fifty years later, the arrangement still works well for all.

The foundation decided immediately to sell 12 million shares to the public, and it was the "hottest" offering ever. It seemed that every American family wanted to own a few shares of Ford. The offering price was set at $64.50 a share, for a total offering of $774 million. Before the first day was over, the stock had climbed to $70. It was by far the largest initial public offering in history. Every investment bank in the country was involved in it except Morgan Stanley, which declined to participate because of its close involvement with General Motors. When the offering was announced in January of 1956, the *New York Times* ran the story on the front page above the fold, with Sidney Weinberg's face smiling out from the accompanying photograph. Goldman Sachs had arrived.

And, to a degree, so had I. Shortly after our big coup with Ford, I started hearing from other companies interested in my services. I'd given up on the thought of becoming some company's treasurer. That seemed like small potatoes now. So I was willing to listen—to one offer in particular. It involved a new venture-capital firm headed up by the glamorous film and publishing magnate Jock Whitney. That intrigued me, I have to say.

10

NEW-BUSINESS MAN

———ᴧᴧᴧ———

"Jock" Whitney was formally John Hay Whitney, the son of Payne Whitney and one of the richest men in America. He was a champion polo player, a horse breeder, and a frequent backer of Broadway shows and Hollywood movies, including *Gone With the Wind*.

When he returned from a three-year stint in the Army, he was eager to use his time and resources as constructively as possible. He was concerned that neither commercial banks nor investment banks provided a source of capital directed toward financing new ideas—ideas that might have great promise but also carried substantial risk. So he founded what was the first venture-capital firm, with an invested capital of $10 million. He persuaded several highly successful businessmen to join him and to share the profits. The founding partners were Jock, Benno Schmidt (the father of Benno Schmidt, the recent president of Yale), Dick Croft, Webster Todd (Christie Todd Whitman's father), Malcolm Smith, and Sam Park.

The new company was highly successful from the start. Their first investment was to back Kenneth Spencer in converting a government-owned munitions plant to make fertilizer; within a year the Spencer Chemical Company was worth more than the capital of J. H. Whitney itself. Minute Maid frozen foods was another early success, and they were off to the races. Other partners were added, including Bill Jackson, and my friend Wrede Petersmeyer, who had called me with the proposal that I join the firm as a partner.

This was 1956. I was thirty-four and I'd been at Goldman Sachs for nearly nine years. I had no particular reason to be unhappy, but I thought I'd done well for the firm and still I had not been made a partner. So I was restless, and maybe a little resentful. Also, I was afraid that, despite my efforts to be my own man, I'd possibly ended up being tied too closely to Sidney, which might damage my prospects. The offer from Wrede seemed like a good chance to establish an independent identity. I told him that I couldn't commit to anything, but I would be happy to explore the idea.

I had a series of meetings with him and the other partners, all but Mr. Whitney himself. The partners all seemed bright and capable, and the business was going well. The new enterprise's objective was to buy companies, improve their operations, and sell them at a profit. It had already had several successes, the most notable being the acquisition and sale of Spencer Chemical and Bird's-eye Frozen Foods. It was a great compliment to have been sought out by such a firm.

As I say, I had not yet met with Mr. Whitney. That event was set to occur at a big luncheon in the firm's private dining room, which would be the final test to see whether I was the right man for the job. I sat at one end of the heavily laden dining table, the very elegant, urbane Mr. Whitney at the other, and the other four partners on the sides. Dessert was a large bowl of delicious-looking strawberries. I was served first, as befitted the guest of honor, and I helped myself to a generous spoonful. Determined to make a favorable impression during the wide-ranging table conversation, I had not noticed that a waiter had placed a finger bowl in front of me. I mistook it for my dessert bowl. I spooned my strawberries into it—and then watched, horrified, as they floated about in the water.

As I wondered what on earth to do, a friendly waiter whisked away the polluted finger bowl, and replaced it with another one. Then he served me the strawberries again. I carefully placed them in the correct bowl this time, and tried to carry on as if nothing had happened. Around the table, no one seemed to notice my faux pas, although I'm sure everyone did. I felt quite humiliated, every inch the small-town boy.

But it didn't matter. At the end of the luncheon, Mr. Whitney declared that he would be delighted to invite me to join his firm as a partner. The pay would be higher than what I was receiving from Goldman Sachs, and the prestige of *being* a partner would be far greater, too, for at Goldman Sachs I bore no title whatsoever. I told him I'd be very pleased to accept.

As I returned downtown to the Goldman Sachs building on Broad Street, I knew I'd have to tell Sidney immediately what I'd just done. If I delayed, I would only have a harder time later. So as soon as I entered the building, I went directly to his office and told him I had to speak to him about something important right away.

"Yeah, what's that?" Sidney did not take the cigar out of his mouth.

I blurted it all out: "Jock Whitney has just offered me a job as a partner at J. H. Whitney, and I've accepted."

Finally, Sidney removed the cigar and looked at me. "Are you kidding me?" he asked. "You're going to leave Goldman Sachs?" He seemed completely incredulous.

"Yes, that's right," I told him.

"That's ridiculous," he shouted, and he picked up the phone and barked at Mary Burgess, his long-suffering secretary, "Get me Jock Whitney."

I was appalled that he would consider interfering with a done deal, but it was never possible to restrain Sidney once he'd gotten it into his mind to do something.

The moment Mr. Whitney came on the line, Sidney started shouting into the receiver. "Jock, I hear you've just offered my young assistant a job at J. H. Whitney." He was absolutely breathless with indignation. "You can't do that, Jock. He's too important to me here, and I'm sorry, but I just can't spare him, and that's that."

I was astounded that even Sidney could be so brazen with such a man as Jock Whitney, one of the richest men in the country, who I was sure was sputtering in astonishment at the other end of the line. But that was Sidney. I could not conceive of standing up to him, and I guess neither could Mr. Whitney. The offer was withdrawn. Sidney did, somewhat bashfully, say he'd raise my salary to match Whitney's offer.

So it was agreed: I would stay on at Goldman Sachs, and at the end of the year I was made a partner.

———————

As I returned to my rounds, it became increasingly apparent to me that the firm had become heavily dependent on one man, Sidney Weinberg. We did almost no investment banking business except with company clients who dealt only with him. For Goldman Sachs, he was the ultimate "rainmaker." But I had to wonder: What would happen to the firm if he retired or died? He was well into his seventies by now. But Sidney didn't seem concerned about the future of the firm, and neither was anyone else. To me, though, it was apparent that our greatest strength was also our greatest weakness.

I decided to draft a formal report to Sidney on the sources of the firm's income to show what a high percentage of the total he was bringing in. Because of its blue cover, indicating "confidential," this report later became known as Whitehead's Blue Book. I pointed out that it was very unlikely that Goldman Sachs would ever again have a single partner as productive as Sidney was. Instead—and I hoped Sidney would find this somewhat gratifying—I suggested that we try to supplement him with ten people. I did the math: If, in time, each of the ten could average just twenty percent of the income that Sidney brought in at present, the firm's income would double. Further, I proposed that each of these people be assigned to one of four geographic regions of the country—East, Midwest, South, and West—and that each of the ten be responsible for soliciting business from 250 of the 1,000 largest companies in the country. It would be up to each new man to pick which of the 250 companies to concentrate his time on.

Sensible as such a proposition might seem nowadays, this was a completely revolutionary idea in the somewhat hidebound investment banking industry of the 1950s. In those days, marketing consisted of little more than waiting for the president of a major company to drop by to discuss additional financing. No one solicited business. That was undignified. The way to attract business was to act prestigious and important—and somehow that would lure the better sort of customer the investment banker was trying to attract. That was, in fact, the way Sidney did it. He established himself as the man to see for a corporation's financial needs. He rarely traveled, in fact, because everybody came to him. That was the way everyone else in the industry did it, too.

The report languished. A couple of months went by, and I didn't hear a word from Sidney.

It was about then that I heard I was to become a partner, with a salary of $25,000 and one quarter of one percent of the profits. It was the happiest day of my life, and a huge relief to me. Being a partner at Goldman Sachs wasn't exactly lifetime tenure, but close. Now I figured that the only thing that would endanger my continued employment was the demise of the firm itself. And, quite honestly, I was afraid of just that, if Sidney retired or died and no provision for bringing in new business was made. I suppose I could have thought, well, what we need is another Sidney. But there would never be another Sidney, I could see that. None of the other partners seemed likely candidates, and certainly I would never be one. Sidney was extraordinarily flamboyant and personable. You just could not help liking Sidney Weinberg. No, the firm needed to go about the acquisition of business in a whole new way.

Now that I was a partner, I screwed up my courage and circulated my report to all fifteen other partners, including Sidney. Once again, nothing came of it. After about a month, I asked Sidney if he'd had a chance to look at it yet. He pulled it out of the drawer. "Oh, this?" he said.

"Yes," I told him.

"Haven't read it."

And I'm not sure he ever did read it. After a few more weeks, though, I finally heard that Whitehead's Blue Book was becoming the subject of some discussion among the other partners. Then I heard that my observations had met with some approval. Not much. Just some. To me, though, the important thing was that no one, not even Sidney, said I should *not* proceed.

So I went ahead, very cautiously. I put myself in charge of what I called the New Business Department, creating new business, just as the name suggests. I couldn't see my way through to hiring a full ten "new-business men" right away, as I had proposed. I settled on four as a first step, one for each of the four sections of the country. Since not too many of the people who were already at the firm dared venture into anything untried, I had to hire one of these men myself from outside the firm. He was Dick Mayfield and had been a jazz pianist at a nightclub in the city earlier in his career, but he seemed like a good salesman. Another was a rather correct, white-haired gentleman named J. B. Walker, who was in his early sixties and had been hired by Sidney but had never found a real place for himself in the firm. The two others, the energetic Fred Weintz and Alan Stein—a former basketball star at Columbia—had been in Corporate Finance, and were both Harvard Business School graduates. I persuaded them to switch over to my New Business Department. I selected these men because they all had a bit of the extrovert in them, a characteristic that wasn't otherwise particularly prized at Goldman Sachs, but one that I knew was essential to being the successful salesmen we needed. And we needed them to have a lot of self-confidence, for I knew that they'd likely have the door slammed in their faces more than a few times.

Meanwhile, I continued with the kind of investment banking work I had been doing—public offerings, private placements, mergers, and the like. On some of these deals, I was still working with Sidney, some not. If it was another deal for Ford, Sidney always had me handle it, since I knew all the people there. "Ford Motor Company wants another $100 million bond issue," he'd say. "Would you work on it?" And he would expect me to get it done. In time, I became a decent producer myself, although nothing like Sidney, of course. I developed relationships with high-ranking officers, often the CEOs, of a number of top companies and persuaded them that they should turn to Goldman Sachs the next time they needed an investment banker. Most CEOs look to their friends in such situations, and I did my best to become a friend. For them, the choice was a very personal one, a matter of trust and confidence. They had to feel I supported them, understood their objectives, and was capable of accomplishing their objectives. In those days, the CEOs often turned to investment bankers they'd grown up with, or known in college, or had played golf with. But gradually, the process became more professional and more businesslike, which left openings for someone like me or my new-business men to develop fairly impressive client lists.

But I also put in a lot of time with the further development of the New Business Department. At first, it was excruciatingly slow going. It took an entire year before any of the men earned his first fee. That was J. B. Walker, who finally produced a $25,000 fee for advising a company on its dividend policy. I think it actually had more to do with how much they liked J.B. than with the quality of our service, but that was a lesson in itself. Salesmanship sells. It was a red-letter day for him, and I gave his accomplishment a lot of internal publicity.

Once the sale was made, the work on the project was not done by the new business man, but by the staff in what we called the Buying Department, now Corporate Finance. This was new. It used to be, at Goldman Sachs as at most firms, that whoever won the business did the job. I noted that at Procter & Gamble and other market-driven companies, the sales department and the manufacturing plants were separate entities. After making a sale, a Procter & Gamble salesman continued on his rounds to make another. He'd keep an eye on all his customers, to make sure they were happy, but not to the point of involving himself with actually making the soap. So we did the same thing at Goldman Sachs. The new-business man was responsible up to the point where Goldman Sachs had been hired to handle a project, and then the responsibility of getting the job done passed to the people in Corporate Finance who were most experienced in that particular kind of project.

Before too long, a Goldman Sachs new-business man was calling on every large company in America, whether or not it was already a client. Many had never been called on by an investment banker from a Wall Street firm before. We undertook training conferences to address basic questions like "How to Get an Appointment with the CEO" and—a matter that proved to be closely related—"How To Treat the CEO's Secretary." Such topics may sound elementary, but they were essential. Should the new-business man give the CEO's secretary flowers to ingratiate himself? We spent a long time batting that one around, and finally left it up to the discretion of the individual salesman.

Getting a foot in the door of the top companies whose business we were seeking was a very difficult problem. At that point, few people outside of New York had ever even heard of us. Goldman Sachs was still only the fifteenth largest investment bank. So we had a great deal of sales resistance to overcome, and a lot to do to make the most of the few sales opportunities that came. "What to Talk About When You Do Get an Appointment" was another big topic.

To clarify our objectives, I set down this advice to new-business men in a memo, one that one of our all-time best new-business men still has on the wall of his office:

- Don't waste your time going after business we don't really want.
- The boss usually decides—not the assistant treasurer. Do you know him?
- It's just as easy to get a first-rate piece of business as a second-rate one.
- You can never learn anything when you're talking.
- The respect of one man is worth more than acquaintance with 100.
- When there's business to be done, get it!
- Important people like to deal with other important people. Are you one?
- There's nothing worse than an unhappy client.
- If you get the business, it's up to you to see that it's well handled.

Again, this may all seem obvious, but it was revolutionary at the time. And within a couple of years, the new system finally began to pay off, as the extra income that the new-business men brought in exceeded the extra expense of hiring them. At that point, two of the original four new-business men left. J. B. Walker, being older, decided to retire and the jazzman Dick Mayfield returned to piano playing. But Weintz and Stein stayed on, and grew into outstanding investment bankers. Weintz in particular was an extraordinarily dedicated new-business man. He once had a late-morning meeting with a company president in Cleveland that went unexpectedly well. The man invited Weintz to stay on for lunch at his club, and then well into the afternoon. It was only when he returned to his car that he realized that he had left his wife in it since ten o'clock that morning! That's the kind of new-business man we wanted.

Over the years, the New Business Department became something of a mecca for talent at Goldman Sachs. Many rising stars wanted to join, and older partners were eager to help with the client companies the new-business men found for us. Gradually, we were able to divide up the 1,000 top companies so that a new-business man handled not 250, an impossibly heavy load, but 100, and eventually just 50. As before, it was up to each man to determine the best prospects on his list. And as the number of new-business men increased, the territory that each man covered got smaller. Of course, the new-business man who covered that smaller area got better known within it. The fellow who covered Cleveland, for instance, became very well known in Cleveland. It all went so well that Walter Sachs himself once boasted that "Goldman Sachs *is* a New Business Department."

It just showed the value of an organized, highly structured sales effort and a sensible delegation of responsibility for carrying out the project. By the time I retired, there were about fifty new-business men, two of them women. Now there are over a hundred around the world. The department is now called Investment Banking Services, or IBS, a far more distinguished title.

But when I think of my major contribution to building Goldman Sachs, I don't think so much of the new business I helped develop, or the sales techniques I tried to implement. Rather, I believe the most important thing I did was to set down in writing what Goldman Sachs stood for. I did it out of necessity. By the early 1960s, our business was expanding so rapidly that new people were coming into the firm faster than we could fully assimilate them. I once calculated that if the firm continued to increase its staff by 20 percent every year, as we were doing, and only 5 percent of the employees left and were replaced, as was in fact occurring, then in two years, nearly half of our employees would be practically brand-new, having been there less than twenty-four months.

I wondered how they would ever get inculcated with the Goldman Sachs ethic, which we old hands had learned over time by osmosis. We did our best to impart these values in new hires through fairly extensive training sessions, but I thought it would be helpful to identify our core values—this was long before that became a vogue term—in a short document that all employees could have, to read and to remember. Values like putting the customer's interests first, emphasizing quality, and working as a team.

I did not want these to be lost. So one Sunday afternoon at home, I sat down with a pen and a yellow pad and tried to write down all the things that

I thought made Goldman Sachs distinctive and a unique place to work. I tried to avoid sounding too schmaltzy about it. But I did want our employees to share the pride I and many others felt about working at Goldman Sachs.

I came up with twelve essential points, which I termed "Our Business Principles." Over the years, the lawyers got hold of the principles and there are now fourteen. Copies of the original version have disappeared, but all of the concepts and most of the original language survives. The careful reader can surely identify the additions.

1. Our clients' interests always come first. Our experience shows that if we serve our clients well, our own success will follow.
2. Our assets are our people, capital, and reputation. If any of these is ever diminished, the last is the most difficult to restore. We are dedicated to complying fully with the letter and spirit of the laws, rules, and ethical principles that govern us. Our continued success depends upon unswerving adherence to this standard.
3. Our goal is to provide superior returns to our shareholders (Goldman Sachs went public in 1999). Profitability is critical to achieving superior returns, building our capital, and attracting and keeping our best people. Significant employee stock ownership aligns the interests of our employees and our shareholders.
4. We take great pride in the professional quality of our work. We have an uncompromising determination to achieve excellence in everything we undertake. Though we may be involved in a wide variety and heavy volume of activity, we would, if it came to a choice, rather be best than biggest.
5. We stress creativity and imagination in everything we do. While recognizing that the old way may still be the best way, we constantly strive to find a better solution to a client's problems. We pride ourselves on having pioneered many of the practices and techniques that have become standard in the industry.
6. We make an unusual effort to identify and recruit the very best person for every job. Although our activities are measured in billions of dol-

lars, we select our people one by one. In a service business, we know that without the best people, we cannot be the best firm.

7. We offer our people the opportunity to move ahead more rapidly than is possible at most other places. We have yet to find limits to the responsibility that our best people are able to assume. Advancement depends solely on ability, performance, and contribution to the firm's success, without regard to race, color, religion, sex, age, national origin, disability, sexual orientation, or any impermissible criterion or circumstances.

8. We stress teamwork in everything we do. While individual creativity is always encouraged, we have found that team effort often produces the best results. We have no room for those who put their personal interests ahead of the interests of the firm and its clients.

9. The dedication of our people to the firm and the intense effort they give their jobs are greater than one finds in most other organizations. We think that this is an important part of our success.

10. We consider our size an asset that we try hard to preserve. We want to be big enough to undertake the largest project that any of our clients could contemplate. Yet small enough to maintain the loyalty, the intimacy and the *esprit de corps* that we all treasure and that contribute greatly to our success.

11. We constantly strive to anticipate the rapidly changing needs of our clients and to develop new services to meet those needs. We know that the world of finance will not stand still and that complacency can lead to extinction.

12. We regularly receive confidential information as part of our normal client relationships. To breach a confidence or to use confidential information improperly or carelessly would be unthinkable.

13. Our business is highly competitive, and we aggressively seek to expand our client relationships. However, we must always be fair competitors and must never denigrate other firms.

14. Integrity and honesty are at the heart of our business. We expect our people to maintain high ethical standards in everything they do, both in their work for the firm and in their personal lives.

When I was done, I showed the twelve principles to the management committee, which suggested a few small changes, and then approved distributing them to everyone at the firm. We included a copy with the annual report and sent it to each employee at home, in hopes that the family would see it, too, and be proud of the firm where Dad (or in a few cases, Mom) worked, and spent so much of his time.

The principles seemed to make a big hit. We asked each department head to hold a meeting with their staff to discuss how the principles applied to their day-to-day work, and to report back to the management committee on their findings. We inserted several sessions on the principles into our employee training programs. To this day, the booklet, still titled "Our Business Principles," is still used and I believe respected throughout the firm.

I always believed in our people at Goldman Sachs. I was convinced that if we hired the best people, which we always tried to do, we would become the best investment banking firm. Conversely, if we didn't have the best people, we would never be the best. If this sounds like a simple truism, it was. But it was also key to our success.

Our professional employees came principally out of the leading business schools. At the beginning, this was mostly Harvard, but gradually we spread out our recruiting to more than twenty schools, some of them overseas. By my last years at the firm, we took people directly out of college for a two-year analyst program, to give them a taste of investment banking at Goldman Sachs before they went off to business school. This gave us a first look at some of the best people before the competition heard about them. Eventually, we even reached down to high school, with summer internships.

We were quite aggressive. Instead of waiting for prospective employees to come to us for an interview, we often sought out the best candidates by asking finance professors at business schools to single out for us the most able students in their classes. We got advice from new employees about the best students in the next business school class behind them. We held "open house" sessions at each of the top business schools to cast our net wider. When we decided we really wanted someone, we made it very hard for them to say no. Even after I was a senior partner, I spent a lot time twisting the arms of twenty-year-olds, and that was very likely one of the most important things I did.

We did not compete for employees on the basis of salary. Each year we set the starting salary of a new person at the average starting salary of the school's previous graduating class. We hardly ever made an exception to that. Most of our recruits could make more money elsewhere, and we knew that. We wanted them to choose us for other reasons. We figured that the people who were only looking for the highest salary were eventually likely to leave us for a better financial offer that came along. We depended on long-term loyalty, and rewarded it long-term. The worst thing we could do was hire someone, train him for a few years, and then see him walk out the door. That would have been a tremendous waste of our investment.

What constituted the best people? That was a key question. Everyone at Goldman Sachs had their own answer. We always left the final hiring decision to the head of the department where the new recruit was going to work. The department head knew better than anyone in personnel, or "human resources," as it's now called, just what skills, attitudes, and potential were needed to succeed in that particular department.

My own definition of "the best" consisted of brains, leadership potential, and ambition in roughly equal parts. Brains could be demonstrated by grades (from high school as well as college), test scores, SATs, GSATs, and the like. Leadership potential was harder to assess, but evidence came from extracurricular activities in high school and college and summer jobs. During interviews, I always looked for "take-charge" people, ones with energy and initiative, which are so critical to leadership. And to me, ambition was essential as well. We depended on people who were absolutely driven to succeed at everything they did.

11

THE TWO JOHNS

—〜〜—

SIDNEY WEINBERG DIED in the summer of 1969 at the age of seventy-eight. It happened just as the first astronauts were returning from the moon, but Sidney's obituary still ran on the front page of the *New York Times*, and deservedly so. He had done an enormous amount to pull Goldman Sachs back from the dark days of the Depression and secure it a position in the first tier of investment banking firms.

Sidney had retired as chairman four years before, in 1965, and selected as his replacement Gus Levy—or Gustave Lehmann Levy, to give him the full name he never used. He'd been the second highest money-maker at the firm (Sidney was the highest), and everyone agreed that he was the right choice. Sidney always looked down a bit at Gus, probably because he was a trader, not an investment banker, forgetting that he himself had once been the assistant porter. But Sidney had believed that the title of chairman and senior partner should go to the leading producer, and he had himself chosen Levy to be his successor on that basis. Despite his Brooklyn roots, Sidney had an Old World style: His office had the finest walnut paneling, and it was absolutely silent, at least when Sidney himself wasn't talking. Levy was no less working class than Weinberg; His father had been a manufacturer of wooden crates in New Orleans. But the trading floor where he worked was a fast-action, noisy, brutal kind of place, and Gus thrived there. There was the joke that people called him Gus because it took too long to say Mr. Levy. By the time they'd gotten the words out, he'd be gone!

Gus's great contribution to the firm was to prepare Goldman Sachs for an increasingly cutthroat marketplace, and more growth occurred under his leadership than under Sidney's. Sidney was primarily concerned with establishing the firm's reputation, because it had suffered so much. Gus wanted growth. He did not bother with strategic planning. To him, short range covered what was happening this morning, and long range extended forward to this afternoon. He did pick up from Sidney an interest in serving on corporate boards of directors. And he added to that a serious interest in nonprofits. Gus was on the board of about a dozen charities and cultural institutions, and was deeply involved with Mount Sinai Hospital as president of its board of directors. In those days, the stock market closed at three-thirty, and Gus was often out of the office by four o'clock and heading uptown to chair a two-hour meeting of the staff at the hospital before going out to dinner with a client.

Wall Street was not an easy place in the early 1970s, and not just because the Dow had dropped from about 1,000 in 1973 to just a little more than half of that at the end of 1974. It was also a time of significant upheaval. In February 1970, Goldman Sachs faced its first serious crisis since the Depression, when the Penn Central Railroad headed into bankruptcy. Even though Goldman Sachs had reason to wonder about the railroad's creditworthiness, it was unable to get truthful answers from Penn Central's chief financial officer, Dave Bevin, and the firm continued to try to sell Penn Central commercial paper right up to the day the bankruptcy was announced. When the announcement was made, it caused some disruption in the whole commercial-paper market.

In the aftermath, some of the Penn Central commercial-paper holders took Goldman Sachs to court, accusing the firm of withholding negative information from its customers. Although Levy testified that Goldman Sachs had never suspected that the railroad would ever go bankrupt, the courts concluded that the firm had not done enough to keep its customers fully informed. Its ruling declared that even if the firm did not know, it should have known. I always thought this certainly established a dangerous precedent in securities law. Who is to say what anyone should have known?

Penn Central had defaulted on $87 million in commercial paper, much of it sold by Goldman Sachs, whose partners' capital was barely $50 million at the time. A number of lawsuits were brought against the firm. It was scary for all of us, because the total claims at one point exceeded the firm's capital, and the partners would be personally liable for the remainder in the unlikely event that all the suits went against us. We eventually settled with many of our investor customers, buying back their Penn Central paper at a discount. The value of the paper subsequently rose when the railroad reorganized, limiting our losses some more. Nevertheless, it was a difficult time for the firm.

It's curious how well we remember the problems that the firm had rather than the details of the far more numerous triumphs. It's because management often has to spend such a large portion of its time on the problems with little time left to create the triumphs. In our case, we were deep enough with good people to be able to assign a small group to work quietly on the Penn Central problem, leaving all the others to work uninterrupted on the future successes. As a result, the five years after Penn Central were very exciting, successful ones for the firm, as markets recovered, important new clients were added, and new activities prospered.

But the next serious problem did occur one day in October 1976, when Gus Levy, who seemed to work twenty-four hours a day, seven days a week, and rarely relaxed, suffered a sudden stroke while attending a board meeting of the Port Authority of New York and New Jersey, one of the many organizations he served. As it happened, he was taken to Mount Sinai Hospital. When I got in to see him a day or two later, I could tell he was obviously a very sick man—weak, frail, and ghostly pale. Even if he survived, I couldn't imagine he would ever come back to running Goldman Sachs.

That was a terrible blow to the firm, as well as to me personally. He was almost as imposing a character as Sidney Weinberg had been. He was such a public figure, too, being a director of so many companies, and trustee of so many nonprofits. He was chairman of the New York Stock Exchange and was very active in the Republican party, not just in the city but statewide and nationally.

While Gus lay dying at Mount Sinai, John Weinberg and I sat down to-gether at the Goldman Sachs office to decide what to do. John was Sidney's son. In fact, he and I had made partner the same year, and we had talked together often about what was wrong with the firm. Whereas Sidney had se-lected Gus to succeed him well before his own death, Gus had made no such decision. It may have been because he could not choose between what became known in the firm as "the two Johns" (John Weinberg and I). More likely, it was because he had no thought of retiring. Because of his contribution, Gus received the greatest percentage of the firm's profits, but John Weinberg and I were tied at second behind him. It was clearly up to us to take strong leadership in this sudden crisis and make a clear recom-mendation to the management committee and all of the partners about who would succeed Gus.

I was several years older than John, and had been at the firm three years before he arrived in the summer of 1950. He'd gone to Deerfield and Prince-ton, and then served in the Marine Corps during World War II. That first summer he'd just finished the first of his two years at the Harvard Business School. Somehow the firm managed to squeeze another desk into that swel-tering squash-court office where I did my work—in fact, it faced mine. The idea was that I'd take him under my wing and do what I could to train him in the art of investment banking. Actually, he didn't need much training from me, having grown up with Goldman Sachs at home in Scarsdale as Sidney's son. John stayed with the firm and, six years later, made partner the very same day I did. Ever since, we'd moved up in the firm in lockstep, receiving iden-tical increases in compensation at every stage.

We were very good friends from the start. In the early days, we'd often have lunch together at Scotty's Sandwich Shop. Scotty's made the largest egg salad sandwich I had ever seen, and I ate my share of them. John and I would com-plain to each other about all the things wrong with Goldman Sachs, and talk about how things would go if we ever had a chance to run the firm—never dreaming that this would ever be an actual possibility.

Now, as we looked across the room at each other, we had to size each other up. I considered myself slightly more established than John was. I'd done a bit more to shake up the way the firm ran, and I was also better known in

Washington, an increasingly important criterion because I'd been heading up the Securities Industry Association for a year or two. I floated the idea of my becoming chairman, and of his taking the job of vice chairman, to succeed me when I retired.

John's face fell. I could see he didn't take that too well. As Sidney's son, and a proud man in his own right, he was not inclined to settle for being my number two.

I suppose we could have thrown the matter open to a vote of the management committee, or even of all the partners. But that sort of semipublic process would have been messy, with factions forming on each side. It was hard to imagine a resolution that would have yielded the united front the firm needed at such a difficult time. Plus, neither of us wanted to risk being labeled the "loser" while the other one was hailed as the "winner."

So we talked about the possibility of sharing power as co-chairmen. The more we discussed it, the more we could see that this was by far the best way to resolve what might otherwise be a troublesome situation. Neither of us had any compelling desire to be the sole chairman but it would not be good for Goldman Sachs or for either of us to end up as number two.

Still, it was an entirely novel solution. No Wall Street firm had ever had two co-chairmen before. What if we disagreed? There were many potential problems, but we thought then only of the positives, that it would extend the reach of each of us. Every client wanted to meet with the top man. If we shared the job, we could meet with twice as many clients. Each of us could cover for the other, too, if one of us had to be traveling. It got exciting as we thought about it. By pooling our abilities, we figured we would make the top of Goldman Sachs that much stronger.

As a practical matter, we decided that we would not divide the job up by responsibility, with John running one half and me running the other. Rather, we'd run the whole thing jointly. A decision by one of us would be a decision of both. If we felt a need to consult with the other before deciding, it would be up to us to do so.

We resolved that wherever either of us might be in the world, we'd try to talk to each other every day to keep up to date. We'd set ourselves up in adjoining offices, with a little conference room in between.

After we'd decided, we both felt relieved. Neither of us had to shoulder the entire responsibility of running Goldman Sachs alone, and neither of us had to settle for being number two. We'd each be free to travel without worrying too much about what was happening back at the office. The arrangement seemed ideal.

Gus faded quickly, as we'd feared, and when he died two days later, we told the Management Committee of our decision. The idea met with its approval, and so we informed the other partners. With their okay, we drafted an announcement to the firm and to the public. As far as we could tell, the news was greeted with universal enthusiasm. No one wanted to see the two of us fight it out. If anything, I think people were surprised that we were willing to share the position so amicably.

When the news was released, the public reaction was generally favorable, but not entirely so. Marvin Bower, the president of the management consulting firm McKinsey & Co., came to lunch in the partners' dining room a few days after the announcement. He congratulated us, told us of his deep admiration for us and the firm, and then declared that power-sharing arrangements never work. Every organization has to have a single boss. Period. Then he smiled. "Fortunately, when you realize that it isn't working, we'll be around to help you fix it." About a year later, we had Bower back. I'm sure he expected that we'd invited him to take him up on his offer. But instead we simply wanted to tell him how well this supposedly unworkable system was going.

And it did go well. In the eight years that John and I ran the place together, I don't believe we ever spoke a harsh word or had a significant disagreement. We both were devoted to the firm, and neither of us had an inordinately large ego. We complemented each other well. I was better at making plans and getting things organized. He was better working out disputes involving people. I could sometimes be harsh and demanding, or so I'm told. John had a more soothing, reassuring manner. If we had different views on an issue, we talked them over openly, each of us listening well. If I felt very strongly, he would usually defer to me. And I would yield to him on issues he was passionate about.

It worked remarkably well. Two heads were better than one. And we needed two heads to face the challenges before us.

12

THE FIRST *TRULY* INTERNATIONAL
INVESTMENT BANKING FIRM

———

TODAY, ALL THE LEADING American investment banking firms operate all over the world. But back when I started at Goldman Sachs in 1947, we did almost nothing outside of the United States. We had no offices or staff overseas, nothing at all. We had no company clients, no investor clients. In our entire history, we had managed only one public offering in Europe, and that was a $10 million bond issue for an Austrian Bank, Credit Anstalt, in 1929. The bank had gone bankrupt a few months later. This was not auspicious.

If any of our clients asked us to handle a foreign transaction, we'd have to decline, although for some especially promising deals we would sometimes refer the client to a "correspondent bank," a foreign bank with whom we had an exchange agreement. We'd give them business in their country on the assumption that they would give us their next piece of business in ours. Kleinwort, an old family firm not unlike Goldman Sachs, was our correspondent in London. If a client needed something done in London, we always recommended Kleinwort.

Edgar Baruc handled the referrals for us through our Foreign Department, which consisted entirely of . . . Edgar Baruc. An old friend of the Sachs', he looked very much the foreign officer, as he dressed in a formal, old-fashioned style, with celluloid collars, and had a waxed mustache. There was precious little for him to do, though. Sidney Weinberg's contacts were all American and, later on, so were Gus Levy's. I don't think Sidney ever left the United States, even for vacations. Asked once by FDR if he would serve as the U.S. ambassador to the Soviet Union, he replied, "In *Moscow?* I wouldn't have anybody to talk to!" When Gus had to fly to London one time for a business meeting, he flew back the next day. There was nothing more for him to do there.

By the 1960s, though, Morgan Stanley had opened an office in London, which was the principal financial center for all of Europe. Merrill Lynch had opened an array of offices across the continent; Salomon Brothers was doing a brisk business in bonds overseas; First Boston had a European office—and many lesser firms did, too. By that time, Goldman Sachs was generally considered to be in the "big five" investment banks, but we had no overseas presence at all, and I considered that dangerously parochial.

Just as ten years before, I had feared we had become over-reliant on Sidney, I now thought we were focused too exclusively on the American market. In 1964, Congress had imposed a corporate interest equalization tax that made it relatively more attractive for American companies to borrow overseas than in the United States. Since we had no operation to sell bonds overseas, this meant that our company clients had to turn elsewhere for those services. The best we could do was exploit a legal loop-hole that counted Canada as "overseas." We had an office in Toronto, through which we had sold a few bond issues for Owens-Corning Fiberglas and General Foods, but that was it.

In 1967, shortly before he died, Sidney received a call from the chairman of General Electric, still one of our most important clients, to say that GE was going to turn to Morgan Stanley to sell a bond issue for them in Europe. *Morgan Stanley!* Sidney managed to salvage a joint-manager position on the deal for Goldman Sachs, but still, that was a dark day for the firm. We had to get into Europe or else.

Finally, at the end of 1968, shortly after Gus took over, I managed to persuade him to ask a new partner named Michael Coles to take charge of our foreign activities. Coles was a British citizen, and had been well educated in American business as a top Harvard Business School graduate and had worked for some years in our buying department. His talents seemed well suited for the challenge of getting us into Europe.

Mike had almost nothing to work *with*, though. He began by opening an office in London in early 1970. A few partners grumbled that this might offend our old correspondent, Kleinwort, but Mike prevailed, and the firm installed a promising young man named Powell Cabot to run the operation there, and also serve as its sole employee.

To me, it was important that this not just be the reincarnation of the old foreign office of the Edgar Baruc days. I saw it as the overseas version of the New Business Department we had started domestically. Just as we had branched out across the country in the fifties, I thought we should branch out across Europe, and ultimately around the world. I never saw this as anything particularly inspired, though. I saw it as purely defensive. I had a terrible premonition that we would lose out badly if we *didn't* do it.

Like the intrepid new-business men spreading out across the United States, Mike found progress painfully slow at first. The Bank of England, which has oversight over the British banking industry just as the Federal Reserve does here, had to approve everything we proposed to do there, and neither the British merchant banking firms (their version of our investment banks) nor our American competitors exactly welcomed us into the fray. Our handler at the Bank of England was an eager young man named Eddie George. It was his job to make sure we obeyed the stringent regulations that had been laid down, and he was very strict with us. (He eventually rose to become chairman of the Bank of England at about the same time I became co-chair of Goldman Sachs. Unlike me, he was eventually knighted for his efforts.)

But thanks to Mike Coles, we managed to get a handhold in London, and then grab on more firmly. We added staff to the commercial-paper operation in the persons of Paul Goldschmid and Dick Rogoff, both very talented men, and then we hired an ambitious young man named Dusty Rhodes to move into corporate new-business activity. Rhodes paid calls on the top British companies just as our new business men had done with the top American ones. Mike Coles added his weight to the corporate side, too.

I thought that we should handle the international banking operation just the way we had gone after new business in the United States, by dividing up the territory. Once we had London nailed down, I thought we'd assign what amounted to a new-business man to France, and another one to Germany, and another to Scandinavia, and so on.

The problem was, because of our accounting procedures, the revenues and expenses for what was termed the International Division were always listed separately from those of the main Investment Banking Division, and for the first few years after Mike Coles started that first office in London, the International Division lost a considerable amount of money. Other partners at the New York office would complain to me that it was the fourth consecutive year that I'd lost $1 million on the London office. How could the firm continue to afford those kinds of losses? We were making very substantial profits everywhere in the United States, while I was blowing serious money on this ill-considered gambit in London. If this were the Chicago office, or Denver, or Los Angeles, they'd say, we'd fire the manager and close it down. "And that's what we should do here before we all go broke." People really spoke to me like that in the management committee when I went to them to approve the annual budget.

I had a hard time persuading them to stay the course, but I was absolutely convinced that Goldman Sachs had to internationalize or the consequences for the firm would be dire.

Finally it occurred to me that if people were complaining about the London office losing money, the thing to do was to change the accounting system, so they couldn't just blame it on the London office. The simple fact was, any new office would lose money the first few years of operation, whether it was London or Los Angeles. When you're starting a new activity in a new place you have to add people before you can expect revenues. That's what we'd learned with the New Business Department, which had taken a long time to produce a substantial return on our investment. And that's what was happening here.

So I decided to eliminate the new International Division as a separate profit center. From then on, all foreign investment banking income and expenses would be absorbed into the Investment Banking Division as a whole. Same for foreign income and expenses of our London equity sales activities: They would be credited and charged to the Equity Sales Division. And so it went throughout the firm.

Almost like magic, attitudes toward the new upstart International Division swung around 180 degrees. Every division head now felt some new responsibility for what happened in London, and the results began to show it. The red ink was easily absorbed into the black ink of the other divisions, and department and division heads began to see new opportunities for their departments and divisions outside the United States. They were determined to make sure that that part of their business would not be a loser for them.

It made me realize that internal accounting is more than just a way of keeping score. It can be a tool for changing incentives and direction.

In spite of the new incentives from the accounting change, it was tough going in London for a pretty long time. Not only did we have the competition of the traditional London banks and merchant banks, but the leading American firms had already become pretty well established. British corporate officers were reluctant to change bankers for fear of offending some old classmate from Harrow or Eton who now worked at Morgan Grenfell or Shroeders. In time, though, the different style of our new-business men began to catch on in London and throughout Europe. They were younger, seemed brighter, were better informed, had new ideas, sometimes were a little brash but didn't waste time talking about their golf game. Every once in a while some company "took a chance on Goldman Sachs" and word got around that our people were worth talking to. In the end, we worked our way up to the top or near the top in Europe faster than we had in the United States.

Once the incentives started turning in our direction, and every department in the firm recognized the opportunities for them, the globalization of the firm proceeded more quickly. Every year, it seemed, we added another country, or more than one. We quickly spread out across Europe, and advanced toward Asia.

Besides bringing a more open style to investment banking—which was old-fashioned in many other parts of Europe besides the U.K.—we also had attractive products to sell. A key one was commercial paper. American-style commercial paper was largely unknown to European companies, and it made an excellent door-opener for our new business men there, just as it had been for them in the States. The prospect of borrowing money at lower rates than what was charged by banks was eye-catching for companies that desperately needed money to grow.

We quickly persuaded several leading British companies to issue commercial paper through us, and it proved an attractive product on the Continent as well. One of the very largest new European companies that issued commercial paper through us was Electricité de France, the giant French electric power company. After several years, it had more than $2 billion of commercial-paper borrowings outstanding. And so it went across Europe. As we expanded, we also deepened our service within each country. Eventually, there would be no distinction whatsoever between the services we offered domestic clients and ones we offered overseas. The London office, just a one-man show when it first got going, now employs several thousand people, more than 80 percent of them European.

The move into Japan was truly a serious challenge, though. We had managed the initial public offering of Honda Motors of Japan back in 1962, and a partner named Charlie Salzman had visited Japan a few times. But otherwise we had no experience operating there. As in London, other American investment banks had made significant inroads in Tokyo by then, and they were beginning to compete successfully against the well-established Japanese investment banks, led by Nomura Securities. We had no clients in Japan, neither corporate nor investor ones.

As in London, we started small. The first member of our two-man team was Bill Brown, who'd attended a Jesuit seminary before graduating from Harvard Business School, and worked in Japan for Fuji-Xerox and as a business consultant. Bill's wife was Japanese, he spoke fluent Japanese, and having lived in Japan for many years, he was intimately acquainted with Japanese customs. He knew who was important in the banking world, how we should handle ourselves, whom we should get to know in the government, and how we should go about it. He had no banking experience per se, but we figured we could provide support in that area from other offices.

Bill's background made him an unusual choice, but he proved a perfect fit. He quickly managed to acquire for us a number of the necessary licenses and clearances from the Japanese minister of finance, clearing the way for us to become, in 1974, what the Japanese termed a "representative office," a designation that permitted us to conduct limited banking activities. The following year, we selected Gene Atkinson, an experienced vice president in corporate finance in the New York office, to join Brown in Tokyo. Together, they attracted such leading companies as Mitsui, Canon, and TDK as corporate clients.

After our experience in London, we recognized that it was important to staff the Tokyo office with as many Japanese bankers as we could. The problem was that there weren't many capable, experienced Japanese bankers available because all of them wanted to work for the five major Japanese banking firms. They were afraid that if people saw them working for an American firm like Goldman Sachs, it would be assumed that they had been fired by a Japanese bank, or why else would they have gone over to the other side? Other American firms like Merrill Lynch were staffed primarily by Americans for just this reason. But we felt it was essential to attract gifted Japanese bankers, and so we persisted and eventually prevailed.

We also had to put up with high barriers to entry if we wanted to do business in Japan. As I recall, as a foreign firm we had to pay $5 million to join the Japanese Stock Exchange, which we needed to do. It was like an initiation fee at a country club. If you wanted to play, you had to pay.

I was personally involved in the Japanese expansion only on a few occasions. One of the more notable ones was through my friendship with a retailer named Masatoshi Ito. One day in the early 1970s, he telephoned me at my office and said through his interpreter that he was in New York and wanted to pay me a visit. I had never heard of him at that point, but I made it a practice to see everyone (or nearly everyone) who wanted to see me, so I arranged for him to come in the following day.

When he arrived, I found Mr. Ito to be exceedingly deferential, a trait he shares with many of the Japanese I have come to know. He very politely explained that he was in the retail business in Japan and that his family operated a single small store in Tokyo called Ito Yokado. I tried not to look at my watch, but all I could think was, this was not a very likely candidate to be a client of Goldman Sachs. But the ambition shone through. He said his role model was Sears Roebuck, then the largest retailer in the United States, and that his dream was to become the Sears of Japan. He'd come to see me because he knew that Goldman Sachs had managed the first public offering for Sears. That was way back in 1906, but it obviously impressed him.

For fun, I pulled out of the firm archives the handwritten 1893 balance sheet of Sears, signed by "Julius Rosenwald, Treasurer," the one that is now on my wall at home. Their net worth then was $258,000. The next year's balance sheet was typed, and showed under "Current Liabilities" the item "$40,000 Notes Payable." I pointed out to Mr. Ito that that item represented the commercial paper Goldman Sachs had sold for them in 1894. I also noted the firm's growth, to a net worth of $350,000, an increase of about 40 percent in a single year.

Mr. Ito was very pleased with all this, and left with the promise that he would come by for a visit whenever he returned to New York City. And he did. Before long we became good friends, and when we opened our Tokyo office, I told Bill Brown to be sure to give Mr. Ito a call. He did, and he signed up Mr. Ito's company as one of our first corporate clients. As fast as the Goldman Sachs Tokyo office grew, Mr. Ito's business grew even faster. From that one small store in Tokyo, he assembled the second largest group of retail stores in Japan, with a total market value four times that of Sears. According to the annual Forbes tally, he is now one of the 150 richest men in the world.

In 1984, we expanded to Hong Kong, opening a two-man office there. I was co-chair by then and, before making the final decision, I flew over to get the advice of John Bainbridge, Hong Kong's chief financial officer, on what we should do to become a good corporate citizen. I expected him to say something like, "Join the Chamber of Commerce and contribute to the United Way." But he surprised me by saying that we didn't really need to do anything at all. "It's easy," he told me. "Just rent a room, get a phone, and start making money." We did all three, and he proved to be absolutely right.

I am not the hero of this story of our international expansion. In business no less than in sports, sometimes you play offense and sometimes you play defense. Taking Goldman Sachs international was not at all a bold, offensive stroke. It was pure defense. I was afraid of what would happen if we didn't do it. I would go further and say that, in general, I'm disinclined to play offense at all, at least in the sense of being the first one to try some bold new initiative. That raises the chances of being the first to make some very expensive mistakes. I'd much rather let someone else be first, try it, see how it goes—and if it goes well, then take full advantage of their experience. Same thing for new products: Goldman Sachs has innovated any number of new financial products through the years. Certain aspects of the first common stocks were a Goldman Sachs invention. I believe we had a role in the first initial public offering, the first preferred stocks, the first convertible bonds. Nevertheless, when I was co-chair, if somebody came to me and said, "Bear Stearns is about to come out with something, and we should hurry up and beat them to it," I was always inclined to say, "Go ahead and let them. And let's see how they do." If it worked and there was a market for it, we had a marketing organization that could introduce the idea to a hundred companies in a week. If the product was good, nobody would remember who came out with it first. In fact, because of our marketing skill, a lot of companies would think we were the first ones because we were likely to be the first to bring it to their attention.

As for globalization, I was not the only one pushing for it. There were two other distinguished figures at Goldman Sachs who contributed heavily. The first was Henry J. Fowler, who'd been secretary of the treasury in the Johnson administration. In 1968, when Nixon came in, Joe—as everyone called Fowler—talked to Gus about working for Goldman Sachs. He said that Sidney had offered him a partnership when he was through at Treasury. But Sidney had died without ever mentioning the offer to Gus. Joe told Gus that he shouldn't feel bound to a commitment that he hadn't made himself, and left the matter there. Gus consulted me and John Weinberg about what to do, and we both thought Sidney's instincts were sound, and Joe would be a tremendous addition to Goldman Sachs. I thought it would give our international efforts a great boost to have a former treasury secretary such as Joe with us. So Joe came on, and served as chairman of the new International Advisory Committee just as it was gathering steam under Mike Coles. With his political and financial contacts around the world, Joe proved a tremendous asset.

The other figure I'd single out in the globalization effort was Henry Kissinger. The day after President Ford lost the 1976 presidential election to

Jimmy Carter and it was clear that Kissinger would no longer be secretary of state, I flew down to see him in Washington to try to persuade him to join Goldman Sachs. He had already received a few offers by then, he told me, and he'd decided to hold off on all of them. After that, John Weinberg and I as co-chairmen met with him at least a dozen times to try and win him over. We both could see that Kissinger, one of the country's great statesmen, would be a terrific boon to the firm just as Joe Fowler was.

Henry was somewhat chary of becoming a partner for fear that people would think he was using his government service for commercial gain, but in the end he did agree to become a consultant to the firm on a two-day-a-month basis. Before long, he created his own consulting firm and devoted himself to that as his principal activity. To Goldman Sachs, though, he gave tremendous advice about the political side of world affairs. His judgment was invariably sound, and our consulting arrangement lasted eight valuable years. He headed our International Advisory Committee, which included other international figures like Bob McNamara, the former president of the World Bank and—as many people forget—of the Ford Motor Company; Akio Morita, the founder and president of Sony; and several others. I do take some joy in teasing Henry about how rich he would have been if he'd only become a partner back then. But I have no complaints, and he remains a good friend of mine and the firm's.

Even though I think of myself as fairly mild and easygoing, I also recognize that I had an ambitious side, too. And this came out at Goldman Sachs in a constant push for the company to move faster and further. I was determined that the firm extend its reach around the globe. I was always telling people I wanted to see Goldman Sachs become "the first *truly* international investment banking firm." It became something of a well-worn phrase. I meant that we should not just serve our domestic clients when they had objectives outside the United States, although that was most of what we did at the beginning. Rather, we would go toe to toe with all competitors, not only our U.S. competitors but the local competitors as well, to win clients everywhere in the world. It has taken several generations of management to do that, but it has largely happened. In most parts of the world, Goldman Sachs is now considered one of the leading investment banking firms, if not the leading one. That has been the fulfillment of a dream for me. It took a lot of work from a lot of different people, but by the time I retired, I could honestly say Goldman Sachs was at least beginning to be "the first *truly* international investment banking firm."

I was also keen to push up profits. Perhaps I got that from Gus. Back when I headed the Investment Banking Division, I'd instituted the concept of budgeting and planning in an organization that had done precious little of either. We could project expenses, but not revenues. So we began, long before I was co-chairman, to urge those in charge of various activities within my investment banking division to begin to forecast revenues, too. That was very difficult to do with any accuracy. Essentially, it was a matter of setting a particular goal, while recognizing that it might not be achieved because of unforeseeable changes in market conditions. Still, there was, at first, a tendency to set goals very conservatively so as to exceed expenses by only a little. I urged my colleagues to set higher goals, to challenge themselves, and to do better than just cover expenses. When a department head accepted a higher goal, he worked harder and smarter to achieve success. This is another way that accounting can change perception: the move boosted revenues and margins substantially.

When I became co-chairman, I pushed to institute the same process companywide. It was even harder for traders to forecast profits than it had been for investment bankers. But the forecast became a target, and an excellent incentive to improve performance throughout the firm.

The culmination of this forecasting process occurred on two weekends in January every year, since no one wanted long planning sessions during the week when they would interfere with business. The first weekend, the department heads appeared before the Management Committee to present their plans for the year. The next weekend, the branch managers followed suit. Our fiscal year began in December, and so by January we were into the new year, which made the annual forecast somewhat easier.

In January of 1984, I faced my eighth annual weekend of forecasting as co-chairman and I found myself, for the first time I could remember, feeling bored and tired. Normally I could summon up a reasonable amount of energy to get through the process, but not this time. Late on the final Sunday afternoon of the branch office review, we spent over an hour reviewing the budget of the Detroit office, whose annual revenues amounted to less than a tenth of one percent of the firm's total. I found myself getting uncharacteristically snappish, and I remember thinking, "By God, I don't think I can do this one more time." That's when I began to think seriously about retiring.

I'd been at Goldman Sachs for thirty-seven years by then. I loved the work, but it was hard and intense, and it took every ounce of energy I had, and I was getting worn down. I'd also found myself saying no to people more than ever before, and I sensed that my decision-making had turned cautious and conservative, and I didn't want to hold the firm back.

I was only sixty-two, certainly too young to retire altogether. I had more money than I'd ever dreamed of possessing, but I didn't have any interest in turning my attention to yachting, racehorses, golf, or any of the other usual pastimes of wealthy retirees. So I kept on for a few more months without confiding in anyone, lest any rumors force my hand. Then in May, I decided the time had come, and I told John Weinberg I wanted to retire.

The news caught him by surprise. Our partnership had worked so well, I think he imagined it would go on forever. He tried to talk me out of it, but soon saw that I had really made up my mind. We agreed that he would stay on as sole chairman for a couple of years, and that Steve Friedman, in investment banking, and Bob Rubin, in trading, should become vice chairmen and, in due course, co-chairmen. I supposed I could have stayed on in some sort of part-time, honorary position, but I always think that when you're out, you're out, so I didn't want to hang around to interfere with my successors. We made the announcement in August, with the decision effective in November, at the close of our fiscal year.

That final year, profits were up again, as they had been for every year of my tenure as co-chair. I was happy to go out on a high note.

I can't conclude this chapter without noting that Goldman Sachs went public in May of 1999 for $53 a share, representing a total market value for the firm of $23.6 billion. It's now more than twice that. I am proud of the excellent management performance of my successors and of the continued spectacular growth of the firm. Yet I worried that, with the transformation to a publicly owned company, some of the intangible special things about Goldman Sachs that I had treasured and tried to follow might be lost: the emphasis on always acting in the client's interest, on the importance of teams, on holding to high ethical standards. As I see what's happened, I think I was wrong to worry. If the firm had not gone public, it would not have had the capital to compete against the giants, including the $2.7 billion it raised from the public offering, and I would not have been happy with that. As to the intangible values that were and are so important, I believe the firm has maintained them pretty well; better than my fears had led me to imagine and, on the whole, better than the others. It has been twenty years now since I retired and Goldman Sachs is much bigger and much better than it used to be. I'm still terribly proud to have had a role in its development.

13

TROUBLES AT HOME

—⁓—

W HILE THE GOLDMAN SACHS YEARS were wonderful ones for me, they were hard on my wife, Sandy. Because of the demands of my job, I became too often an absentee husband and father. Anne had been born in 1953 and Greg in 1955. It wasn't unusual for me to stay on in the city for an important dinner with a client after work, so that I wouldn't get back to Essex Fells until ten o'clock, when I was so tired I nearly always went to bed soon after. There were many times when she urged me to come home earlier. I remember one meeting of the local PTA that she was particularly eager for me to attend but, inevitably, there was an important client for me to see that night as well. I thought that it was a better use of my time to attend to the client and not run the risk of his defecting to another investment banker, rather than swelling the crowd at the PTA. That was a typical decision on my part, although I was much better about being home on weekends, and I always reserved the entire month of August for a vacation with the family in a beautiful summer house we had bought on the ocean in Nantucket.

Sandy did a wonderful job raising Anne and Greg, and I feel bad, looking back, that she had to do so much of it on her own. But habits are hard to break, and I continued to log long hours at the office, and was off traveling a lot as well. It all came to a head at the end of the summer in 1970. It was time for Anne to return to California for her second year at Stanford, for Greg to come back to Essex Fells for his last year at the Pingry School in New Jersey, and for me to go back to work. Sandy decided she didn't want to come back to New Jersey, but rather to stay on in Nantucket, and so, reluctantly, we parted ways. After twenty-four years of happy marriage, we both knew it was the end. A few months later, the divorce was final. My parents, at that point retired in Connecticut, were reaching their fiftieth anniversary, and I had always hoped and expected to get there myself, but it was not to be. Sandy stayed on in Nantucket and lived the rest of her life year-round there, becoming a much-beloved and useful citizen. Fortunately for all, we had reestablished a friendly relationship several years before her death in 2002 from congestive heart failure.

After finishing at Stanford, Anne, our oldest child, went on to George Washington Law School and a legal career at Shearman & Sterling and Skadden Arps, two distinguished New York law firms. She was married to Bernard Crawford, a heart and lung surgeon, for twenty years and now lives in New York City and Millbrook, New York.

Greg, her younger brother, graduated from Haverford and is a writer doing radio plays for PBS and television plays for the BBC. He lives in Lenox, Massachusetts, with his wife, Lillian, and their two wonderful children, Morgan and Blake. I was surprised when they named their first daughter Morgan and made them promise that if the next one was a boy, they wouldn't name him Stanley. Morgan, age ten, is planning on becoming a prima ballerina, and Blake, nine, an Olympic soccer star.

After Greg went to Haverford, I remained in the Essex Fells house, even though it was way too big for one person. I had a housekeeper to take care of things. But it was a lonely life and, two years later, I met Jaan Chartener, whose late husband, Bill Chartener, had been a classmate of mine at Haverford. We'd recruited Bill to come to Goldman Sachs as our in-house economist; in the early seventies he took a year off to be assistant secretary of commerce in the Nixon administration. He'd been married to Jaan for only two years before he died suddenly. He'd named me his executor, and I found myself spending a fair amount of time offering financial counsel to his bereaved widow, who was pregnant besides. She was a serious academic whose interest in economics would soon take her back to Princeton for an advanced degree. We fell in love and married two years later.

Bill's son, Bob, twelve, and their new daughter, Sarah, two at the time of my marriage to Jaan, became part of my family. I adopted Sarah, and she is now Sarah Whitehead. Bob, who kept his father's name, went on to Hotchkiss, Princeton, Cambridge, and Harvard Business School, worked at Goldman Sachs for ten years, and is now a partner at J. H. Whitney. He is married to Kate, and they have two wonderful boys, William and Jaspar, and live in Washington, D.C. Sarah went to Bennington College and attended the Naropa Institute in Boulder, Colorado, where she now lives and practices alternative medicine with a group of other women.

Jaan was busy teaching economic history from Plato and Aristotle to Reagan, and I was more involved with Goldman Sachs than ever as I rose to become co-chairman in those years. I was again too much the absentee husband, rarely able to give Jaan the attention and companionship she deserved. After obtaining her degree, Jaan devoted herself to a regional theater company in Montclair, which she served as chairman of the board. Gradually, and sadly, we drifted apart. She had her academic friends, and I had my financial friends, and there was little overlap. The marriage officially ended in 1984, just before I retired from Goldman Sachs, but it had probably been over some time before.

14

"HAVE YOU TOLD HIM YET?"

—⁓—

SEVERAL MONTHS AFTER I HAD RETIRED, I was still using my old office at Goldman Sachs on Broad Street while I worked on a book tentatively called *The Social Responsibilities of Business*, which was intended to present case studies of companies doing good works while they made money for their stockholders. I'd finished one chapter and even received a modest retainer from McGraw-Hill, which wanted to publish it.

Late one afternoon in April, the phone rang. My secretary had gone home for the day, so I picked up the receiver myself and discovered Secretary of State George Shultz on the line. I'd known George slightly from his days at Treasury. Over the phone we greeted each other with a friendly hello, and then George got right to the point: "Can you be in my office in Washington at eight tomorrow morning?"

I made a quick calculation. To be there at eight, I'd have to take the shuttle that evening, which meant revising various plans. I was due to leave for a trip to the Far East the morning after that, so there wasn't much room to maneuver. But I could not say no to the secretary of state. "If you'd like me there, of course I'll come," I told him.

"Good." I could tell he was about to hang up, but my curiosity was burning. What could he possibly want so urgently? I figured it had to be some advice for some policy decision. "But George," I prodded, "if you can tell me what it's about, I can be thinking about it overnight."

"It's not something I can discuss over the phone," he replied. "I'll see you at eight." And then he hung up.

The other times I'd talked to him on the phone, he'd also been a man of precious few words. So I wasn't overly surprised.

So that was that. I called my housekeeper at home to say I would not be home for dinner, and then arranged to get a room at the Madison, my usual Washington hotel. As I pondered the matter, I decided Shultz had to be calling about Latin America. At the time, that whole region was beset with serious economic problems that had everyone on Wall Street concerned. American banks had taken on a lot of loans that were in serious danger of default. The economies of Argentina and Brazil were at particularly dangerous points. All I could think was that one or the other was on the verge of bankruptcy, and Shultz wanted advice on what to do when a sovereign nation goes bankrupt.

I called down to our Goldman Sachs library and, although it was after six P.M., I found a young assistant librarian still at her desk. I told her I needed all the latest economic and financial information we had about Argentina and Brazil right away. In a few minutes, two large manila envelopes arrived at my office. One was marked "Argentina," the other "Brazil." Each was filled with newspaper clippings, magazine articles, and our own Goldman Sachs analyses.

I tucked the envelopes under my arm, grabbed a small suitcase that I keep packed for just these sorts of emergency trips, and rushed off for the airport. Once I was in the cab, I started to dig in to the manila envelopes. I spent most of the trip studying up on Argentina and Brazil.

The next morning I arrived in Shultz's office at the State Department promptly at eight. He gave me a brisk hello, then started to pull off his comfortable cardigan sweater in favor of a proper jacket. "We're going over to see the President," he told me.

Well, this must be a serious crisis. It must be that *both* Argentina and Brazil are going bankrupt. I followed George to the elevator and descended with him to the basement garage. There, we climbed into his government limousine. As we emerged to the street, a Secret Service car followed behind us. I continued to clutch my manila envelopes, and my head was still brimming with facts about the endangered economies of Argentina and Brazil.

The whole way, though, Shultz said not one word to me, merely turned his head to the window to look at the cherry trees, which were in bloom all over Washington.

We pulled in through the gate to the West Wing of the White House, and in moments we were inside, headed up the stairs. The West Wing is very crowded, with a lot of people packed into small offices; there is no long formal corridor to walk through. We wove our way through to the door of the Oval Office. I've been there many times now, but it always gives me a this-can't-be-me feeling. It is, in fact, quite modest, at least by international standards. There are no uniformed guards by the door, no ceremonial flags. Just the President's secretary sitting behind a desk outside. We waited only a moment or two before the door opened, and Shultz ushered me in.

The Oval Office is smaller than you'd imagine, but it is still tremendously august. You can't escape thinking this is the power center for virtually the entire world. Inside, the President reached out a hand to greet me. He was very jaunty and warm. I'd met him years before when I'd hosted a large dinner in New York for his 1980 election campaign. He'd sat beside me, and I'd been very impressed by his confidence and conviction. Now, he directed me and George to seats on the two couches in the middle of the room.

"Have you told him yet?" the President asked George.

I got a slightly queasy feeling in my stomach. I still didn't know what this was about, but I sensed that my manila envelopes might not be needed.

Shultz shook his head, and Reagan sat down on the couch across from me. "We understand you've retired from Goldman Sachs," he began, "and we want you to come to Washington to join the State Department as deputy secretary of state."

Then Shultz turned to me and added, "I want you to be my partner."

I was floored. Usually I have a decent instinct for what's about to happen, but not this time. I fumbled around for a bit, saying how honored I was, but how surprised. I started to blurt out to the President that I really didn't know very much about foreign policy—until a frown from Shultz told me to back off from that. Still, I had to tell the President that I would feel more comfortable at Treasury, the World Bank or the Fed—financial institutions I'd developed a feeling for over my many years as an investment banker.

"But John, there aren't any openings there," the President interrupted.

I didn't accept on the spot. I'd learned never to make big decisions without giving myself time to reflect. I told the President that I would be leaving the next day for three days in Hong Kong, and then a week in Japan. I was scheduled to make several goodwill appearances there, and give some speeches, a kind of last-hurrah farewell tour to see Goldman Sachs friends and clients. "I'll have an answer for you when I get back," I told him. "Would that be all right?"

That was greeted by silence. Finally, the President said, "Gee, ten days is an awful long time, John. Why don't you just go to Hong Kong and skip Japan? We'd really like to get an answer from you sooner."

The Japan visit had been long planned, and I felt rotten at the prospect of canceling it at the last minute, since quite a number of important people were planning to turn out. But this was the President of the United States, and I simply could not say no to him. "All right," I said.

"Fine," he replied. "I'll see you back here early next week." He stood up and went to his desk to make a note on his calendar.

I hadn't realized I would be expected to come back to give him my answer in person. "Very good," I said, all the same.

And that was it. George and I left the room. Fortunately, no one asked about my manila envelopes.

As I thought about it afterward, I realized that George had been so secretive about the true purpose of the meeting because he and the President wanted to preserve maximum impact. They didn't want me to spend any time thinking up reasons to say no. Shultz also didn't want the political people at the White House to be coming up with other names.

I had never thought of taking any Washington job. I was very committed to my life in New York, and I had that book to write. Still, I talked over with my children the prospect of my moving to Washington. Anne was married now and living in New York, and Greg was writing radio plays for PBS on Nantucket. Neither had any objection to my taking the job. All the same, I did brood about it a little on my trip to Hong Kong. While I was there, I asked the U.S. chargé d'affaires what it was like to work for the State Department, and he gave reassuring answers. Nevertheless, I think the question puzzled him, since I couldn't tell him why I was asking.

By the time I returned, I'd decided to tell the President I would accept. For our meeting we repeated the same ritual as before. I met Shultz at his office and rode with him and his Secret Service entourage to the White House. In the car I told him my decision. He seemed very pleased and relieved. He let me know that he was indeed looking for someone to be a true partner. As secretary of state he had to be out of the country a lot, and he wanted to have someone who could act in his place whenever he was away. Ken Dam, the deputy I was replacing, had had the role more of an assistant. An economist who had written a book with George, Ken was very capable but was much younger than George, and he was not inclined to take it upon himself to make the important decisions, leaving them all to the secretary. George wanted someone who could handle things in his stead.

That was appealing to me, since at that stage of my life I didn't want to be anyone's assistant. I'd had enough of that years back with Sidney.

In the Oval Office, the President was completely charming. "It's exactly three o'clock," he told me after a glance at his watch. "I've reserved fifteen minutes for this meeting, but I've told my secretary that if it takes longer to convince you to take the job, she should cancel my next appointment. In fact, I've told her to cancel all my meetings right through till ten o'clock tonight, if necessary. So I figure I've got seven hours to persuade you. Where do we start?"

"Mr. President," I replied, "I told George on the way over that if you both still want me, I'll do it. I have a lot to learn, but I'll get right at it."

"Good," the President replied. He checked his watch again. "Well then, we still have twelve minutes left. Why don't we go for a walk in the Rose Garden?"

He opened up the French doors, put his arm around my shoulder, and we went for a little walk outside. It was a beautiful April day, and the spring flowers were all in bloom. He told me how, when he finished his second term as governor of California, he'd wanted to retire to his ranch. All he wanted to do at that point was go riding, chop wood, and enjoy life with Nancy. But a group of old friends had persuaded him to run for President, and he was glad they had. Now he was glad I'd made a similar choice and agreed to join his team.

If I had not already been a big fan of the President, I would certainly have been won over by our little walk in the garden. He was so charming, so kind and relaxed and comfortable with himself. It was an enormous pleasure to be in his company. People tend to scoff at him and say he was just an actor, but I thought he was a wonderful human being. I practically floated out of the White House all the way back to New York. (As for that book, I returned the advance to McGraw-Hill. The first chapter is still lying in my bottom desk drawer.)

The next morning, I started paying special attention to the foreign news in the *New York Times*. And a few days later, I was startled to see my name on the front page after the White House announced my appointment, pending Senate approval. There was a picture of me, too.

If my head swelled at all that morning, it was brought back down to its original size when I pulled in to Ed Peeler's gas station in Essex Fells. It was my habit to fill up on Saturdays for the week of commuting ahead. Ed was something of a local institution, and I always liked chatting with him. "Morning, Mr. Whitehead," he greeted me. He was always quite formal.

"Morning, Ed."

He tucked the nozzle into the gas tank, and stepped closer to my open window. "I see you're gonna leave Essex Fells."

"Yes, that's right."

"Gonna work for the government."

"Yes."

"Too bad." He shook his head sorrowfully. "If Goldman Sachs had a better pension plan, you wouldn't have had to."

I've told that story many times, and it always gets a laugh. But I treasure that exchange. As I met world leaders, and struggled with some of the larger problems around the globe, and started to feel self-important, I always brought myself back to earth by remembering my conversation with Ed Peeler.

I moved to Washington the very next day, Sunday, taking up what I thought would be temporary residence at the Watergate Hotel, not far from the Watergate office building where the famous break-in occurred, just a few blocks from the State Department building. Even though I went immediately on the federal payroll, I could not legally assume either the title or the duties of deputy secretary until I had been confirmed by the Senate. I had to be careful about that, since the Senate was quite protective of its prerogative of confirming all presidential appointments. Ken Dam very graciously offered to let me share his office until I was confirmed. He also showed me the ropes.

I discovered that the position of deputy secretary came with a small staff of its own. Ken had filled all of the spots. I could have changed any of them if I'd wanted to, but I elected to keep them all on, and was glad I did. Wes Egan was my chief of staff for a brief time, until he left to become ambassador to Portugal. I then signed on Marc Grossman, who'd been the executive assistant to Peter Carrington, the secretary general of NATO. My only addition was Sharon Matthews, who'd worked with me at Goldman Sachs, whom I hired to serve as my liaison to the business community. I'd had only one personal staff assistant and one senior secretary at Goldman Sachs, even when I was co-chairman, and was impressed to see how much more I could accomplish with the extra help.

I quickly got a sense of the State Department's organizational structure and its high-quality Foreign Service staff. I had a lot to learn from them. I was not just being modest when I told the President that I was not all that well versed on foreign policy. Over the next month, I tried to get up to speed by setting up daily briefing sessions from regional assistant secretaries and various department heads to tutor me on geopolitics. I found these cram sessions tremendously helpful. You couldn't beat the faculty–student ratio, which ran about a hundred to one. I learned a lot from the experts, and they got to know me better, too.

My daughter Anne was amused at the prospect of her banker father trying to become a foreign policy expert, and she gave me two sets of flash cards to further my education. One set listed the capitals of each country; the other the political leaders. With 185 countries recognized by the United States, it isn't easy. I was proud that I could soon rattle off the capital of the tiny South

American nation of Surinam. It's Paramaribo, of course. And the president of the west African country Burkina-Faso? None other than Captain Blaise Compaore. Possibly to her surprise, I found the cards very helpful, and I carried them around with me, so I could quiz myself in spare moments.

George Shultz had great respect for the professional Foreign Service officers in the Department, too. Every morning between eight and nine, he squeezed in four fifteen-minute meetings, each with a different group of about a dozen senior staff people. That way, within an hour, he could meet with the fifty top people in the department. If he had a message to get out, or if any of the fifty had something important to tell him, that was the time to do it. Eventually, I chaired these meetings when Shultz was away. I wished we'd used a similar technique at Goldman Sachs.

Some secretaries bypass the Foreign Service professionals in favor of their own hand-picked staff. Jim Baker, when he became secretary of state under George H. W. Bush, operated this way, moving a small group of his people with him from one problem to the next. George Shultz took the opposite approach, relying heavily on the in-house staff of experts, and I followed his lead, always drawing on the State Department's specialists to work on whatever problem was at hand. State Department people were marvelously loyal to Shultz as a result; it made a big difference to them to sense they were being listened to and counted on.

I thought it made a lot of sense to use the people we had. They were all eager to help, deeply knowledgeable, and very responsive to the leadership. They didn't expect George or me always to agree with them. They recognized that, obviously, the secretary and his deputy had a right to decide issues for themselves. They were equally effective in carrying out decisions whether they agreed with them or not.

In the month before my confirmation hearings, I took the opportunity to meet with each one of the Senate Foreign Relations Committee members who would be deciding my fate. And not just a courtesy call, either. First impressions are important, and if I was confirmed, I would be working closely with these senators for the next four years; I wanted to get each of these relationships off on the right foot.

When it finally came time for my confirmation hearings, I was flattered to be introduced to the Senate Foreign Relations Committee by four senators, rather than just one from my home state, as is the custom. Both senators from New York, where I'd worked for Goldman Sachs all those years, and both senators from New Jersey, where I'd lived, showed up to do the honors. As it happened, an old friend of mine, Senator Claiborne Pell, a Democrat from Rhode Island, was the chair of the committee, and he was a little amused to see the four senators, first Bill Bradley and Frank Lautenberg of New Jersey, and then Pat Moynihan and Al D'Amato of New York, all talking me up in their introductions, each one's rhetoric exceeding the one before. This didn't leave much time for me to testify. I said a few very safe things about the importance of bipartisanship in foreign policy. When I was finished, there were no questions, and I was approved on a unanimous voice vote.

That was a relief, but I still needed to be approved by the full Senate, and here is where I hit a snag. I joined a select group of thirty-seven presidential appointees, most of them would-be ambassadors, whose appointments were being held up by Senator Jesse Helms, a Republican from North Carolina, as a point of personal privilege. Helms found it to be good politics to express his general disapproval of the State Department this way.

When I reported to Shultz that my hearings had gone well, and that my only problem now was Senator Helms, he said, "Well, good. You're a good Republican. You're just the person to take this up with him."

So I called up Senator Helms and asked if I could come up and see him. (I'd learned by then that one always goes "up" from the State Department in Foggy Bottom to Capitol Hill, even though I'd never detected any incline.) He said to come the next morning.

I knew Jesse Helms just well enough to call him Jesse, which distinguished me from practically everyone else at State. He was very scornful of the department, and invariably complained that it was filled with that tired old government troika, "waste, fraud, and mismanagement," and he was convinced that the career Foreign Service officers were soft on Communism besides.

Although I disagreed with him on most points, I rather liked Jesse personally. I enjoyed his courtly southern manner, and admired his backbone. He was one of the strongest personalities in the Senate, and possibly the key senator to the State Department, since he often opposed what we tried to do, and was often quite vocal about his objections.

When we met at his office, we greeted each other warmly but warily. I told him that I'd become the thirty-eighth presidential appointee to be held up by him. "This is a terrible embarrassment to the President," I said, "and I've come here to seek your advice as to how all this can be resolved."

This brought a sly smile from the senator. "Well," he said, "I am glad to see you. You're the first person from the administration to ask me that. All the rest do nothing but berate me."

This was encouraging.

"Actually," he went on, "it's not a difficult problem to solve. I have a young man on my committee staff who I consider to be very knowledgeable about foreign affairs. He's been in his current job for six or seven years now, and I think it's high time for a change." He looked straight at me. "I believe he'd make a fine ambassador somewhere."

He mentioned the man's name. I'd never met him, but I did recognize him as experienced and reasonably well regarded.

"Well, where does he want to be ambassador?" I asked. I thought for sure Jesse would say the Soviet Union or Great Britain.

Jesse waved a hand in the air nonchalantly. "It doesn't especially matter. He just needs a little practical experience out in the world. Develop himself a little."

"Would Barbados be all right?" I asked, knowing that post was about to open up, and it wasn't a particularly sensitive spot politically.

"Barbados sounds very nice," Jesse replied.

I couldn't believe my ears. "Just so we understand each other, am I right in thinking that if I can get the President to appoint your staff officer to be ambassador to Barbados, you will let all thirty-eight of us out of the penalty box?"

Jesse smiled again, more broadly this time. "You know, John? I think you'll make a damn fine deputy secretary. I really do."

Back at State, I checked around and found out that Jesse's staffer was actually better qualified than I had thought. I went to the White House to talk the matter over with Bob Tuttle, the son of one of Reagan's closest personal friends. Bob was assistant to the President for personnel. He saw the beauty of the arrangement, and the President made the announcement the next day. A day later, Jesse released his thirty-eight hostages. I called him right up to thank him, and he said, courtly as ever, "No, thank *you*."

As it turned out, a background check developed some negative information that put the kibosh on the staffer's candidacy. I braced myself for an irate phone call from Jesse for double-crossing him. He did call, but when I told him how sorry I was, he said, "Oh now, don't you be sorry. You did everything you said you'd do. I like doing business with you. You keep your word."

Inevitably, I had a few other disagreements with Jesse during my tenure, but we always got along, which is more than most people can say.

For me, the key lesson was the value of speaking directly to an adversary in an effort to work things out. In this particular case, Jesse's obstructionism was taken as a fact of life. No one made the effort to understand what he was trying to achieve. As it happened, he enjoyed all the attention that came with causing such a logjam. But more deeply, he wanted respect. And I showed him respect by asking what he wanted. I am not convinced he cared about his staffer's ambassadorial career all that much. He wanted only to be taken seriously, to be asked. The other point is the importance of trust. "Trust is the coin of the realm around here," Shultz told me often. And it is true. If your adversary trusts you, he is far less of an adversary.

I was sworn in two weeks later. George Shultz performed the ceremony at the State Department. I was only sorry my parents had died a few years before, and so were not there to see that their once-mischievous son had indeed made something of himself after all.

I came to appreciate and admire George Shultz enormously. It was clear he truly meant to make me his partner. Every secretary can use his deputy whatever way he chooses. Some secretaries prefer to be the "outside" person who specializes in overarching policy decisions while the deputy is the "inside" person running the department. Others divide up the world by territory, the secretary reserving, say, Europe, Asia and the Middle East, and leaving everything else to the deputy. Or a secretary might carve it up by subject area and devote himself to political and strategic issues while ceding economic ones to the deputy.

For Shultz and me, the partnership was similar to what I had developed with John Weinberg at Goldman Sachs. When he was out of town, I would handle everything that came up at State in his place, which freed him to devote himself to whatever he needed to attend to elsewhere in the world. And it worked very well. We agreed on all the basics. We were both middle-of-the-road Republicans; I was probably a little more middle-of-the-road than George, sometimes impatient with the right-wingers in our party as well as with the ultraliberals among the Democrats. We tried to keep each other fully informed so there would be no unwelcome surprises. Like me, he had come out of the business world—he had been president of the international engineering and construction firm of Bechtel. But he had infinitely more political experience than I, having been secretary of labor, chief of the Office of Management and Budget, and secretary of the treasury. He helped me avoid some of the more hazardous political pitfalls. He was wonderfully loyal to me, never hanging me out to dry, as superiors sometimes do in Washington. He was a wonderful boss, and I am only sorry he didn't run for president. He would have been a great one.

15

EMERGENCY DIPLOMAT

※

A FEW DAYS AFTER I WAS SWORN IN that October of 1985, Shultz was off in Latin America, so the President turned to me to handle a piece of international diplomacy stemming from the *Achille Lauro* hijacking, which had taken place on October 7. The *Achille Lauro* was an Italian cruise ship that, while sailing in the Mediterranean off the coast of Egypt, had been seized by a terrorist group headed by the notorious Abu Abbas, with four hundred passengers on board. One was an American in a wheelchair, Leon Klinghoffer, and he was murdered and thrown overboard. Abbas later claimed that Klinghoffer "was inciting and provoking the other passengers. So the decision was made to kill him." Abu Abbas was captured, arrested, and imprisoned by the Italian authorities, but then summarily released on the grounds that there was insufficient evidence to hold him.

President Reagan despised terrorists above all else, and he issued a sharp criticism of Italy's president, Bettino Craxi, for having let Abbas go. Craxi reiterated the Italian legal position that their laws did not permit him to hold a suspect more than two weeks without making specific charges. Furthermore, Craxi then declared that he was so insulted by Reagan's remarks, he could not bring himself to attend the G7 conference of representative of the seven leading industrial democracies, which Reagan was hosting the next week in Colonial Williamsburg. Reagan did not want to be embarrassed by Craxi's absence from the conference. My assignment: Go to Rome and get Craxi to change his mind.

I flew to Rome the next night. I'd sent off a cable asking Craxi to see me, and I'd spoken to the Italian ambassador in Washington, Rinaldo Petrignani, whom I knew socially, and he assured me that Craxi was serious about not attending. When I arrived at the Rome airport, I was met by our ambassador, Max Rabb, who said I had an appointment at noon with the Italian president. That was just a few hours off.

When Max and I arrived at the presidential palace, we were ushered into an ornate room where a small table stood in the middle with two chairs on each side. In a moment, Craxi appeared, accompanied by his foreign minister, Giulio Andreotti. The atmosphere was extremely stiff and chilly. They both shook hands with us, but didn't say a word. We sat down, Craxi and Andreotti on one side, and Rabb and I on the other. Craxi placed his briefcase on the table, opened it, and pulled out a yellow pad filled with many pages of handwritten notes.

Obviously, he had a lot to say. I thought it best to let him speak first. But he opened the session by saying that *I* was the one who had asked for the meeting, so I should begin by saying what was on my mind. I explained that President Reagan had asked me to find out President Craxi's thoughts on the *Achille Lauro* matter. Craxi was eager to speak, and quickly plunged into his notes, describing in great detail his version of the *Achille Lauro* incident.

At various points, Max would try to interrupt to disagree with Craxi's version of events, but each time I pinched his knee under the table and managed to quiet him, so that Craxi could say his piece without interruption.

He did go on. The gist of it was that, if it hadn't been for him, all four hundred of the cruise ship hostages would have been killed, not just one. And there was some truth in that.

I made notes on a yellow pad of my own, so that I could brief the President on Craxi's remarks upon my return.

When Craxi finally finished, well over an hour later, he heaved a great sigh of relief, and then returned his notes to his briefcase. It was as if an enormous weight had been taken off him. He no longer seemed tense. He turned to me with a smile, offering me a turn to speak, but it was clear that from his point of view the meeting was over. This was certainly not the time for any rebuttal from me. I could tell that none of the differences mattered anyway. I

*(Right) My parents,
Eugene Whitehead and
Winifred Kaufmann, on their
wedding day in 1918.*

(Below) On my tricycle at age four.

*(Above) With my younger sister,
Margaret, at the beach in New
Jersey.*

*(Left) By my parent's house in
Montclair, New Jersey, at age 12.*

(Above Left) My childhood home at 110 Summit Avenue in Montclair.

(Above) My graduation portrait from the Montclair High School yearbook. I'm the class of 1939.

(Above)
My parents in 1976.

(Right)
With my wife, Sandy, and our children, Gregory and Anne, at our house in Essex Fells, New Jersey in 1957.

(Right) With my shipmates from the Thomas Jefferson *in Oran, Algeria, just before coming to Scotland to train for the Normandy landing. I'm in the middle of the top row.*

(Above) With my colleagues from the first Management Committee at Goldman Sachs.

(Left) After returning from Saudi Arabia during the oil crisis of 1974. I don the traditional garb for a photo with Goldman Sachs chairman Gus Levy.

(Left)
With John Weinberg,
my co-managing partner at
Goldman Sachs from 1976
to 1984.

(Right)
With Solidarity leaders
Lech Walesa and Bronislaw
Geremek during my visit
to Poland as Deputy
Secretary of State in 1986.

(Left)
With President Reagan
in the Oval Office
discussing U.S. policy
toward Eastern Europe
in August of 1988.

(Right)
With Frank Sinatra and
the Reagans at a
New York fundraiser for
Ronald Reagan in 1980.

(Left) With Lesley
Stahl in April 1986
to discuss American
policy regarding the
Soviet Union on
Face the Nation.

(Right) With Soviet President
Mikhail Gorbachev at the
Russian Embassy in
Washington, D.C., in 1987.

(Above)
With President Reagan in the White House Library in 1988.

(Left)
Trekking in Nepal after a meeting of regional foreign ministers and ambassadors there in 1987.

(Right)
Meeting Mujahedin refugees in Pakistan during an International Rescue Committee trip in 1984.

(Right) Greeting Li Peng, Vice Premier of China, during a trip to Beijing in July 1995. Henry Kissinger looks on, along with Nancy Dickerson Whitehead.

(Left) President Bill Clinton welcoming me to a White House dinner in October 1995. Also pictured: Vernon Jordan and James Wolfensohn, President of the World Bank.

(Right) With Kofi Annan, UN Secretary General, at an International Rescue Committee dinner in 1997.

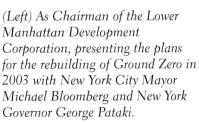

(Left) As Chairman of the Lower Manhattan Development Corporation, presenting the plans for the rebuilding of Ground Zero in 2003 with New York City Mayor Michael Bloomberg and New York Governor George Pataki.

(Right) With my wife, Nancy Dickerson Whitehead, after the New Jersey Devils, of which I was a minority owner, won the Stanley Cup in 1995.

(Left) Sailing off Sakonnet Point in Rhode Island.

(Right) Morgan and Blake Whitehead, the two daughters of my son Gregory and his wife, Lillian. They are two of my sixteen grandchildren.

thanked him for his detailed account, which I promised to report promptly to the President. "This will certainly clear up the misunderstanding," I promised him. "I'm sure the President will want to renew his invitation for you to come to Williamsburg. And I hope I can tell him you'll be there."

"Now that he knows what happened, I will be there," he replied. "Thank you for coming."

The meeting complete, we left with warm handshakes and big smiles, both of us pleased to have repaired a relationship that was important to both nations.

The truth was that, despite the President's aversion to terrorism, it was too late to do anything about the release of Abu Abbas. He was forced to leave Tunisia for Iraq, became general director of the Palestine Liberation Front, but seemed to fade from influence in terrorist circles. He was captured in April 2003 by U.S. special forces outside Baghdad shortly after the American invasion. He died during detention the following year. At this point, in any event, he was gone, and there was no way to bring him back. It was a *fait accompli*. To punish Italy for its actions would only be to punish ourselves. If Craxi had boycotted the G7 meeting, his first, that would have created a big rift between the United States and Italy, and a quite unnecessary one.

I was proud of the way I handled that, which was entirely by instinct. There is no little diplomatic handbook that governs such situations, and Shultz was not one to give how-to advice. But it seemed to me that, in general, listening is better than talking. You never learn anything when you're talking. That was a lesson I had tried to drive home to our new-business men, and it was just as true here. Let the other fellow talk before you do. That way you'll learn what the real problem is, and that is the first step toward resolving it. For years afterward, Max Rabb told me his knee still hurt from my pinching.

Before I left for Italy, word had gotten around the State Department that I was going abroad. Other officials had suggestions for other diplomatic visits I might make before I came home. Eager to please at this stage of my diplomatic career, I had agreed to make two more stops.

The first was to see Hosni Mubarak. He had succeeded Anwar Sadat as Egypt's president after Sadat's assassination in 1981. Sadat had taken an enormous risk at Camp David by being the only Arab leader to recognize Israel, and now it had fallen to Mubarak to make that decision work in a desperately poor country like Egypt. He was trying to incorporate a few elements of the free market into an economic system where the government set most of the prices. He'd been told I was a former businessman who knew all about free markets, so he was eager to meet me.

I found Mubarak to be an earthy, rough-hewn figure who lacked the urbane charm of his predecessor. Politically insecure in the still-turbulent aftermath of the assassination, he was reluctant to take any bold steps that might get him into trouble. Canny and street-smart, he did not have much of an academic turn of mind, and I could tell I would make no progress whatsoever if I tried to discuss economics with him on any kind of theoretical basis. So I turned to a simple example: the price of bread. Bread sold everywhere in Egypt for a very low price, about a penny a loaf, which in no way reflected its true cost. This was, of course, very popular politically, since bread is a staple of the Egyptian diet. But it wreaked havoc with the federal budget. I recommended to Mubarak that the price be raised to the equivalent of ten American cents, which was much closer to its free-market price.

He looked at me, amazed. If he did that, he would meet the same fate as Sadat.

"Well, how about to two cents a loaf, then?"

Mubarak pointed out that even to double the price of bread could be catastrophic. But he did acknowledge that the bread subsidy was a huge drain on the government's resources. He made no concessions to me at the time. He was a proud man, a tough negotiator, and a survivor. And I would lose many arguments with him in my years at State. But our ambassador to Egypt, Nick Veliotes, told me afterwards that he thought I had made some progress with Mubarak on the price question and, sure enough, a few weeks later he did indeed raise the price of bread.

After that, I visited President Habib Bourguiba, the elderly leader of Tunisia. Well over eighty, he had been in office for over thirty years and, for all that time, he had been a tremendously loyal friend of America. Now, though, his faith was being sorely tested. A few weeks before I arrived, Israel had bombed the country in a surprise raid, destroying barracks and other facilities Israel believed were being used to train terrorists. Arafat and the PLO had taken refuge in Tunisia after being driven out of Lebanon by Ariel Sharon. Most Tunisian officials believed that the United States must have had advance word of the attacks, since we had such close ties with Israel, and there was considerable agitation in the country to break off diplomatic relations with us in retaliation. My job was to assure the Tunisian government that, in fact, the United States had been caught entirely off guard, which was the case. Israel had not informed us ahead of time.

A long series of appointments with lower-level government officials had been arranged for me, culminating in a meeting with Bourguiba at the very end. But I thought that was exactly the wrong approach. For I saw Bourguiba himself as the key. After all his years of unswerving loyalty to this country, it would be hard for him to believe that we were complicit in such a destructive act. I figured Bourguiba was not likely to counter what all his other officials would tell me in our meetings but, if I saw him first, and could persuade him of the truth of America's ignorance about the bombing, then he would persuade the others in his government to accept the American position.

Fortunately, I was able to rearrange the lineup and meet Bourguiba first, at breakfast the morning after I arrived. All the ministers in his cabinet would also be there; I would follow up with them personally afterward.

At the breakfast, I addressed myself primarily to Bourguiba as the others listened. I told him that President Reagan had sent me to personally reassure him that, no matter how it might look to Tunisians, the United States did not know in advance about the bombing. Furthermore, he had my word that we would have stopped it if we had known. I reminded him that we had publicly criticized Israel for the raid after it took place.

I saw Bourguiba nod his head in agreement. I was gratified to see he was accepting my explanation.

In reply, he launched into a long oration, reciting his love for America. He recalled how General Patton had freed Tunisia from Rommel's army in the Battle of Madanin during World War II.

When the breakfast was over and we all stood up, Bourguiba, clearly moved by his memories of American troops liberating his people, reached over to me to clasp my hands in his. He was a small man, no more than five foot three, near-sighted and quite deaf. As he moved closer to me, still clasping my hands, I could see tears streaming down his cheeks. "I believe in America," he said, his voice quaking. "They would never betray us. You tell your President I understand." I was so moved by this profession of faith in our great country that a tear or two trickled down my face, too.

As I glanced around to his other ministers, I could see that none of them were in any mood to disagree. Bourguiba turned and walked away from me. But I'll never forget his parting words: "Please give my best regards to President Eisenhower." I was taken aback by that, but decided it was further proof of his undying loyalty to our country. To him, Eisenhower—the liberator of Europe, and of North Africa, from the Nazis—would always be President in his mind. Eisenhower was also much admired in the Arab world for having put an end to British and French imperialism in the Middle East, opposing their plan to recapture the Suez Canal in 1956, and because he was perceived to have been the last American president to have stood up to Israel.

I flew back that night, very happy with the result. I had batted three for three. I returned to Washington, and in the morning gave a report to President Reagan, who was delighted by what I had been able to accomplish on my first diplomatic foray. He also got quite a chuckle out of President Bourguiba's exit line.

16

PRESIDENTIAL MISSION TO
THE EASTERN BLOC

———

AFTER I'D BEEN IN THE STATE DEPARTMENT about a year, I began to
look for a particular area—either a region of the world or a geopolitical
issue—to focus on. Whatever it was, I wanted to be able to take personal responsibility, while leveraging my effort to make a significant difference.

I had been enjoying my work at State a great deal, much more than I had
expected. True to his word, Shultz had left me to be his alter ego when he
was out of Washington, which was often. It was a daunting challenge for me,
with my background, to be acting secretary of state, especially with George
as a point of comparison. But I worked hard, and learned a great deal from
the professionals around me. And George was very open about showing me
how things were done. I was always welcome to sit in on every meeting he
attended.

Since George was unable to attend to a lot of administrative details, I took
some responsibility for running the department, with a particular emphasis on
its budget problems, which were even more serious than usual. While most
Americans certainly prefer peace to war, they do not budget for those objectives accordingly. Our government's appropriations for peace efforts are less
than a tenth the size of appropriations for war. Most Americans believe we
should not go to war until we have exhausted every possible diplomatic effort
to maintain the peace—and yet the machinery for maintaining that peace is

grossly underfunded year after year. The Department of Defense does a vastly better job of making its case to Congress than does the State Department. We lacked the staff to keep the key members of Congress and their staffs regularly informed about foreign policy issues we considered essential, and so we suffered at budget time. I was sorely tempted to take on this budgetary shortfall as my major responsibility and, looking back, I often wish I had.

But I did handle the more routine budgetary matters, and I also took charge of relations with our embassies around the world, and had oversight over our many ambassadors. A few got themselves into trouble of one kind or another, and I had to spend a fair amount of time straightening things out. And there were many routine matters that I ended up attending to as well. Problems with diplomatic passports, visas, and the like.

I didn't want to spend all my time at State on such minor details. As I say, I wanted to make a difference in the world, much as I had at Goldman Sachs in their world. There, with just a little insight and some persistence, I had been able to get the firm to spread out across the country and around the globe. What might be similar opportunities in my current position? I thought about the various geopolitical hot spots where I might get involved. Latin America? With all its economic problems, that seemed too complicated for me to take on. Despite the emergence of Japan as an economic powerhouse in those years, Asia was not an area of much American interest in those days, and most of the problems concerned trade, which were handled by the Departments of Treasury and Commerce. We seemed to have no serious issues with China. A large delegation of Chinese dignitaries had come to Washington the previous year, and absolutely no one in the administration had wanted to meet with them. I'd quickly get lost if I tried to change that. By the same token, the entire continent of Africa was off the map then, too. The president of Mali would come, and nobody would see him, either. The Middle East? That seemed infinitely too intricate for a neophyte like me.

It was the Cold War that was our most serious foreign relations problem, and our relations with the Soviet Union and its allies were an essential strategic issue. Two years before I arrived, Reagan had famously called the Soviet Union the "Evil Empire" and had committed the United States to developing a Strategic Defense Initiative to shield the nation from Soviet missiles, and to deploy our intermediate-range missiles to counter the Soviets' SS20s. It was abundantly clear that the President was bent on ending the Cold War with a victory for the West. How could I help with that problem?

A great deal of attention at the State Department was focused on the Soviet Union itself, but I thought its satellite nations in Eastern Europe—Poland, Hungary, Czechoslovakia, East Germany, Romania, Bulgaria, and maybe Yugoslavia—were being largely overlooked. Occasionally, Shultz might be able to stop off for a brief visit to an Eastern European capital on his way to or from Moscow, but that was all. I thought that if Shultz was going to concentrate personally on Moscow as he had to do, it might be better to have someone else take on the job of trying to pry these Eastern European nations loose from Soviet control. Anyone encouraging these Eastern Bloc countries to break away from the mother country was likely to be *persona non grata* to the Kremlin.

This seemed to me to present a major opportunity for the United States. Both the people and the leadership of these largely oppressed Eastern European nations had to be dissatisfied with their total dependence—political and economic—on the Soviet Union. Each of these nations, after all, had its own proud history, with its own culture and traditions, entirely independent of the Soviet Union. In fact, Eastern Europe had much more in common with *Western* Europe than with the Soviet Union. Surely, those countries would prefer to orient themselves in that direction, if they only could. What if we gave them an alternative to Soviet domination? Perhaps they would begin to inch away. And perhaps then the whole Soviet empire might start to crumble. Already, there were reasons for hope. The Solidarity movement in Poland had a million members who opposed the Polish Communist government, and in Hungary, a number of economic reforms had been tolerated by the Soviets.

When I brought the matter up with George Shultz, he quickly agreed. He was frustrated that he'd been unable to pay more attention to Eastern Europe himself, and doubted that he would be able to any time soon. He had his hands full with Mikhail Gorbachev, who'd taken over in the USSR on the death of Konstantin Chernenko in 1985, and Gorbachev's foreign secretary, Eduard Shevardnadze.

Ever since the Yalta Conference, in February 1945, when Stalin, Roosevelt, and Churchill agreed to the partition of Europe, the United States had been reluctant to interfere in what the Soviets regarded as their sphere of influence. The Warsaw Pact bound the countries of the Eastern Bloc tightly together militarily, and a trade agreement called COMECON (an acronym standing for Council of Mutual Economic Assistance) did the same for their economies. The Soviets had installed strong, ruthless Communist leaders in each of the Eastern European countries, with only token opposition from the United States. I thought it was shameful the way we'd stood idly by while Soviet tanks crushed the Hungarian Revolution in 1956 and then the Prague Spring in Czechoslovakia in 1968, and again when martial law was imposed in Poland in 1981. But the American government didn't want to risk a potential nuclear confrontation with the Soviet Union over such repressions.

Because so much attention was focused on the Kremlin, Eastern Europe was still regarded as a backwater at the State Department in 1985. The European Bureau was busy with a range of activities for improving our relationship with the Soviet Union, but Eastern Europe was not on anyone's radar. It took me some doing to even discover what our current policy was toward the region. It turned out it was one of "differentiation." That meant that, officially, we did not regard the Eastern European countries to be part of any "bloc." Rather, they were all to be considered as distinct and individual countries.

As policy, I thought this was rather thin. The U.S. should have been much more aggressive in wooing these countries away from the embrace of the Soviet Union. I was convinced that if we just showed these countries what they were missing in terms of economic growth and personal liberty, they would begin to rethink their position. I regarded a love of freedom as universal, a love that becomes all the more desperate for those who, as in Eastern Europe, have had freedom taken away, first by the Nazis, and now by the Soviets.

My plan was to visit those countries, survey the scene, tell the governmental leaders our concerns about their undemocratic conduct and their human rights violations, listen to their concerns, and, of course, dutifully show them we regarded them as "differentiated" countries in accordance with official policy. When I ran this by Shultz, he approved wholeheartedly, but I encountered trouble elsewhere in the department. Standing in the hallway outside

Shultz's office, I had a long argument with Roz Ridgeway, our former ambassador to East Germany and now the very able assistant secretary for Europe. I can't say I won her over, but she did give me her blessing to go. (I would never have undertaken the effort otherwise. Political appointees may have the authority, but it is unwise to ignore the seasoned judgment of the best Foreign Service officers, of whom Roz was definitely one.) State Department opposition gradually faded, although few people developed any particular optimism that I would actually succeed.

At the White House, though, I encountered more resistance from the numerous hardliners there on the National Security Council staff. Their line was that it was a mistake to give these leaders in the Evil Empire the prestige boost that comes from a high-level American visit. They thought it was essential that we isolate the Soviet Union's satellite nations, ignore them in hopes that they would simply wither away. We should not dignify these Communist regimes by paying attention to them.

I never understood this. Why then was it appropriate to have meetings and summits with Soviet leaders? Didn't such contacts encourage *them*?

Don Regan, a competitor of mine on Wall Street from his days as chief of Merrill Lynch when I was at Goldman Sachs, was now the President's chief of staff, and he took a very hard line. For a time, he even refused to let me use a government plane for the diplomatic trips to the region I was planning.

Finally, I got a chance to discuss the matter with the President himself, and he thought an overture to Eastern Europe was a wonderful idea. When Regan saw that his boss was on my side, he came around and agreed to have the trip officially designated a "presidential mission," which upped its diplomatic significance substantially.

I took pains to consult various congressional leaders as well, and found them much more sympathetic to my effort. I neglected to check with Senator Helms, though, and he blasted the idea of my trip practically the moment it was announced. That was my fault. If I'd taken the time to talk to him first, I think I could have convinced him the plan had merit.

17

MR. STEP-BY-STEP

———∿∿∿———

WHEN I FINALLY TOOK OFF for my first swing through Eastern Europe in November of 1986, I made Hungary my first stop. As far as I knew, I would be the first high-level American official to visit there since the 1956 revolution. Janos Kadar had been installed by the Soviets as the nation's Communist party leader in the aftermath of that brutal crackdown, and he was still there. At first, Kadar had been received by most Hungarians as a hated tyrant, but he had become more moderate over time, relaxing the usual Communist strictures against basic human freedoms and allowing small, privately owned family businesses to exist if they had less than twenty employees. I found that encouraging, and I chose to start with Hungary precisely because of Kadar's political evolution. I figured his evolving views would give me my best chance of success, and I wanted to begin the trip on a positive note.

To my distress, though, Kadar refused to see me. Whether this was purely his decision, or the Soviets', I didn't know. All I was told was that Kadar "did not see deputy secretaries." I was disappointed, but I had to recognize that, from his point of view, he would be taking a big risk with his Soviet bosses if they were displeased with the results of my visit.

Instead, I was referred to their number two leader, Belok, a longtime party functionary who had previously been a tailor specializing exclusively in pants. Apparently, he never qualified to handle jackets, and I could see why. He was a dedicated Communist, fiercely loyal, terribly narrow-minded, and completely unwavering. When we sat down together, he subjected me to a nonstop diatribe for a full hour, going on and on about the glories of Communism, the wonders of the USSR, and the many sins of the United States.

This was not a good start for my trip. In fact, on three subsequent visits to Budapest, I received the identical lecture from him, in the same words. Every time I tried to respond, he would talk over me. Eventually, I simply excused myself.

If it had been up to Belok, change would never have come to Hungary. But change did come, of course. And it came so rapidly that it was hard for me to keep up with, and impossible for poor Belok. For much of his party career he was feared. But by approximately the time I arrived on the scene, he was merely tolerated, and he would soon be laughed at as an embarrassment. He died a broken man in 1990.

I felt the change on my second trip to Hungary the next November, in 1987. An economic reformer named Karoly Grosz had taken over by then as prime minister, and he himself sounded astounded as he told me of the progress his country was making. "Do you realize that we have now announced that other political parties besides the Communist party are no longer illegal?" he asked, almost breathlessly. I had, but it was nonetheless a major step. In the parliamentary elections the following June, non-Communists would be campaigning against Communists, and Grosz thought it likely that the non-Communists would win a majority of the seats in the Hungarian parliament. This was a surprising opinion, coming from a Communist prime minister.

"But if that happens, what will your friends in Moscow say?"

"I wondered the same thing myself," Grosz said with a smile. "So last week I went to Moscow to ask Gorbachev what I should do if that is the result of the election."

Gorbachev had already decided that he would let Grosz allow the results of the election to stand, however they turned out. He was remarkably sanguine about it; Grosz found that astonishing. "The most I expected was that he'd say, 'It's your country. Do what you think best,'" Grosz told me. "But Gorbachev went further than that, and instructed me to allow Communists to be voted out of office in Hungary."

As I say, this was a year later, in November of 1987, but it was the first evidence I heard that Gorbachev was encouraging democracy in Eastern Europe. A single word from him to an Eastern European leader would have slowed progress significantly, but that word never seems to have come. Gorbachev was content simply to let these countries go.

Unlike his more idealistic successors, Miklos Nemeth and Imre Pozsgoy, Grosz seemed at first to favor democracy on the practical grounds that it simply seemed inevitable, not because he had any particular appreciation of its virtues. But he became a complete convert when he later visited the United States for the first time in 1988. He experienced the same kind of transformation that occurred in virtually all the Soviet and Eastern European leaders who came here, although some of them were reluctant to acknowledge it publicly. All their lives they had been fed so many exaggerations about the States that when they finally visited our country and saw for themselves what it was actually like, they were simply overwhelmed. Grosz himself happened to visit Chicago first before flying on to New York and Washington. When he came to see me at the State Department, he could not stop raving to me about Chicago as "the most beautiful city in the world," with "so many tall buildings." I found his enthusiasm infectious.

But back to that first trip. From Hungary I went on to Poland. That initial visit was considerably more harrowing than my Hungarian visit, but also more successful.

We arrived in Warsaw on a Tuesday night and were met at the airport by my Polish counterpart, their deputy foreign minister, Jan Kinast, and by John Davis, our very able deputy chief of mission, who later became ambassador when we reestablished full diplomatic relations with Poland in 1987. Kinast directed us to the airport's VIP arrival lounge, where we anxiously sipped coffee while our baggage was being unloaded from the plane and Polish officials cleared us through customs and immigration. As we sat together, Kinast went over the schedule for our visit.

He said that unfortunately he had some "disappointing news" for me: Lech Walesa would not be able to come to Warsaw on Thursday, as had been scheduled.

I was more than disappointed. I was surprised and angry. My staff had made it very clear to General Wojciech Jaruzelsky, the Polish president, that any visit to Warsaw to meet him was contingent on my meeting with Solidarity leaders, including Walesa, and with Cardinal Glemp, the leader of the Polish Catholic church. Without these other meetings, our visit would merely give credibility to a repressive Soviet-backed regime, just as the hardliners back at the National Security Council had feared. We had received every assurance that Walesa would be available for a meeting with me.

"Why can't he come?" I asked.

"He works in the shipyard in Gdansk, and he has used up all his vacation days," Kinast airily replied.

It was obviously a phony excuse, but not completely unexpected. The Communist authorities would have much preferred that we not meet with him at all. Just as we were afraid of giving Jaruzelsky credibility, he was afraid of our giving Walesa credibility, both in the West and in Poland. At this stage, Solidarity, the organization he headed, had been declared illegal. To the government, in fact, it simply did not exist. Walesa was restricted to Gdansk and was not permitted to travel. The government had decided to make no exception for me.

What to do? In my anger I was tempted just to get up, collect my bags, and leave, and then explain to reporters that the Communists had welshed on their agreement. At that moment, such action would have been satisfying, but I knew it would ultimately be unproductive.

Then I had a better idea. I told Kinast, "If Walesa is not permitted to come to Warsaw on Thursday, I will fly to Gdansk on Friday, instead of meeting here in Warsaw with Jaruzelsky, as I am currently scheduled to do." Without waiting for a response, I stood up, shook hands, and left the room. I made my way to a waiting car for the drive to our hotel.

That was a bold, possibly even rash, thing to do. Others in my party were nervous about it, and I will admit that I was a little nervous, too. We were playing hardball, which can be dangerous in world politics. But I had a significant advantage over my adversaries. I knew it would be a serious embarrassment to the Communists if the chosen representative of the American President came for the first high-level visit to Poland in many years but visited only Solidarity's President Walesa and left without seeing Poland's President Jaruzelsky. It seemed to be a reasonable gamble on my part that they would be determined to avoid such ignominy.

I was right. They were bluffing, and they folded. By the time we arrived at the hotel, Kinast was already in the lobby waiting for me. I cannot imagine how he got there so fast.

"Everything is okay," he said. "You misunderstood me about Walesa. He's on his way now from Gdansk. He left a day early to be sure to be here on time for your meeting."

It wasn't the most graceful concession, but it was all I wanted. And it told me that, just as I suspected, Jaruzelsky was very eager for a dialogue with the United States, although he could not admit it. No doubt this was true for the other Communist leaders as well. It was the first confirmation of the validity of my original argument: We could wrest some concessions from these leaders solely in return for the meetings themselves. It made me realize that I could move a little faster than I had planned, and made me less fearful that my discussions would result in more repression from Moscow.

The process of weaning Eastern Europe away from the Soviet Union had begun.

I met with Lech Walesa at John Davis's residence on the outskirts of Warsaw. It was meant to be a private meeting. To publicize the event heavily would have needlessly embarrassed the Polish government, and possibly jeopardized Walesa's safety. We had agreed that we would not hold a press conference, but Walesa and I both wanted it known that the meeting was occurring. So we arranged to let press photographers onto the grounds to record Walesa's arrival at Davis's door, where I greeted him warmly.

Those pictures were in newspapers around the world the next day, and indicated strong U.S. support for Solidarity without anyone in the American government having to say a word. The photos did not make the Polish newspapers, needless to say.

Walesa brought along half a dozen of his closest colleagues: Bronislaw Geremek, his top adviser, who later succeeded Walesa as president of Poland; Jacek Kuron and Karol Modzelewski, who had cowritten the famous "Open

Letter" in which Solidarity challenged the Soviets; and Adam Michnik and Janus Onyszkiewicz, who had just been released from prison, having been charged with publishing antigovernment material. They made a point of traveling in a group, one of them explained, in the belief that, while the Communists might arrest any one of them individually, they wouldn't dare arrest all of them at once.

Although martial law had been lifted in 1983, it was illegal to be a member of Solidarity, and anyone who belonged to it risked a jail term. Membership had dropped as a result, from five million at the union's peak to about one million. But that one million was still an impressive figure under the circumstances, and a great tribute to Walesa's leadership.

Lech Walesa himself was a simple electrician, working a regular eight-hour shift, with only Sundays off, in the main shipyard at Gdansk. He lived in a humble row house in a working-class section of that grim port city (I visited the house on my next trip in 1987). The house had only three bedrooms for his wife and eight children. Between his job and his family, he still somehow found the time and energy to run the vast, illegal union, publish five hundred underground newspapers, appear frequently on radio and TV, fend off Communist interference, and present a solid enough figure to the world that he'd earned the Nobel Peace Prize in 1983. I admired him tremendously. Gruff and tough, a fiery speaker with enormous courage who was rightly idolized by his followers, he will surely live in history as one of those most responsible for the ultimate collapse of Communism, not just in Poland but throughout Eastern Europe and around the world.

The meeting itself was held over dinner, and it was almost an anticlimax. In many ways, it mattered more just for me to be seen with Walesa. There wasn't much for us actually to discuss. There were about twenty of us present for the dinner—ten members from the American delegation, and ten Poles. I sat next to Walesa at the dinner table. He looked like the tradesman he was: a hardy, thickset fellow with a handlebar mustache. That night, though, he seemed tired and discouraged. He'd been fighting an uphill battle for many years, and he told me he sensed little progress. I tried to buoy his spirits, reminding him that he was a hero not only to his countrymen, but to all Americans, especially to the 10 million Americans of Polish descent.

He asked me if the American government could provide financial assistance to Solidarity. I told him that I would try to arrange some assistance, but I couldn't promise anything, given the delicate international situation. At the end of the meal we exchanged laudatory toasts, each of us with tears in our eyes. I was moved to be on the front lines in the battle for freedom.

When he left, I saw that the Communist police had surrounded the cars of his Gdansk group, but they allowed him to leave without incident.

It was a few years afterward that Walesa let on to me what a significant meeting it had been. Being allowed to leave Gdansk to come see me in Warsaw had set an important precedent, and the Communists did not dare restrict his travel after that, for fear that it would put them in a bad light in the West.

Fresh from the successful dinner with Walesa, the next morning I met with Cardinal Glemp, the principal leader of the Catholic church in Poland. Because nearly all Poles are devout Catholics, the Communists did not dare try to stamp out Catholicism in Poland as they attempted to do with virtually all religious activities in other countries. Nevertheless, the party did restrict the Church severely. Priests were required to have government-issued licenses, and these could be withdrawn at any time for any activities that the government considered improper. The Communists also closed down all the Catholic seminaries, starving the Church for new priests, and held up the appointment of new bishops and cardinals as well. Sometimes they went further. On a later visit, I laid a wreath at the grave of Father Jerzy Popieluszko, a young Catholic priest who was murdered by the Polish police on October 13, 1984, for speaking out against the Communist regime. His body was found in the Vistula River, outside Warsaw.

It fell to Cardinal Glemp to preside over the Church during this difficult time. He saw his role as being a mediator between the Communists and Solidarity, trying to keep a semblance of peace between them. Leaders in Solidarity and the Church were sometimes disappointed that Glemp did not come out more strongly against the Communists. Some thought that the Communists were using him to neutralize any opposition that might otherwise grow up in the Catholic church against the regime.

I pressed him on that point of view in our meeting. He bristled when I told him that several people felt he was too sympathetic to the Communists. He replied that he considered it his first duty to see that the Catholic church survived. A more extreme leader would only bring more oppression—and more violence—against the Church and its members. The Church had, he said, been a dominant force in Poland for centuries, through every kind of government, and it would survive this one. He let me know that the Pope, who was himself a Pole, was not unsympathetic to this view. But Glemp was clearly not inclined to challenge the Communists in any case. He even described Father Popieluszko's death to me as an "unfortunate political incident," rather than the brutal assassination that it was.

As I sat there listening to this drab, uninspiring churchman, I couldn't help thinking that his accommodating approach played into the hands of the Communists. Looking back, I suspect a more assertive Church leader might have brought the Communists down in Poland sooner. But of course we will never know for sure.

I met General Jaruzelsky the next morning as planned. The meeting was scheduled to last thirty minutes, but it lasted nearly three hours, for I had a lot to say, and so did he. From the first, the meeting was tense and confrontational.

Jaruzelsky was a forbidding figure. As befitted his rank, he carried himself with a military bearing, very stiff, with his chin in tight and his shoulders erect. He never once smiled. He wore mirrored sunglasses with a silvery tint, which concealed his eyes from view. I found that very disconcerting. I was told his eyes were sensitive to the light, but I was sure that he found it convenient to be able to see my eyes without revealing his own.

He said not a word of greeting as we shook hands and we were directed promptly to two straight-back chairs in which we sat facing each other across a small table. Once we were in place, he gestured for the news photographers present to record the scene. (I was discovering that the "photo op" before such high-level diplomatic meetings is a standard feature around the world, not just in Washington.)

When the press departed, he tipped his head toward me to indicate that, since I had initiated the meeting, I should speak first. I considered that an advantage in this case, since it let me set the agenda and, to a degree, the terms of our dialogue. I explained as I always did on these trips that I was appearing at the request of the President of the United States, who had asked me to assume special responsibility for my country's relations with the countries of Eastern Europe. I was there to begin a process of improving those relations. We found it "unnatural" that Poland, with its long history as a proud, independent nation, had become so closely coupled to the Soviet Union, and that its relationship with the United States, with which it had so much in common, had become so distant. We'd like to change that, I told the General, and find a way to build up relations between the United States and Poland, and to allow Poland to be less dependent on the Soviet Union.

This was powerful stuff, and I paused for a moment to see if I could get any reaction. But Jaruzelsky was stone-faced, his eyes hidden behind his mirrored sunglasses. With a flick of the hand, he gestured for me to continue.

"There are, however, a number of things going on in Poland now that concern us deeply," I told him. "They involve human rights." I reminded him of our own country's history, rebelling against British rule and creating a democracy that guaranteed various personal freedoms like the right to vote, to own property, and to worship. I did not have to tell him that these rights were not much in evidence in Poland. I concluded: "These rights are very dear to us, and it is hard for us to have good relations with other countries that do not share our basic beliefs."

I went on to mention specific instances of human rights violations in Poland, some of them quite extreme. I spoke of political murders, of imprisonment without trial, of the closing down of dissident newspapers, and of widespread religious repression.

This was too much for him. "Mr. Whitehead," he declared angrily, "I cannot allow you to continue. You are interfering with our internal affairs. I cannot allow you to do that. You have your system. We have ours. I do not interfere with yours, and you must not interfere with ours."

I feared for a moment that he would end the meeting right there. But the Soviet Union had responded to American questions about human rights in almost exactly the same words, and yet it had continued its dialogue with us. I sensed that that would be the case with Jaruzelsky, for he had a great deal to gain from improved relations with the United States, or he would not have agreed to meet with me in the first place.

I decided not to back down one inch. "You are right, Mr. President. We have no right to interfere in your internal affairs. But we do certainly have a right to choose our friends. And in choosing our friends, we prefer to be friendly with countries that treat their people decently. What I am here to propose is a simple, step-by-step process in which you will agree to make some small concessions to our concerns in the human rights area, and we will respond by making equivalent concessions to your concerns in the area of trade and investment. By this process, we would expect that our relations would steadily improve, just as fast as you are willing to go."

That seemed to hit a responsive chord. At least he seemed willing to continue the discussion, which was more than before. He wanted to know what I had in mind, and I told him that I would be happy to sit down later with his foreign minister to get more specific.

Later, I turned the conversation to Solidarity, but he interrupted me. "That is a word we don't use any more," he snapped. "Solidarity is an illegal organization. Therefore under our law it does not exist and we don't talk about it. And its leader, Walesa, is a nonperson, and we don't use his name either." That said, he proceeded to rip into Walesa with tremendous anger and venom.

Then he turned to what I realized was his true subject: his ill-treatment by the Americans. "I know that I am hated in your country," he told me. "Two years ago I went to New York but I was not allowed to go to Washington and the President would not see me. Your secretary of defense said last month that I was 'a Russian general in a Polish uniform.'" I remembered the incident, and I'd thought it was very rude and shortsighted at the time. "For me," he went on, "there could be no worse insult. I am a Pole for many generations. I have served my country starting with World War II, fighting against the Germans. I am now the top general in my country. I am president of my country now, and I am trying to run it as best I can. It is not easy. We would not survive if we tried to be independent of the Soviets. Who do you think is responsible for keeping us still a separate country and not just another Soviet Republic?"

He looked at me. "Someday you in America will realize who is the real Polish patriot who has kept his country alive all these years."

He added that he understood that Walesa had received twelve honorary degrees from American colleges and universities. "Including one," he declared, "from Harvard, which I understand you attended." I was impressed he had done his homework on that point. "Maybe someday it will be my turn," he concluded.

These last personal remarks were bitter but revealing. It was clear he was eager for approval from the outside world. It was also clear that he was devoted to his country, and wanted the best for it. He did not want to be under the thumb of the Soviets, but feared that he had no choice. Our job was to provide him a choice. I had the feeling he would cooperate with a step-by-step process, and indeed that proved to be the case. Several years later, after I was out of the State Department and he was out of power, we met again. He greeted me: "Here comes Mr. Step-by-step."

And progress did indeed come step by step. I would complain to them about a particularly outrageous human rights violation—maybe the imprisonment of a certain political dissident—and propose that if that person were released I would use my best efforts to lower our tariff on the importation of Polish ham from 40 percent to 35 percent. They never promised anything, but a couple of weeks later I would find that the dissident had indeed been released, and I would then persuade our tariff commission to adjust the tariff rates. Since we were eager to develop trade with Eastern Europe, both sides of our little deals benefited the United States. Most important, though, the Poles, Hungarians, and Czechs discovered they could deal openly and confidently with us without getting the Kremlin's permission. Before too long, at first jokingly and then seriously, we found ourselves discussing their obligations to the Warsaw Pact and COMECON. Change was in the air in Moscow—and in Budapest, Warsaw, and Prague.

18

WARS OF WORDS WITH
TWO DICTATORS

———

THE THING I REMEMBER MOST about my first visit to Romania was the old woman I saw waiting in line to buy a chicken. It was a Saturday morning on the third and last stop of my initial swing through Eastern Europe in October 1986. I'd taken a walk around the capital city of Bucharest, accompanied only by a young woman interpreter from the embassy. Most of the stores were closed, but in front of a few there were long lines. The old woman was at the very end of one of them.

When I asked her why she was there, she told me this was the chicken store.

"Last Saturday they got a delivery," she told me through the interpreter, "and so I'm hoping they might get one today, too."

"This is the only place to buy a chicken?"

She nodded her head. She lived six miles away, but she walked here once a week to buy her food.

There was another long line about a block away. Unlike this one, that line was moving, and I asked her why she didn't get in that one. "Oh, that's the fish store," the old woman said. "I've gotten a fish the last three weeks. This week, I decided I'd try for a chicken."

"But if the chickens don't come, you won't get anything," I told her. "You'll have waited here all day, and the fish will be gone."

She shook her head sadly, and could only agree. "That's Romania," she said.

That was Romania, and it was a terrible thing to see. There was hardly any food anywhere, just a few wormy apples and some green peppers in the market. Long lines of cars were parked on the street by the gas station. There was no gas. It was illegal to use more than a single twenty-five-watt light bulb inside an entire house. At night, everyone huddled around a single lamp scarcely brighter than a candle. Much of the beautiful old city had been torn down to build a complex of palatial public buildings lining a long promenade. Romania's autocratic President Nicolae Ceauçescu boasted that it was longer than the Champs-Elysées. I wasn't looking forward to dealing with a man who would force his people to the edge of starvation so that he could build public monuments to his own supposed glory.

The government secret police were everywhere in Romania, and this posed a problem for me. Before I arrived, our embassy security service removed a tiny TV camera from the chandelier in the bedroom the government selected for me at the hotel. I'm not sure what they expected to see. We had to assume that every room was bugged; all Romanians operated that way. Government informers were everywhere. Nobody trusted anyone. There were terrible stories of children informing on their parents, and vice versa. It was all very distressing.

Whenever any of us left the hotel, we were immediately followed by secret police, who tailed us everywhere. When we complained, we were told it was for our own protection. I couldn't help toying with them on one occasion. With a few members of my staff, I'd been looking around a department store that offered hardly any merchandise on the racks. The police were following me, as always, so for fun I slipped into the women's lingerie department, which was quite empty. In seconds, the room was filled with a half dozen bodyguards, all of them red-faced as they pretended to appraise different pieces of intimate ladies' apparel.

I succeeded in shaking these tails only once, when I was walking along the sidewalk with my little group, and we all suddenly doubled back and darted down the subway steps and into a departing train. It was something to see the police thugs chug down the stairs after us as we escaped down the track. The look of terror on their faces when they realized they had failed in their duty!

The matter turned more serious one evening when I tried to meet the daughter of Ion Mihai Pacepa, the former head of the Romanian KGB, who had attracted the government's ire by defecting to America and then publishing detailed information about Ceauçescu's brutal regime in a book called *Red Horizons*. Pacepa hoped that his daughter might be less at risk if the Communists recognized that the Americans were in touch with her. She didn't dare go to the American embassy herself for fear that Ceauescu's men might intercept her en route. Sure that her phones were tapped, she was afraid even to telephone. With a few staffers, and the two bodyguards who always accompanied me, I set out to pay a call on her myself.

As I approached her building, though, an enormous policeman loomed up out of the shadows to block my path. Obviously, she was a prisoner under armed guard in her own apartment. We realized that a potentially violent confrontation with this policeman was in no one's interest, and we reluctantly withdrew. Happily, a few years later, she was able to escape from Romania and join her father in the United States.

Romania was different from the other countries of Eastern Europe. Ceauçescu had distanced it from Moscow, especially in regard to its military commitments under the Warsaw Pact. And unlike the other Eastern European countries, Romania had recognized Israel. He considered Romania—and himself—superior to his neighbors, more cultured and better educated, and remembered fondly the "many times" he and President Nixon had met to discuss the problems of the world, man to man. As a result, he had closer relations with the United States than the others did and, despite his appalling human rights record, Romania enjoyed Most Favored Nation trade status with the United States.

Ceauçescu had another peculiarity: He did not believe in borrowing. He considered a country truly independent only if it owed nothing to anybody, and he had pledged to pay off all of Romania's debts over the next several years. Regardless of the merits of the policy, it meant that there was nothing left in the budget to provide services to the people, and they were starving from neglect. It represented a maniacal and egocentric kind of Communism, in many ways more like Chinese Maoism than the Leninism of the Soviet Politburo.

My first meeting with President Ceauçescu produced nothing of substance. It followed a pattern that would be repeated in the next two visits in later years. I brought along our ambassador, Roger Kirk; the Romanian dictator brought his foreign minister, Totu. The meeting lasted several hours, but the whole time, through all three meetings, Totu never uttered a word. He merely nodded vigorously whenever Ceauçescu turned to him for confirmation of whatever point he was making.

Ceauçescu himself was a terribly smug character. Unimpressive in height and build, he looked to be in reasonably good health (contrary to rumor), but he suffered from an odd speech impediment that caused him to seize up periodically in midsentence, seemingly struggling to compel his mouth to obey his brain. He never looked me in the eye when he spoke, but always off into space, sometimes at right angles to me, as if he were posing for a profile. And he had an annoying superior smile on his face—or was it a sneer? He seemed to be making an effort always to appear perfectly serene. Laughably, he regarded himself as one of the world's great leaders, and several times, he claimed to me that other heads of state called him for advice.

The lack of progress in the meetings reflected the lack of progress in the relationship between our two countries. Whereas most other Eastern European nations responded to our overtures with at least some interest in improving the lives of their citizens, not so Romania under Ceauçescu. He was an evil man who was completely uninterested in the welfare of his people.

When I came to Romania for the last time in 1988, Ceauçescu had perpetrated his latest outrage on the citizenry through what was termed the Rural Rectification Program, which amounted to a vast vendetta against the poor who lived in small farming villages well away from the cities, which were appalling in their own way. The plan was to destroy those villages by the thousands, and force the residents to relocate to sterile new housing in larger, more centralized towns. This was done in the name of improving the efficiency of the nation's farming. The result, however, was simply punitive.

Western reporters were not permitted into Romania, and travel was severely restricted, so few people in the country had any idea what the Rural Rectification Program actually entailed. I arrived in the country with my usual small staff on the Sunday before my Monday meeting with the president, and our ambassador, Roger Kirk, thought we might drive out into the country to see what we could discover about Rural Rectification. He had heard rumors that there had been some activity well to the northeast of the capital, so we drove in that direction for about an hour, pulling off the main highway near the village of Balotesti. On the road into town, we were confronted by a large red sign: "Road Closed by Order of the Police. Violators Will Be Prosecuted to the Full Extent of the Law." I was tempted to continue on regardless, but I realized that, as an official representative of the United States, I shouldn't simply ignore such directives.

As the driver started to turn the car around, however, he told Ambassador Kirk that he knew another road into town. That was the best news I'd heard all day, and I told him to take us there. That road approached Balotesti from the other direction, and it had no "Road Closed" sign.

As we came in to what should have been the center of town, we discovered that the village of Balotesti was no more. Evidently, there had been about thirty houses standing there, but every last one of them had been bulldozed to the ground. They'd been simple peasant cottages with thatched roofs and dirt floors. Not much, but everything to the families that lived there. Most likely those families had owned them for generations—centuries, even. There had been little vegetable gardens beside some of them, and a small pen for a cow or a few chickens. All gone, plowed under by enormous yellow bulldozers that were parked along the road, waiting, it seemed, to go on to level the next town in the morning.

The whole place was deserted except for a couple of elderly peasant women dressed in black who were silhouetted against the setting sun as evening came on. They were picking through the rubble, looking for anything that was left of what had been their homes.

Sadly, there was nothing we could do about it, though. We returned to the car and continued on a few more miles, and found another village that had been plowed under in similar fashion. We kept on and, finally, we reached a larger town called Cioflicenti, where a spare concrete slab of a building rose up four stories, obviously brand-new. This was where the displaced peasants had been forced to move to. We climbed out of the car to take a closer look; inside we found that the rooms were just bare, raw, unheated spaces. There were no proper kitchens with stoves or refrigerators or even running water. There were no bathrooms, either. Residents were expected to relieve themselves outdoors, like animals. All the rooms were a uniform ten by twelve. A married couple was assigned one room, unless they had children, in which case they received two. There was no place to raise cows or chickens or grow vegetables in a garden.

I was still smoldering with anger over the terrible injustice of what I had seen when I met Ceauçescu the next day. I began by handing him a letter from President Reagan, explaining that, under our laws, our government is required each year to determine whether Romania is making progress in human rights and in its emigration policies. If not, we were obliged to cancel Romania's Most Favored Nation trade status. The President added that Romania was in danger of that outcome.

The letter had been translated into Romanian, and Ceauçescu read it through slowly and carefully. When he finally finished, he set it aside. "I cannot accept this letter," he said indignantly. He delivered to me the now-familiar line about how outsiders like Americans must not intrude in his country's internal affairs. Then he grew stern. "I do not want to have our policies 're-viewed' by your President and your Congress. Therefore, I will voluntarily give up your Most Favored Nation treatment."

That surprised me, but it was probably a sensible position for him to take. After all, he was bound to lose MFN status anyway, but it would be only after a long, highly publicized exposure of his human rights abuses. By surrendering it on his own, he avoided the bad publicity. What's more, the designation probably didn't much matter to him—assuming he cared about any aspects of the economic circumstances of his country at all. Our imports of Romanian oil were exempt from MFN regulations, and the other imports probably didn't amount to more than $200 million a year. Still, he would have felt the loss of MFN politically. We'd just granted Poland MFN for the first time, and relations with the rest of Eastern Europe were thawing. Romania alone was being left out. All the same, if he felt any shame or embarrassment to be singled out for condemnation in this way, he didn't show it.

I told him I would report his decision back to the President. He said he'd prefer to write the President himself (and did so a few weeks later).

Now came the moment I had been waiting for. "Mr. President, there's one other aspect of our relationship that you should be aware of." I paused, to get his full attention. "And that's the very negative reactions that Americans have had to your Rural Rectification Program."

"Oh yes," he interrupted. "I realize there has been a lot of misunderstanding around the world about that program. So several months ago we suspended action on it."

That, of course, was a complete lie, and I called him on it.

"Well, Mr. President, I'm a little embarrassed to have to tell you this, but yesterday afternoon Ambassador Kirk and I drove out to Balotesti and it had been destroyed only last week." I told him what I had seen there.

He showed no emotion, but said he would look into it. Then he turned to Foreign Minister Totu, the one who never spoke, and asked him in Romanian how this could happen. "Wasn't it a closed area?" he demanded.

The foreign minister sputtered, but got no words out. For once, Ceauçescu had nothing further to say. In the often ambiguous world of international diplomacy, I took this as a clear win for the good guys.

We turned to other topics. I asked about the Romanian economy, and he proudly told me that for the fifth straight year, the gross national product had risen by 8 percent. This was a startling figure for a country in such obvious decline. Either he was simply deluded, or he was being given phony statistics by his retinue of yes-men, or some combination of the two. I'd previously heard him assert that the value of the peasants' property had increased by 50 percent once they'd been relocated to those barren new concrete barracks in the Rural Rectification Program. It looked to me more like they'd *fallen* by 50 percent. But if he was going to use statistics like that, he could argue anything.

As we were finishing up, he turned to me and said: "Mr. Whitehead, you seem to think I am not popular here in my country." That was an understatement, of course, but I said nothing. "Do you know that every time I stand up to make a speech, every time I appear in public, the people cheer and cheer until finally I have to signal them to stop clapping and sit down?" He repeated the point for emphasis: "Mr. Whitehead, I am very popular here."

Many people in Washington asked why I would want to go to Bulgaria. Of all the countries in the region, it was the most corrupt and brutal, and it seemed the least likely to change. It adhered strictly to the Communist party orthodoxy and seemed to be completely loyal to the Soviet Union. This general assumption challenged me a bit, particularly when I discovered that no high-level U.S. official had visited there for many years.

Tudor Zhivkov of Bulgaria was the oldest and longest-serving of any of the Eastern European Communist leaders. He was seventy-six when I first met him and had been in office thirty-seven years. Despite his age and many years in power, he was still a hands-on manager: He knew everything that went on in his country, far more than his subordinates did, and he made all the decisions.

As a dictator, he was ruthless, and had no patience for human rights niceties. In person, though, he was self-confident and jovial with a feisty, loud manner and an unusual laugh. It was more of a joyous shriek, and it erupted most frequently when he was describing one of his many supposed triumphs over his enemies. His stories weren't very funny, but his laugh was.

We met that first time in the enormous reception room of his palace. The room could have housed a basketball court; it must have been at least fifty yards long. It was absolutely empty, though, except for a small table with four chairs in the very center. Ambassador Mel Levitskey and I sat on one side; Zhivkov and an aide on the other. At least, I assumed he was an aide. Zhivkov never introduced us. The man might have been a bodyguard. He never spoke in any case. After a while, I noticed that a woman was seated at the far end of the room. She wore headphones and, at intervals, reached down to change a tape in a recording machine. In the corners of the room up by the ceiling, a pair of TV cameras were trained on us. I could spot no microphones anywhere around us, but the meeting was obviously being recorded all the same.

Zhivkov did not observe conventional rules of diplomacy. As soon as I started saying anything, he loudly interrupted me with some objection or other. Still, I did my best to plow ahead with my standard introductory remarks about our eagerness to improve relations with Bulgaria, our distress at Bulgaria's "unnatural" dependence on the USSR, and our concerns about human rights. When I started to mention specific human rights abuses in Bulgaria—a case of false imprisonment, the murder of a dissident, the destruction of a certain church—Zhivkov could not contain himself.

"I will not tolerate this," he exploded, pounding his fist on the table for emphasis. "If you insist on going on like this, the meeting is over. Over!" He was shouting at the top of his lungs, filling the huge room with his voice.

Having now heard similar threats from the other dictators I'd been dealing with, I was not going to be intimidated by Zhivkov, no matter how loud he yelled. So I simply began gathering up the papers in front of me, as if preparing to leave. "I'm sorry you feel that way," I told him calmly. "It seems to me that if two countries are interested in improving their relationship, each should be able to talk freely about what concerns them. If you find that unreasonable, I guess there's nothing left for me to say." I stood up, and started to place the papers in my briefcase.

At such tense moments, there is sometimes only a hair's breadth difference between boldness and folly. I was being bold, no question. But I had already achieved a great deal from Hungary and Poland in this first diplomatic mission. No one expected much out of Bulgaria, so that I figured if worse came to worst and it ended right there, the total mission would not be considered a disaster. Further, I sensed that Zhivkov did not want me to leave on that note. He knew it would not look good for him if I departed and told reporters that he'd simply refused to discuss the human rights issues that concerned us.

And I was right.

"Sit down," he told me. "Sit down." He gestured with his hands, but I remained standing, not sure I was ready to oblige him. "You misunderstand me. I was only telling you what I thought you were saying. I wasn't telling you the meeting was over. Actually, I was enjoying our conversation."

With that, I had heard enough to feel we were making progress, and I settled back into my chair.

"You were actually going to leave, weren't you?" he asked, obviously astounded that anyone would do such a thing to the great Zhivkov. Then he broke out into his raucous, shrieking laugh. The room rang with it.

Our relationship improved markedly. I'm sure I was the first person to challenge him in a very long time, and I think he found that intriguing. We talked a great deal that day, and quite freely. It was clear he disliked being subservient to the Soviets. No doubt the Soviets were troubled by him, too. All the other Eastern European leaders boasted to me about their closeness to the Kremlin leadership, as evidenced by their frequent travels to Moscow. Zhivkov never went to Moscow at all. He said he didn't like to travel. The Soviet leadership had to come to him.

We became almost friendly, although I never forgot for a moment how cruel and rotten he was. He took me to hunt wild boar with him. That was a surreal affair in which he and I sat in a field in upholstered wing chairs, while the boars were paraded across in front of us so that we could take potshots at them with rifles that attendants handed to us. And we chatted a little about the free-market system. I had thought he was just making conversation, but when I returned several months later, he returned to the subject and asked, almost conspiratorially, "Now, tell me again about the New York Stock Exchange." He was fascinated by the whole notion of public ownership of corporations through the stock market, about the pricing of equities, of compensation systems by which employees get paid more for accepting more responsibility, and the whole system of free-market capitalism. To him, it was a matter of intellectual curiosity. He had never been told about it before. But he seemed to be intrigued by the notion of getting rich. A year after my last visit, there was a revolution and he was succeeded by his foreign minister, Petur Mladenov. It was the end of a very long era.

When I returned to the United States after that first trip, I described Bulgaria to the press as a "sleeper," meaning that the country should not be written off as being committed forever to the Soviet Union. The Bulgarian ambassador, however, was not familiar with American slang, and he thought I was dismissing Bulgaria as being permanently asleep. It took two meetings to straighten that out.

Eastern Europe continued to preoccupy me for the remainder of my tenure as deputy secretary of state. With each passing month I became more confident that the view I had had from the first—that most, if not all, of these countries were itching to break free from their dependence on the Soviets—was absolutely correct. I became all the more convinced of the ultimate failure of the Soviet system when I finally had a chance to travel to Moscow to see the Soviet economy up close in 1987. I had not had a chance before because Secretary Shultz properly claimed that as a priority of his own, and there was no need for us both to go there. But I finally arranged a trip, and one Sunday while I was in Moscow, I asked the liaison officer who was in charge of my visit if he could arrange for me to see a typical Soviet factory. I had been seeing wild estimates from the CIA about the purported success of the Soviet economy, and I wanted to see evidence of it for myself.

The officer arranged for me to see a toaster factory in the countryside outside Moscow. It was a genuine working factory, not a show factory to impress visiting dignitaries, and it was a remarkable thing to see. It looked like something out of the nineteenth century, before Henry Ford. The factory produced just one kind of toaster, which may well have been the only kind of toaster available in the entire Soviet Union. I hadn't seen one like it since I was a small child. It didn't have the slots on the top that you'd expect, but rather two flaps on either side that folded up to hold the slice of bread near to the heating element. It toasted only the inside of each slice, so when one side was done, you had to flip down the flaps, turn the bread over, and toast the other side. There was no timer, and no switch. You had to plug it in to start it, and unplug it to stop it.

The factory did not employ a modern assembly line as you'd find in the West. Instead, each toaster was rolled around from one work station to the next on a little trolley. There was no accounting for the costs of the parts, either. The factory manager told me he had no idea how much the heating coils, knobs, and pieces of aluminum might cost. It didn't matter to him anyway, since he had no alternatives; the parts would arrive at the factory whether he wanted them or not. He was expected to produce a few hundred toasters a day. At the end of the week, he delivered them all by a flatbed truck to a warehouse in Moscow. What happened to them after that, he had no idea. He was also expected to employ four hundred people, whether he had a use for them or not. So he had all the extra personnel sweeping the floor at half-hour intervals. The floor was spotless.

This was during the period when Gorbachev was trying to modernize the Soviet economy, and the manager told me he had recently received a new edict saying that, since the country was now going to operate on the principles of a free market, he should do his best to cut costs. Of course, the exact same materials—the knobs and so on—continued to arrive just as before. There was no reducing it. He tried to let all the extra floor sweepers go, but they complained to Moscow higher-ups and had to be reinstated. At one point, the distribution warehouse returned his truck full of finished toasters saying they had enough and couldn't take any more. The whole system broke down, and complaints were going every which way, and so the manager said that they had no choice but to go back to the old approach. The new edict was revoked.

This told me that the Soviet system wasn't working in the Soviet Union, just as it wasn't working for its client states. It seemed to me only a matter of time—and a fairly short time, at that—before the whole thing would collapse under its own weight. And of course that is exactly what happened. I'd been out of office for just under a year when the Berlin Wall finally fell in November 1989, and ended the Cold War with a clear victory for our side. It gave me a good feeling to think that my work in Eastern Europe had played a part. Afterwards, Gorbachev was asked what he thought were the decisive factors in the breakup of the Soviet Union. He said there were two—one military, and one geopolitical. First, the overwhelming strength of the U.S. military. He noted that although the military expenditures of the United States and the USSR were roughly the same, our economy was so much larger that our defense budget represented only 6 percent of our gross domestic product, whereas it represented a full 20 percent of theirs. Further, if we were to increase our military by another 25 percent, it would push our defense budget to only 7.5 percent of our GDP, but if the Soviet Union were to try to keep up, it would have to go to 25 percent, an overwhelming percentage that would shrink consumer expenditures more than the Soviet people could bear. Gorbachev also expressed enormous respect for our ability to develop new military technology, including Reagan's Strategic Defense Initiative. He conceded that many of his scientists doubted the United States would succeed with SDI, but he was afraid that if they were wrong and we did succeed, there was no way the Soviets could ever afford to match us. Second, on the geopolitical front, Gorbachev feared he could no longer count on the Eastern European nations to fulfill their military obligations to the Soviet Union under the Warsaw Pact. That sense of vulnerability was decisive in leading him to conclude that the old Soviet Union would never be able to compete with the West.

And I like to think that I played a role in that.

19

TARGET: TRIPOLI

—*∿∿*—

I N EARLY 1986, while I was busy with my forays into Eastern Europe, terrorism returned as a major preoccupation of the State Department as it became increasingly evident that Muammar Qadhafi, the president of Libya, was training and financing terrorists throughout the world. He seemed to have been behind the 1975 explosions at the Rome and Vienna airports and the bombing in April 1986 of the La Belle discothèque in West Berlin. Although I was often skeptical of CIA conclusions, there seemed to be no doubt in this case. The CIA showed us at State the evidence: forged passports, photographs, even copies of checks drawn on Libyan banks and paid to known terrorists, one of the checks signed by Qadhafi himself. He must not have realized that a check delivered to a terrorist leaves an incriminating paper trail.

Along with other nations, the United States had undertaken a variety of diplomatic efforts to change Qadhafi's conduct, all to no avail. The terrorists he was backing were likely to harm Americans and damage our interests around the world. This was unacceptable. The White House had been considering military action against Qadhafi for some time, but we had not settled on the timing or the type of strike. The issue came to a head on a Sunday evening when the President called a meeting of all his top advisers at eight o'clock.

Since Shultz was overseas, I was expected to attend the meeting in his place. Unfortunately, I had not heard about it. I was taking a rare break from Washington to spend the weekend in Colonial Williamsburg, which I had never seen before. I'd driven myself there in my own car, leaving behind my chauffeured government car, with its excellent communication equipment for staying in touch with the White House. I did call in every few hours, though, and when I called at six o'clock, the State Department officer on duty told me that he'd been frantically trying to track me down. I was due at a high-level White House meeting at eight.

I'd been following the Libyan developments closely enough to know instinctively what the meeting was to be about, and I simply had to be there. I dashed back to the hotel, frantically packed up and checked out, and then drove back to Washington faster than I'd ever driven before or have driven since. I arrived at the meeting in the upstairs quarters at about 8:10 and slipped into my seat, embarrassed to be even that late for such an important meeting. I vowed never again to leave Washington when I was "on duty."

President Reagan and Vice President Bush were there, along with Defense Secretary Casper "Cap" Weinberger, Joint Chiefs Chairman Colin Powell, CIA Deputy Director Bob Gates, and eight top congressional leaders—four from the Senate and four from the House, four Republicans and four Democrats. As I'd guessed, the subject was Libya. The presence of congressional leaders indicated that action was imminent and that the President was now consulting with them as to what that action would be.

When I arrived, Gates was describing what intelligence information we had on Qadhafi and his terrorist activities. I was asked to speak next from the State Department perspective. I hadn't had time to pick up my materials on the subject but I was familiar enough with the matter to be able to describe in some detail the various diplomatic efforts that had been made to get Qadhafi to reform, and also to summarize the evidence that Libya was a terrorist haven. I also reviewed the details of the West Berlin bombing, and the previous history of Libyan involvement in terrorism.

It fell to Weinberger to describe the proposed military plan. It was to involve a surgical bombing attack on some barracks near Tripoli. In fact, the planes were already en route from Britain, but there was plenty of time to order them to return to their bases if that was the decision tonight. Cap added that France had refused to permit overflight, which substantially lengthened the trip for our bombers. The planes would have to be refueled in the air five times.

President Reagan picked up the discussion, summarizing the information that had been given. He said he didn't want to make a final decision until he had received the views of the members of Congress who were present. He went around the room asking for those views now.

The representatives raised questions about the plan. They worried about the risk of civilian casualties and the accuracy of the bombing. They wanted to know if we had informed other nations. We hadn't yet, but would once the decision was made. Would it be better to give Libya further warning, they wanted to know.

Because so many of the observations of the representative had a somewhat negative slant, I was unsure how the President would respond. He answered most of their questions himself, occasionally directing the more technical ones to the relevant cabinet member. When the discussion ended, he betrayed no uncertainty. "Well," he said, "we're at the point of decision. I've listened carefully to your questions and comments. I think we've had good answers to all of them." Then he turned the question back to the representatives. "I'm ready to decide that we should move forward, but before I do, I'd like to ask—do any of you advise me that I should cancel the operation and send our planes back to Britain?"

The President then locked eyes on each of the congressmen in turn. None of them spoke. There was dead silence around the room.

Finally, after what seemed like a very long time, the President said, "All right then. Let's go."

It was Reagan at his best—cool, decisive, relying on his aides, but perfectly ready to make the big decision.

Before we adjourned, the President stressed the need for total secrecy. He said the attack would not take place until six A.M., and any leaks before that time would jeopardize the mission's success. The existence of this unusual late-night meeting had somehow gotten out, though, and by the time the meeting was over, a large number of reporters had assembled on the White House front lawn to see what they could find out about it. To avoid them, we were all spirited outside through a rarely used exit. I'm glad to report that six of the eight congressmen complied with the President's request for secrecy, a high ratio for such a valuable secret that could win a politician plenty of favorable coverage from any reporter he chose to tip.

The attack was a success. The barracks were destroyed along with several other targets. One plane was lost and one bomb went astray, damaging the French embassy in Tripoli. Qadhafi himself was not a target, but without our knowing it, he had pitched his tent in the courtyard of one of the barracks and the blast had knocked down the tent pole and killed a two-year-old child whom Qadhafi claimed was his adopted daughter.

After announcing the military strike, the United States declared the imposition of heavy sanctions on Libya, designed to restrict the sale of their oil. All American citizens living there were required to leave, and no American firm would be allowed to do business with the country. The announcement concluded by saying that Deputy Secretary Whitehead would be leaving immediately for a round of visits to Europe to persuade other countries to follow suit. This was news to me.

It proved a difficult mission. No country wants to be considered a lackey of the United States, and it didn't help to declare ahead of time that my job was to persuade them to follow our lead. My first stop was supposed to be Great Britain, our most reliable ally, but before I set out, Margaret Thatcher, Britain's prime minister and President Reagan's great friend, declared, "Mr. Whitehead would be wasting his time to come to Britain. Sanctions never work." The fact was, I agreed with her. She was right: Sanctions never do work. Well, hardly ever. Sanctions are usually imposed impetuously by a government, acting in anger, in response to an aggressive act by an antagonistic government. Little care is taken to carefully analyze exactly the likely results of the sanctions, and how to maximize the desirable ones, while minimizing the others. The problem is compounded when the sanctions are intended to restrict the sale of a particular country's oil, for once a barrel of oil leaves a Libyan well, it is nearly impossible to identify it as Libyan.

Nevertheless, my job was not to philosophize about the merits of sanctions but to get others to impose them. All the same, I couldn't ignore Mrs. Thatcher's comment.

So I changed plans and decided to go first to Canada, where I thought I'd have a chance of success. Brian Mulroney, Canada's young prime minister, was also a close friend of the President's. They had almost a father-son relationship. I armed myself with a letter from Reagan that said in effect, "Brian, we need your help on this one" and took off for Ottawa early the next morning.

After a brief discussion, Mulroney agreed to support us and made the announcement right away. With at least one favorable vote in my pocket, I flew back to New York in time to catch the overnight plane to London to work on the prime minister. I checked into Claridges when I arrived the next morning.

Charlie Price, who was serving as our ambassador to the Court of St. James, tried to persuade me that any meeting with Mrs. Thatcher would be pointless, given the prime minister's stated position. But I persisted and asked him to set up an appointment all the same, leaving word that Canada had signed on and that the matter was now pressing, as I had to leave for Paris that night.

For some hours there was no response. Finally, at about four P.M., when I was just about to give up, I received the following message from the prime minister's office: "There is no room today on the official schedule, but would Mr. Whitehead be good enough to come for tea this afternoon at five o'clock?" I accepted with alacrity and showed up at 10 Downing Street at five on the dot.

Mrs. Thatcher led me into the Italian room, an intimate spot well suited to taking tea. Charles Powell, the prime minister's chief of staff, was also present. Mrs. Thatcher served the tea herself in a very ladylike fashion. Once our teacups were filled, she reiterated to me her view that sanctions never work, and explained why in great detail. She was gracious and friendly but very firm.

When my time was almost up, I said that I could see that her mind was made up and I would not presume to try to dissuade her. She seemed relieved at that. But I sensed she didn't want to send me away completely empty-handed, and so I added, "I know Ronny"—as I knew she called him—"would be delighted if you would just ask British Petroleum"—which was then owned entirely by the British government—"to buy a little less oil from Libya. As you know, there's lots of oil available elsewhere."

I watched her mind work on that for a brief moment. Then, with a slight smile, she said she'd see what she could do about that. True to her word, within days, British purchases of Libyan oil dropped to almost nothing.

I had achieved my objective, though I could not boast about it. And she had achieved hers by not giving in on sanctions. I'm quite sure she knew exactly what she was doing.

A year later, I attended a Bilderberg meeting at Glen Eagles, the famous golf club in Scotland. Bilderberg is an unofficial, informal organization of leaders from Europe and the United States which meets once a year to talk and listen to others about what's happening in the world. When Mrs. Thatcher arrived at the pre-dinner reception where she was to be the featured speaker, she spotted me across the room, caught my eye, and in a loud voice and with a pointed index finger said, "I told you sanctions never work." She was firm about this to the end.

I was less successful with President François Mitterrand of France. A meeting with him was mostly pomp and circumstance. It was then always necessary to meet first with Jacques Attala, his chief of staff, who later became the president of the European Bank for Reconstruction and Development. Attala wanted to know from me, in detail, what I planned to ask the president. Then he would disappear into the president's office for a few minutes, during which time, I assumed, the official response was determined. When I finally took my case to him directly, Mitterrand was noncommittal, which I took to mean no. He said he would look into the subject but promised nothing, and nothing was what I got. France had its own interests. Their Total Petroleum Co. was eager to take over the Libyan concessions that our U.S. companies might have to abandon because of the sanctions.

Other European countries were more obliging. In Bonn, I found Chancellor Helmut Kohl to be a pleasant man and a strong leader, a rare combination. He offered to help, not with the full across-the-board sanctions we sought but with some helpful steps. The Dutch, major oil dealers, helpfully shifted contracts to acquire less oil from Libya. Although Italy, as Libya's largest trading partner, had the most to lose, it agreed to stop buying Libyan oil for a while, even though that meant that Libya would buy less food and other products from them in return. Despite their stand on Abu Abbas, the Italians had become very tough on terrorism, which I appreciated.

In sum, many governments and private companies—although by no means all—tried, for at least a couple of years, to buy less oil from Libya and more from other producers. Oil is a fungible, hard-to-track commodity, but we assembled evidence to suggest that Libyan oil's value dropped by at least $1 a barrel, costing Libya several hundred million dollars in important foreign exchange each year. The Libyan oil businesses are state-run, with the revenues concentrated in relatively few hands, so I doubted the common people of Libya felt the effects appreciably. Qadhafi did stop being a supporter of terrorism—with the important exception of the terrorist downing of Pan Am Flight 103 over Lockerbie, Scotland, on December 21, 1988, which may have been done by Libyans without his approval. We will never know exactly why he stopped. It might have been the bombing, it might have been the sanctions, or it might have been that he just didn't want to be a pariah any longer. But he did stop supporting terrorists—at least for quite a while.

20

"I HATE TO DISAGREE WITH MY PRESIDENT, BUT . . ."

———✺———

THE WORST DAY OF MY DIPLOMATIC CAREER was November 24, 1986, shortly after I returned from my first, highly successful diplomatic foray into Eastern Europe. It began with my usual early-morning meeting in Shultz's office with George and Mike Armacost, the deputy secretary for political affairs and the senior Foreign Service officer in the department. We were discussing the testimony Mike was to give at two o'clock before the House Foreign Affairs Committee on our relations with Iran. It looked as if the questioning might be more politics- than policy-oriented, and Mike wasn't sure it was appropriate for a Foreign Service officer to testify on a largely political matter.

All three of us knew what he meant. The scandal that would become known as Iran-*contra* had broken a few weeks before in a Lebanese paper called *Al Shiraa*. It appeared that the White House and the National Security Council might have been involved in an elaborate, secret, and possibly illegal transaction involving the sale of arms to Iran in exchange for the release of seven American hostages held by Iranian sympathizers in Lebanon. The Nicaraguan *contra* dimension—by which the proceeds of the sale of arms, along with other funds, might have gone to support the *contras* (U.S.-backed rebels fighting to overthrow the Marxist-oriented Sandinista government of Nicaragua) in violation of laws recently passed by Congress—did not emerge for several more weeks.

At the State Department, we were as eager to free the hostages as anyone, but we adhered to a firm policy, established by President Reagan and frequently repeated by Secretary Shultz, never to pay ransom for any hostages, for that would only encourage the taking of more hostages in the future. Still, the air in Washington that November was filled with Watergate-style rumors about who had known about the transaction and when. At the State Department, we had no knowledge whatsoever of any negotiations along these lines, and Secretary Shultz let it be known that he strongly disapproved of any such deal. This, however, had the effect of putting him at odds with the White House, and that Monday morning, the papers were full of speculation about the possible dimensions of the scandal.

When Mike Armacost indicated his reservations about testifying, George turned to me, as if to ask, "Well, can you do it, then?" I couldn't think of any good reason for me not to. After all, none of us knew anything about the rumors, and I did not imagine that it would be difficult for me simply to say that.

I spent the next few hours going over the written testimony that Mike had prepared. It had to do with our current policy toward Iran and our efforts— the legitimate, public ones, not the clandestine ones developed by the NSC—to try to develop contacts with elements of the Iranian government who were more moderate than the Ayatollah Khomeini and his inner circle of clerics, who had taken such a hard line against the United States.

When I arrived at the committee hearing room, I could see that this was no ordinary hearing. The room was completely packed. All across the back of the room and around both sides, at least thirty TV cameras had been set up to record my testimony.

The proceedings started with the standard opening statements by the committee chairman, Dante Fascell (Democrat from Florida), and the minority leader, Ben Gilman (of New York). For about ten minutes, I read into the record the rather bland testimony that Mike had prepared.

And then the fireworks began. Each member of the committee had questions for me. The grilling went on for almost three hours. I did my best to

speak up for Shultz and the State Department, to denounce the idea of ex-
changing arms for hostages, to decry Iran as a supporter of state-sponsored terrorism, and to deny any knowledge of the rumored NSC activities. Then,
toward the end of the day, Representative Bob Torricelli, a Democrat from
my home state of New Jersey, asked this question: "Mr. Whitehead, last week
at his press conference, President Reagan, in defending your policy of trying
to seek out more moderate leaders in Iran, said that he had noted evidence
of some moderation of the hard-line anti-American attitudes of the current
Iranian leadership. Do you agree with that?"

I took a deep breath and replied: "Well, I hate to disagree with my President, but I have seen no evidence that their hard-line policy has changed at
all." I was being completely honest, but, in that charged environment, I
should have been more careful. In all my testimony that afternoon, this was
the only moment where I had suggested there was a sliver of difference between the White House and the State Department regarding Iran. The questioning continued for another half-hour as the Democrats homed in on my
answer, but the reporters and cameramen started to leave. I didn't realize that
it was because I'd given them their sound bite for the day.

In the car on the way back to the office, I turned on the radio. There was
my voice, "I hate to disagree with my President, but . . ." When I flipped on
the television later, I was distressed to see my remark leading the evening
news. The next morning it was all over the front pages of all the newspapers.
My unprepared statement, not very important substantively, had become big
news. I should have said, "Well, it's probably too early for any of us to really
know," and no one would have noticed. But it was too late for "should-have-
saids." If people were already calling for a head to roll, they would probably
be calling for mine now. What should I do?

I sat down and wrote a quick note to the President calling my remark an
"unfortunate slip-of-the-tongue" and apologizing. I had it hand-delivered to
the Oval Office, but I heard nothing back, which worried me.

About four o'clock the next afternoon, I got a message to come over and
see the President right away. I felt like the proverbial dying man who sees his
whole life passing before his eyes. I'd been in Washington a little more than
a year and had enjoyed practically every minute. If I had to leave now, I fig-

ured at least I'd had a good year. Eyes rolled in disbelief as I passed through the President's outer office. When I passed through the open door to the Oval Office, Reagan was on the phone but signaled me to sit down. Soon he put down the receiver and turned his attention to me.

"I understand what happened," he told me, to my immense relief. "I've had my own troubles being misunderstood by the press. Just forget about it. It's a one-day wonder. You've been doing a great job and, of course, I want you to stay on. I'll make it clear to the press that I'm not upset." I'm sure my sigh of relief could be heard all the way to the Hill.

As I started to leave, the President added a little footnote. "Let me tell you how I heard about it," he said. "You know what a busy day I had yesterday. I had a speech in Arlington and a long meeting at the Pentagon and some other things and I finally got back upstairs a little before seven. I fixed myself a drink, put on my slippers and smoking jacket and sat down to watch the evening news."

I steeled myself for what was to come.

He went on: "You know, John, how when you turn the TV on, the sound comes on first and then there's a few seconds pause before the picture comes on?"

I nodded sheepishly, knowing what was coming next.

"Well, when the sound came on, I heard someone saying, 'I hate to dis-agree with my President, but'. . . and I said to myself, 'Now who the hell could that be?' and suddenly there was the picture and it was you. I couldn't believe it."

Once more, I apologized profusely and left quickly, feeling remorseful but relieved.

The scandal continued to grow, but my own employment remained se-cure, as did George Shultz's. In the next three years, I saw the President at least once a week and he never referred to that contretemps again. And nei-ther did I.

The system of identifying the culprits at the National Security Council worked slowly, but ultimately successfully. Those who broke the law and vio-lated American policy were brought to justice, and the State Department's record for integrity remained whole. There was one further repercussion for me, though. When my secretary, Rita Johnson, tried to make the appointments for the regular Sunday afternoon tennis game with George Shultz and Kay Graham, she was told that I was temporarily off the list of eligibles for the White House court. I suspected Nancy Reagan was behind it, but years later when I asked her, she absolutely denied any involvement. It was a small penalty for my transgression. A little petty, perhaps, but not unreasonable. I discovered, though, that I could appear as Shultz's guest without having to give my name, so, appearing incognito, I never missed a match.

Although I suspected Nancy Reagan of being the secret enforcer in that matter, she was an important ally of mine on an issue of far greater significance to me, and to the nation. It had to do with our relations with the United Nations.

At the State Department, one of my duties was to manage our official relationships with world organizations, including the World Bank, the International Monetary Fund, and the U.N. Ever since high school, I have been strongly committed to the dream of bringing the entire world together into a single political body, where any disagreements could be resolved before they escalated into open warfare. To me, the idea of the United Nations is like the idea of the United States. Just as our Founding Fathers persuaded the former colonies to come together and work out a system for resolving individual differences, the United Nations could do that for the various constituent countries around the world, maybe over a period of many years. I knew that the hard-liners in the administration such as my old rival Don Regan, Attorney General Ed Meese and others felt that the United States should not surrender any of its sovereign power to a global body such as the U.N. Back at the time of the Revolution, Americans had similar anxieties about their precious individual colonies' giving up *their* sovereign powers to a new national government. The fact was, many of those powers were retained by the states. The federal government only claimed jurisdiction in the areas of common defense, interstate commerce, currency, and foreign policy. We would never, and should never, cede power to the U.N. over issues that were essential to our sovereign interests. My friend Claiborne Pell, a senator from Rhode Island and chairman of the Senate Committee on Foreign Relations, was such

a strong internationalist that he used to keep the preamble of the U.N.'s charter in his pocket and he'd often pull it out to read the stirring words: "We the
Peoples of the United Nations, determined to save succeeding generations
from the scourge of war, which twice in our lifetime has brought untold sorrow to mankind, and to reaffirm faith in fundamental human rights, in the
dignity and worth of the human person." Those lines, with their deliberate
echoes of our own Constitution, are wonderfully inspiring.

So it was painful for me to see the administration stop paying our dues
to the U.N., running up a "past-due" bill that had reached $450 million by
1988. We were the leader of the free world, and yet we were unwilling to
be a leader of the United Nations? I found that terribly misguided and, as
the State Department official in charge of our relations with the U.N., I
tried to put into our department budget sufficient funds to pay off our back
dues in five installments of $90 million a year, and to put in a procedure
for paying future dues on time. Not surprisingly, this allocation stalled in
the administration's Office of Management and Budget, and in the White
House itself.

President Reagan had told me that if something important came up, his
door was always open to me, night and day. He didn't want to be surprised by
something I had held back out of respect for his time. But I thought the U.N.
dues were a matter worthy of his attention. Other countries such as the Soviet Union were now beginning to follow the U.S. example and withholding
their dues as well. Without these funds, the United Nations was in danger of
failing to meet its payroll. I persuaded Reagan's secretary to get me a few minutes with the President in the Oval Office so I could lay out my case.

Several of Reagan's advisers and staff, including Don Regan and Ed
Meese, joined the President to hear my presentation. From the way Reagan
listened, I sensed that he was more sympathetic to the plight of the U.N. than
they were. Still, he said nothing that indicated a change of heart, and I did
not succeed in freeing up payment. Frustrated, I spoke with George Shultz,
who felt as strongly about our U.N. dues as I did. I then decided to take a new
approach: I would speak to the First Lady.

Nancy had an office in the West Wing, but she could also be reached upstairs in the residential quarters. I'd called her a few times about minor mat-

ters, and she had always been receptive. This time, when I said I needed to speak to her in person, she found a time to meet.

I saw her in the family sitting room. I came quickly to the point, that our refusal to pay our United Nations dues was pushing it into bankruptcy. "I don't think that the President wants to leave that as his legacy," I told Nancy.

"Bankruptcy?" she asked me. "Are you sure you aren't overdramatizing this?"

I assured her that I was not.

"Well," she said. "I don't think the President knows it's *that* serious."

I told her I didn't think the information was getting through to him.

"So, what do you think we should do?" she asked me.

I told her that I was hoping the President could meet with the U.N. Secretary General, Javier Perez de Cuellar, so that he could hear the story directly from the man who knew it best.

"Well, I'll do what I can," Nancy assured me.

I didn't hold out much hope, since I had powerful forces in the White House allied against me. But shortly afterward, I received an invitation to a lunch at the White House with the President and the Secretary General, and several members of the President's staff. I accepted immediately. Not wanting to be outnumbered by the anti-U.N. faction at the lunch, I brought along a State Department colleague who could be counted on to buttress my case for the U.N., and also to provide a record of the meeting if there should be any doubt afterward about what occurred.

The luncheon was upstairs at the White House, and about a dozen people were there. At the end of the meal, Reagan offered a gracious toast to the Secretary General, and then allowed him to speak first.

Perez de Cuellar was not known as an orator, but he delivered a moving speech about the importance of the United Nations to the world and about its precarious financial situation. Reagan was moved by the Secretary General's eloquence. When he rose to respond, he said he hadn't realized the seriousness of the U.N.'s financial problems and, now that he knew, he wanted Perez de Cuellar to know that the United States fully supported his program.

I was immensely heartened, but Reagan's White House staffers were appalled. The next day, I received several calls from them saying the President had misspoken. He had not meant what he said.

"Listen," I finally fired back. "There's no way you fellows can wriggle out of this. You heard what the President said." I was glad I'd brought a witness to corroborate my account.

The hard-liners fought hard, but the President stuck to his guns. The budget we proposed was approved by the White House and forwarded to the Congress with the U.N. money intact. In 1988, President Reagan's last year in office, the United States government finally issued the first of the five $90 million checks that would bring our account up to date.

Gratified, I decided to deliver the money to Perez de Cuellar in person and, after slipping the huge check into my jacket pocket, I took the shuttle to New York. Dick Holbrooke, who at the time, was a partner at Lehman Brothers, happened to be on the plane. When he asked me what brought me to New York, I told him I was making a delivery to the United Nations. Then I pulled out the $90 million check, and took some pleasure in seeing his eyes widen. "Want to hold it?" I joked.

We both laughed; it was the biggest check either of us had ever seen. He did not dare touch it. Once we landed at LaGuardia, I drove straight to the home of the Secretary General. There, with a few flashbulbs popping from news photographers we had alerted, I triumphantly presented the check to Perez de Cuellar.

That was great, but the story has an unfortunate postscript. To my dismay, when President George H. W. Bush succeeded Reagan, he bowed to the hard-liners, returned to our old ways, and did not follow through with the next four $90 million installments during his presidency. Our debt to the United Nations began to grow once more.

In Reagan's last year in office, I was visited one day by Tom Kean, a former governor of New Jersey, and several other Republican leaders from the state. They came to approach me about running that year against the democratic senator Frank Lautenberg. It would have meant leaving the State Department right away and dropping a lot of important projects I had going on. It would not have pleased George Shultz, either. Still, I considered the matter carefully. One doesn't get too many requests to run for the U.S. Senate!

But I turned it down. I loved what I was doing. Pete Dawkins, a former West Point football star and former Army general, made the run instead. He'd never lived in New Jersey, which left him open to charges of "carpet-bagging," and he lost to Lautenberg. I'll never know whether I'd have won — or how good a senator I'd have made.

A few months after that, Jim Baker resigned as secretary of the treasury to run George H. W. Bush's campaign for president. Shultz asked me if I'd like to take Baker's place. It was only for a few months he said, and he thought it would be nice for me to have a full-fledged department secretary's job on my résumé. I wasn't building a résumé, but even so, the possibility was quite tempting. I'd always thought I was more qualified for a job at Treasury than at State. So I said yes, if the President asked me I'd be glad to do it. Shultz talked to Reagan, and Reagan said yes. But Vice President Bush intervened. He told the President that if he was elected, he planned to name his old friend and former Yale roommate Nick Brady, the head of the investment firm Dillon Read and a former interim senator from New Jersey, as secretary of the treasury, and would the President please appoint him as interim secretary to give him a few months' experience in the office. The President could not say no to that. He was nice enough to apologize to me. I was not too sorry. I had plenty more to do where I was. But it did mean that when the Reagan administration came to an end with George H. W. Bush's inauguration in January 1989, my time in Washington also concluded.

21

THE LOLLAPALOOZA OF
WAUWATOSA

———∞———

F OR ME, HAPPILY, Washington was not all work. A few months after I
arrived, I was invited to a dinner party at the Canadian embassy. As the
deputy secretary of state, I was often invited to these sorts of functions. It was
a rare evening that I spent at home. Since I was single, my hostess, Sonia
Gottlieb, the wife of the Canadian ambassador, needed to find a single
woman to "balance the table," and she called up her friend Nancy Dickerson, a well-known television personality in town. Nancy had, in fact, already
been invited and had turned down the invitation and, even though Sonia
called and begged her, she still said no. It was the only evening she would
have free the whole week, she pleaded, and she couldn't face a dinner with
some unknown banker named John Whitehead, even if he was deputy secretary of state.

Sonia called all over Washington, but couldn't find anyone else. So she
called Nancy back at the last minute and begged her to do her this one favor.
Nancy reluctantly agreed to come.

She sat next to me, and I was very impressed. Poised, charming, cultivated,
witty, stylish, bright, dazzling—there were nowhere near enough adjectives
to describe her. I was amazed by all she had accomplished as a small-town
girl from Wauwatosa, Wisconsin. I used to joke with her that she was the Lol-
lapalooza of Wauwatosa. She'd attended Clark College in Dubuque, Iowa,

and then the University of Wisconsin, before returning home to teach school in Wauwatosa for a couple of years. Finally, she set out to conquer the world, and moved to Washington. She got a job on the Senate Foreign Relations Committee writing speeches for Senator "Scoop" Jackson, until CBS discovered her and assigned her to cover the Kennedy White House. She became the first woman broadcaster to cover this beat, and she did it brilliantly. She married a nightclub owner named Wyatt Dickerson. He had three daughters by a previous marriage, and Nancy and he had two sons. But that marriage had ended in divorce, and when we met, she was living alone in an apartment in Kalorama Square. She'd covered the White House for CBS for ten years before moving to NBC for ten more. When we met, she had her own television production company. She knew everyone and everything in Washington, as far as I could tell, and was always way ahead of me on the day's political developments, to say nothing of the gossip.

After I was confirmed, however, I was extremely busy, and I wasn't able to pursue the relationship nearly as avidly as I would have liked. Once again, the job came first, and we both dated other people. As the months passed, though, we found ourselves increasingly drawn to each other. Having been married twice already, I was a bit leery of making that kind of a commitment, and Nancy had her own busy life.

As my time in Washington drew to a close, I assumed that I would simply return to New York by myself. But then, about a month before I was to leave office, a close friend of Nancy Reagan's, Mary Jane Wick, called me, and she put it to me very directly: "John Whitehead," she said, "you are the stupidest man alive. You are about to go back to New York and leave behind this wonderful woman who is very much in love with you. Wake up." I had an early flight to Israel the next morning, so I really didn't have much time to think about what Mary Jane said. It was startling to me, though. Nancy and I had never discussed marriage, and I had assumed that neither of us was ready. On the long plane ride to Tel Aviv, though, I turned the matter over in my mind, and I realized that, by God, Mary Jane was right. I was being a fool. And that very night I called Nancy from my hotel room in Tel Aviv and, with all the passion I could muster over the phone, I proposed.

Nancy said she'd think about it—she always was an independent woman—and I didn't hear from her again for two anxious days. By then, I'd flown on to Ankara, Turkey, and there she reached me at my hotel. She accepted—she would be my wife. Wow! Was I lucky! Conducted over a scratchy, international line, this was not the most romantic exchange. But I was very pleased with the result. We were married the next month.

So when I returned to New York, Nancy came with me as my wife. We bought a beautiful home on Sutton Square, overlooking the East River. The bathroom had a big picture window, and the tugboat operators sometimes tooted at her as she sat up in her bath, which I always rather liked, and I think she did too. I thought it might be a difficult transition for her, after thirty-five years in D.C. But she took New York by storm, just as she had Washington. A few minutes after we moved there, she had more friends in the city than I did. Our marriage was one of those rare occasions when one and one make three. We were both better people for being together. Eight years later, Nancy had a heart attack, then a stroke. She died in 1997, after eighteen months in and out of New York and Mount Sinai hospitals.

I kind of inherited her five children as a stepfather: her three stepdaughters, Elizabeth Sinclair, Jane Dickerson, and Ann Pillion, and her two sons, Michael and John Dickerson. Michael is a venture-capital investor and John, following in his mother's footsteps, is the White House reporter for *Time* magazine. So by spring 2005, my complex family included nine children and sixteen grandchildren, with one more well on the way.

22

FREEDOM FIGHTER

———

THROUGH MOST OF MY YEARS at Goldman Sachs, I had another life outside the firm, and it was one that I returned to in earnest once my career
in government was over and I was back in New York. This other life involved
the world of nonprofits, and it had offered a satisfying contrast to the often
tense world of for-profit corporations I was so devoted to at Goldman Sachs.
Because the nonprofits were concerned with noble causes, they appealed to
the idealistic side of my nature.

Like so many things in my life, my interest in philanthropy developed out
of utter serendipity. It dates back to the fall of 1956, shortly after I made partner at Goldman Sachs, when my first wife, Sandy, and I went to Vienna to
celebrate. We had been taking short vacations in Europe for several years by
then, but we'd never been to Vienna. We'd planned to see the usual tourist
sites like the Kunsthistorisches Museum and Schonbrunn Palace, and maybe
hear some Beethoven and Mozart. We hadn't expected the trip to open up a
second career for me.

As part of the trip, we had looked up an acquaintance of mine, Jan von
Hefton. He managed the Austrian businesses of my old international affairs
professor at Haverford, Edmund Stinnes, a remarkable man from a family of
wealthy German industrialists, who as a young man had chosen to leave Germany when Hitler came to power. Sandy and I met Jan for breakfast one
morning at one of the many fragrant cafés Vienna is known for. As we were
talking, a disheveled young man burst in the door and rushed up to von

Hefton. He gave him a hug, politely shook hands with Sandy and me, and then sat down at our table and poured out a long story to von Hefton in rapid Hungarian. I didn't understand any of it, but I started asking Jan some questions in English, and the young Hungarian spoke English back to me. It turned out he was a freedom fighter resisting the Soviet invasion of Hungary. He had just escaped that night from Hungary by boat across the Neusiedler See, a long, fairly narrow lake in southeastern Austria, whose southern portion reaches into Hungary. The U.S. government had seemed to be encouraging an uprising of Hungarians against the Soviets, but just a few months before, the Soviets had sent in tanks to crush the movement, and the United States had not been willing to intervene. The papers were full of the conflict, and I had been frustrated that our government had not done more to support this heroic popular movement against the Soviets.

This man said that his fellow freedom fighters were now isolated in small pockets, short on food and supplies, yet still fighting valiantly. "But we need help," he told us. "We need radios to talk to each other. We need outboard motors to make faster escapes across the lake. We need medical supplies for our wounded."

I was completely caught up. I had tremendous sympathy for these young Hungarian patriots fighting against such terrible odds. And having encouraged the revolt, Americans had some responsibility to help it succeed. So I decided right there and then that I would do all I could to help this man. I cut short our vacation and flew back with Sandy to New York that night.

Officially, I was still on vacation, but I spent the next two days in my Goldman Sachs office on the phone trying to round up the various things that the Hungarian freedom fighter said he needed. I'd developed a lot of friendly contacts in fairly high places by then, and the name Goldman Sachs helped me with the rest. To get the radios, for example, I called up David Sarnoff, the legendary radio and TV pioneer who was the head of RCA. Sarnoff would appreciate the importance of steady wartime supply lines, I figured, since he'd been Eisenhower's communications consultant in World War II, and had later risen to the rank of brigadier general.

When I told his secretary I was a partner at Goldman Sachs, I got right through. "General Sarnoff," I told him, "I've just gotten back from Vienna

and learned how desperately the Hungarian freedom fighters need communications equipment." I went on to say how much of a difference his help
could make. He agreed right away, and arranged to deliver me a shipment of
RCA two-way radios.

And so it went. I was able to find outboard motors from this company,
bandages from that one, pharmaceuticals from another. It wasn't particularly
easy, but it wasn't terribly hard, either. I was impressed by how many Americans admired the Hungarian resistance and wanted to help.

In two days, I had assembled all the supplies and persuaded Pan Am to
provide a transatlantic plane. The next morning, while Sandy stayed in New
Jersey with Anne and Greg, I climbed aboard a windowless Pan Am cargo
plane that was mostly crammed with supplies and settled into one of the few
seats, which faced in toward the center of the plane.

Many hours later, the plane landed with a thud at the Vienna airport, and
taxied along to one of the cargo bays. I'd alerted van Hefton to what I'd been
able to provide, and he'd arranged for a truck to meet the plane there. They
unloaded the supplies, and then drove them to the docks along the shore of
the Neusiedler See, and they were taken across to Hungary by boat from
there.

But that was the end of the trip for me. I flew back to New York on the
same plane. Around the time that the freedom fighters were receiving their
supplies I was returning to my desk at Goldman Sachs. My contribution was
just a drop in the bucket, but it got me interested in getting more involved in
international relief efforts.

A few days later, I realized that my little escapade had probably broken several laws: interfering in American foreign policy and the foreign affairs of another country; exporting materials without a license; landing at the Vienna
airport without proper clearance. I'd never told my generous donors that I'd
neglected to obtain prior governmental approval.

A little nervous, I called up the CIA to tell them what I had done, and
then, at the agency's behest, took the train to Washington, where I was interviewed about my activities by a couple of agents at my hotel. They wrote
down everything I told them. But I have never been a particular admirer of
the CIA, and I was not overly impressed with those two agents. I expect they

filed their report away somewhere and forgot about it. Still, I tried to avoid telling people anything about the whole incident for several years—until I was sure the statute of limitations had expired!

But I was caught up with the democratic movement in Hungary, and I looked around for an American organization devoted to the cause of Hungarian freedom. John Richardson was a young lawyer at Sullivan & Cromwell, the law firm used by Goldman Sachs, and I knew he took an interest in the Hungarian freedom movement. (He later became head of Radio Free Europe.) When I called to ask what I could do, he directed me to the International Rescue Committee, a small nonprofit on whose board of directors he served. The IRC directed a lot of its efforts toward rescuing Hungarian refugees and helping them resettle in the United States. It had been founded in the mid-thirties by Albert Einstein and a few other people to help Jewish refugees escape Nazi Germany. It was very small, but I found it tremendously inspiring. It was led by a charismatic and courageous chairman, Leo Cherne, a fierce anti-Communist who gave fiery radio appeals on behalf of the organization. He was one of the two or three best speakers I ever heard in my life. He was also an excellent sculptor. When I met him in his office later, I saw the heads he'd done of historical figures such as Winston Churchill, FDR, Mahatma Gandhi, and Abraham Lincoln. At the time, Eric Warburg, a member of the great German banking family, was on the board as treasurer, but he lived in Europe, and John Richardson asked me if I'd be willing to come on as assistant treasurer, and largely take over the finances of the organization. I said I'd be glad to.

The catch was that we hardly had any money. Today, the annual budget is around $160 million, and the IRC operates in twenty-five countries around the world. But at that time, we had only a few hundred thousand dollars. When the Hungarian refugee crisis eased and moved out of the newspapers, contributions slowed to a trickle, and the IRC almost had to close down. Several times, I arranged to set aside money for severance pay for our three staff people in case we had to shut our doors. But our focus soon shifted to assisting refugees from the Soviet Union, and kept us going. Over the years I got increasingly involved, eventually becoming chairman of the board myself. I've been on that Board for forty-nine years now.

Goldman Sachs was very supportive of my nonprofit work. Sidney Weinberg was involved in a broad array of civic activities, and had his own set of institutions in which he was active. Gus Levy, of course, served on the boards of Mount Sinai Hospital and other nonprofits. This set an important example for the rest of the partners. I think that it helped Goldman Sachs's image to be involved with nonprofits. It showed that we weren't just a bunch of crass, money-grubbing bankers, but rather a firm whose people were trying to make a broader contribution to the world.

My involvement with the IRC had the added benefit of bringing me into contact with some important people who became some of my best friends. For a small organization, the IRC attracted unusually interesting people like the Swedish actress Liv Ullman, who was our vice chair and a terrific spokesperson for us, telling heartbreaking stories about refugees in need. I used to tell her she was the only woman that could make me cry in sixty seconds. Senator Claiborne Pell was involved. So was Angier Biddle Duke. The descendant of two distinguished families, he was a Foreign Service officer who served as our ambassador to half a dozen different countries; he was a wonderful free spirit who brought a lot of good cheer to the board. Tragically, he died as he lived—hit by a car in 1995 in Southampton while Roller-blading with earphones on.

Of all the refugees the IRC has served, one of the most famous is Andy Grove, a founder of Intel. He fled Hungary in late 1956, shortly after I conducted my mission in Vienna. I'd certainly like to think I helped him escape. He slipped across the border in the dark and was passed from one safe house to another. His parents didn't dare leave Hungary themselves, but they urged their sons to go. As Jews, they figured their sons would not be safe there.

Andy made it to Vienna, where he found the IRC. I've met Andy a few times, and he has told me how grateful he was to the IRC. In Vienna, it gave him food and shelter, then helped him apply for status as a political refugee and guided him through the immigration process. After a year, he made it to New York, and the IRC looked out for him there, too. Andy had a hearing problem from a bout he'd had with scarlet fever as a small child, and an IRC caseworker helped him get the right hearing aid, and provided the money for it, too. She also got him into the City College of New York, where he learned engineering. Even though Andy was still learning English with the aid of a small dictionary he kept at his side, he got through the four-year program in just three years with almost straight A's, a remarkable accomplishment. His professors said they'd never seen anyone so talented and ambitious. He moved to California and eventually became one of the founders of Intel, one of the great stories of American business. He is now Intel's chairman.

I have enormous respect for refugees, and their willingness to take risks to find a better life for themselves and their families. Not just Andy Grove, but the harpsichordist Wanda Landowska, the painter Paul Klee, the Cubist sculptor Jacques Lipchitz. There are thousands upon thousands of extraordinarily talented, determined people who have come here in this way. And I am very proud of the IRC's role in helping them. Most of these refugees are in desperate straits, lacking food, water, medical care—all the basics of life. But they pick up and move because they have a thirst for freedom. Almost all of the refugees the IRC has helped come to this country have become outstanding citizens.

By now, I've made dozens of trips for the IRC to see refugee camps in places that are far off the usual tourist routes: the Thai-Cambodian border, Laos, South Vietnam, the Ethiopian-Somalian border, Pakistan, Afghanistan, Sudan, Azerbaijan, Soviet Georgia, many parts of Central Africa, Rwanda, Burundi, and the Congo.

One of my most memorable trips was to Somalia in 1979. Somalia is one of the poorest countries in the world, with a population of about three million people and nine million camels. The camels are exported, but the people are doomed to stay, plagued by endless civil wars, relentless droughts, and a largely useless government. In my judgment, it is rivaled only by Sudan as the most miserable country in the world.

With a small contingent from the IRC, we took one of the few planes that land in Mogadishu, the capital city. There, we got into a jeep for a ten-hour drive across the sun-baked desert. There were no roads; we were guided by compass, as if we were at sea. We were bound northwest, to the Ethiopian border, where the IRC had set up some refugee camps along the Juba River. The refugees had been forced to flee their homes in the south, but the Ethiopians had forbidden them to cross the border. In the camps, food, shelter, and medicine were being provided to these swarms of desperate Somalians by the IRC staff, including eleven wonderful young U.S. college students spending their junior year abroad.

I made a lot of IRC trips to visit Afghan refugees in Pakistan during their war with the Soviets. Many of the refugee leaders were mullahs or mujahedin who years later became members of the Taliban, but in 1980, they were our heroes. On one trip to Pakistan in late 1979, I called on President Zia. We always tried to keep in touch with the top-ranking official of any country where we operated in order to assure official support for our relief efforts. For that trip, President Zia was most obliging and gave us the use of his presidential helicopter, and we flew in it from Peshawar to a small town on the Afghan border, west of Chitral, where several thousand Afghan refugees were encamped. As in all the camps, the men were bearded and dressed in long robes, and most of them carried rifles. All the women were in the background, faces covered. Everyone spoke Urdu, and since I fortunately had a translator with me, I could talk with them.

All the refugees gathered around to see this strange man from America. Through the translator, I told everyone that the IRC was going to bring them food, help them drive wells, and supply medical care. The response was the same everywhere. "Thanks for all that, but what we really need are weapons and bullets to fight the Russian invaders. After the meeting, one of the refugees came up and said in British-accented English. "That was a helluva speech."

I was astonished. It turned out he was a Pakistani who had gone to Harvard Law School. I've forgotten his name, but he told me he'd come back to his native country and joined with the mujahedin to try to push the Soviets out of Afghanistan. As if that wasn't surprising enough, he said he would be leading a raid of about a hundred men on a Soviet fort that very night. "You want to come along?" he asked me.

I had to think about that. I wasn't there as an official representative of the U.S. government, so I was free to decide for myself. I was certainly intrigued. I'd never seen anything like what he was proposing, and I thought that it might help me get a sense of the overall situation. The man assured me I would be perfectly safe. "We'll get there at two in the morning," he explained.

"Don't worry, you and I will stay a safe distance from the fort, a good half mile." If Bob DeVecchi, the IRC's wonderful executive director in New York, who usually came on these trips, had been there, he would have advised me to forget it, I'm sure. But he wasn't there, and I couldn't say no.

First, though, I had to dress like an Afghan. At their direction, I took off all my clothes, and pulled on some heavy, tan-colored robes of theirs. I left my wallet, keys, passport, and all my other papers back in the camp. That way, if I was captured, I would be just another Afghan. We ate dinner together, all of these men sitting around on their haunches, eating with their hands, just as men had done there for a thousand years. And I did too, although it was pretty hard on my aging knees.

When it grew dark, they put me on a camel and, together with my new friend and his men, we rode for several hours to the hills surrounding the Russian fort. The camel took big, rolling strides, and I kept getting thrown this way and that. Finally, after I'd gotten thoroughly sea-sick, we reached our hilltop destination. I sat with the Harvard Law leader, and looked down on a stone fort that had been built in the fourteenth century, and had changed little, if at all, since. I was a little frightened, but the leader said not to worry, we would be perfectly safe there. Communicating with his troops by walkie-talkie, he directed his men to tether their camels, take up their positions on the hills around the fort, and wait for his signal. Although there were about a hundred of them, they had just twenty-five rifles—old British Enfields, surplus from World War I. There were, however, plenty of knives to go round. When the leader gave the word, the mujahedin came racing down the hills and as soon as they neared the fort burst into full battle cry, shooting off their rifles, and then stormed over the low wall with short ladders they'd carried along.

It was a breathtaking scene, lit up by occasional flares that they sent off into the sky. I watched, mesmerized, as the mujahedin plunged into the fort, firing away at any Soviets they could find, the rifles making popping sounds in the distance, all the men shrieking to add to the Soviets' terror. The Soviet troops were completely unprepared, and a lot of them were killed. Five minutes after entry, according to plan, the mujahedin charged back out the way they had come, clambering up the same little ladders and then racing back up the hill to their camels. They were exultant when they rejoined their leader, as each soldier tried to outdo the last one with tales of how many Russians he'd killed. "I got six!" one cried out to their Harvard Law leader. "I got eight!" another shouted. If you added up all the claims, the dead would have reached into the hundreds. Then we all climbed back onto our camels and hustled out of there before the Russians could regroup and come after us. We returned in time for breakfast, just as the day was dawning.

That was quite a night. I'm pretty sure I'm the only Goldman Sachs chairman who ever got involved in anything like that. I still have some of the clothes I wore that night, but I didn't tell anyone about that particular adventure for quite a few years. Until that trip, I didn't realize that the Soviets were no longer on the offensive in Afghanistan. In this wild and pretty much unoccupied and ungoverned country, they could roam around a bit during the daytime, but at night they were obliged to seek safety in a place like that old fort, and even that was not safe from the mujahedin. I sensed the war might soon be over. It was remarkable to think that the mighty Red Army, which had captured so much of that part of the world, could be defeated by these brave, primitive, poorly armed Afghans.

Now, of course, those same mujahedin have turned into the Taliban, which became our sworn enemy after 9/11. Since I know a few of these leaders, I really can't condemn them, for I know they aren't all bad. Mullah Omar, the self-appointed leader of the Taliban, was pretty rotten, but he didn't represent all the mullahs, by any means. Some of them were doing very good things in their own part of the country, permitting schools for girls (even though that ran counter to official Taliban policy), setting up a justice system that meted out genuine justice in most cases and didn't just levy punishments such as chopping off hands in accordance with the most extreme interpretations of Islamic law. And I'm proud that today, the IRC finds it possible to continue to work with the people like that. It is so important to continue to have diplomatic relations with the countries we disagree with. I find it so foolish that, whenever there is a disagreement, the first thing we do is close our embassy. That should be the last thing we do! It leaves these places completely in the hands of our enemies, and gives us no voice in the country's future. If the United States had reopened the embassy in Kabul after the Soviets withdrew, it might have made a big difference in the restoration of freedom. Now, especially after the recent elections, I am quite optimistic that Afghanistan is on a favorable course.

I'm happy that the IRC has remained in Afghanistan, helping the Afghans build latrines, distribute food, and dispense medicine and all the other things needed to give their people a better life.

23

INTERNATIONAL MAN

———✧———

THE INTERNATIONAL RESCUE COMMITTEE was my introduction to international politics, a subject that probably came naturally to me as a World War II veteran and as someone who was overseeing the globalization of Goldman Sachs. My work for the IRC led in turn to my taking an interest in other nonprofits in the international arena.

An important one has been the United Nations Association. I have already told about how I tried so hard to restore the country's payments to the U.N. when I was at the State Department. After I returned to New York from Washington in 1989, it seemed natural for me to continue to support the U.N. through an organization called the United Nations Association. The former attorney general Elliot Richardson and Cyrus Vance, a secretary of state under President Jimmy Carter, had been co-chairmen; now, they wanted to step down, and they asked me whether I'd be willing to take their place.

I wasn't all that familiar with the organization, but I quickly found out that with its 30,000 members in 175 chapters in cities and towns across the U.S., it is the strongest proponent of the United Nations in this country. That sounded good to me, and I called Elliot back and said I'd be honored to sign on.

As it turned out, the chairmanship proved very difficult. The organization had a single mission: to rally U.S. support behind the U.N. As I have related, this country still was not living up to its financial obligations to the international body. This was especially frustrating, given that President George H. W. Bush had himself once been the ambassador to the United Nations. But the hard-liners in the administration and in the Congress—people who felt that participating in the U.N. at all and honoring our financial obligations to the international body, compromised our sovereignty—held sway.

I worked hard for the United Nations Association, but I was being stymied by members of my own Republican party. I went around the country giving a speech declaring that we must pay our back dues "in full, on time, and without conditions." That phrase became a mantra to me. But in 1996, when Bob Dole was running against President Bill Clinton, he saw it differently. He was one of those conservative Midwestern Republicans who are suspicious of the U.N., and he had a standard stump speech with a line in it that bothered me a great deal. "You can be sure, my friends," Bob would say, "that if I am elected president, no American soldier will ever serve under the command of Boutros Boutros-G-h-a-l-i." Bob would deliberately draw out the name of the Egyptian Secretary General of the U.N.—who had succeeded Peru's Javier Perez de Cuellar—to make it, and the man himself, seem all the more foreign.

The whole thing was and is a red herring. We have veto power over any actions that the U.N. might take. They simply can't do anything without our approval. And no American participant in a U.N. force would serve under Secretary General Boutros-Ghali or anyone else in the United Nations staff. Any American soldier in a U.N. force is always under the command of the President of the United States, and from him on through the ranking officers on the Joint Chiefs of Staff and down to his own platoon leader.

Bob Dole was a friend of mine. I'd hosted a fund-raiser for one of his Senate campaigns—at Windows on the World on top of the World Trade Center, as it happened. He and Elizabeth "Liddy" Dole lived just a few floors away from me at the Watergate apartments when I was in Washington. He was always fun to talk to and joke with. I used to tease him about how much better a politician Liddy was than he, and he always took that well. When I heard about the speech, I called him up and said, "Bob, when you go after Boutros Boutros-Ghali like that, by name, that's a mean-spirited way of expressing how you feel. I really wish you'd change it."

Bob just laughed. "But John," he said, "it's the one line in the whole speech where I can count on getting a standing ovation."

I had to wince at that, but Bob knew the voters, especially the Republican voters who were suspicious of U.N. leadership. And that line of his stayed in—and I continued with my mantra that we must pay our dues "in full, on time, and without conditions."

In 1999, after ten years, I turned the chairmanship of the United Nations Association over to Bill Luers, a former ambassador to Czechoslovakia and Venezuela and the then president of the Metropolitan Museum of Art. He became both chairman and president.

That was the year that Senator Jesse Helms, the last holdout in objecting to the United States' full participation in the U.N., finally withdrew his objections and we finally paid up our outstanding dues. I'm not quite sure why he finally changed his mind, although I am glad he did. Richard Holbrooke, then the U.S. ambassador to the U.N., negotiated the deal.

In survey after survey, the American people have always voiced strong support for the U.N., and I think that possibly Boutros-Ghali's successor, Kofi Annan of Ghana, did a much better job of making the case that full American participation in the U.N. would do our country more good than harm. Annan studied at the University of Science and Technology in Kumasi, got his B.A. from Macalester College in St. Paul, Minnesota, studied at the Institute for Advanced International Studies in Geneva, and as a Sloan Fellow earned a master's in management at MIT; he had spent his whole career as a U.N. staffer before becoming Secretary General in 1997.

The United Nations has a difficult job to do. Imagine trying to run an organization with no common language, whose employees come from 185 different countries, each of which, from the smallest to the largest, gets a vote in the General Assembly. Ambassadors who often have no experience running anything are put in charge of a multi-billion-dollar organization. It's nearly an impossible situation. But it has gotten a lot better, and I attribute a lot of the U.N.'s improvement to Joe Connor, a former head of the accounting firm Price, Waterhouse, who was brought in as under-secretary general for management in 1994. He has straightened out the organizational structure and tightened up administrative practices there and made the whole thing much more businesslike. A lot of the greatest successes of the U.N. have come in areas that the public knows little about: the work of the World Health Organization, or the control of nuclear weapons, or international drug control.

But I think the United Nations can still be more effective and influential, and I can't see the world achieving any sort of lasting peace without it. In Kofi Annan, we have been blessed with the best Secretary General the U.N. has ever had. He's smart, experienced, and compassionate. Still, Annan needs to be encouraged and supported by the United States, for the Secretary General is only as strong as the members and the Security Council let him be, and they need to realize that a strong Secretary General is in all nations' interest.

There is also a very important economic role for the U.N. as national economies become more linked globally. We've now had a long series of free trade agreements under GATT. Similar favorable results have been achieved in North America with NAFTA. We need now more world negotiations to extend the progress that has been achieved regionally. Certainly there are drawbacks to international trade, but I am convinced that ultimately it benefits everyone, as each country produces what it can with the highest quality and at the lowest cost. The Economic Union in Europe, for example, has brought those nations tremendous advantages as trade barriers have come down among the member countries in Europe. Obviously, certain restrictions are necessary. We need laws and regulations to maintain decent working conditions, acceptable environmental standards, and restrictions on child labor. We don't want to deforest the Amazon to get cheap lumber.

But we shouldn't be paralyzed by these issues, either. Environmental standards can rise internationally as trade restrictions fall away, as can standards for working conditions and child labor laws.

On the international front, I have been chairman of an organization called Youth for Understanding, a foreign exchange program for young people. It was started in 1951 by an American minister named John Eberly, who thought it would help teenagers in Germany get over the bitterness of their country's devastation during the war by coming here to live for a year with an American family in order to see a bit of the United States. Soon, it was taking in young people from other European countries as well, and also providing an opportunity for American high-schoolers to spend a year abroad.

By the time I got involved in 1989, however, Youth for Understanding had serious problems. Part of the difficulty was that the program had become a victim of its own success. The various YFU affiliates around the world maintained different standards and cultural practices, which reduced the general cohesion of the organization. Meanwhile, here in the United States, overloaded public school systems were resisting the addition of temporary students from other lands. Further, as mothers entered the workforce, they were increasingly reluctant to serve as hosts for these international visitors. I had hoped that we could grow our way out of these problems, but unfortunately, the program started to wither instead. Without funds, we had to let go of some of the management and staff, which further upset the organization. This is one case where I did not make a difference for the better. It didn't help that I lived in New York and YFU was based in Washington. It was not easy to find a successor, but I finally turned over the chairmanship with some sadness. The concept is still a great one. It can be a wonderful experience for a child to spend one of his or her teenage years abroad, with a family in a different culture.

My involvement in international nonprofits and my interest in international education was amplified when I took on the chairmanship of International House. International House was founded in 1909, when Harry Edmonds, the head of the YMCA in upper Manhattan, noticed a young Chinese man on the steps of Low Library at Columbia. Edmonds bid the young man good day, and was astonished when the Chinese fellow turned and practically shouted out to him, "Thank you!" He said he'd been in New York three weeks, and Edmonds had been the first person to say a word to him. Edmonds was very disturbed to hear this, and he thought there should be a house of some kind to offer foreign students emotional support during their stay here. Edmonds was well connected in the city, and he enlisted the financial aid of Cleveland H. Dodge of the copper mining family, and John D. Rockefeller, Jr., and in 1924, International House was built at 500 Riverside Drive.

International House is a special residence for graduate students, 60 percent from abroad and the remainder American. It offers to its residents a variety of extracurricular social and cultural programs. I think it's good for young people from other countries to spend time in the United States and to meet Americans and students of other nationalities who can be friends for their entire lives. Ties of this kind help all the countries. International House held dances on Friday nights, and offered sightseeing trips on weekends. There was an orchestra, a newspaper, and many other cultural activities. Over the years, many marriages have resulted from friendships that began at International House events.

Descendants of both those initial backers, Dodge and Rockefeller, have stayed involved in the organization, and one day in 1990, David Rockefeller's niece Abby came to see me. I'd known her for years, ever since I first considered going to work for her father, David Milton. As the oldest member of her generation of Rockefellers, Abby has always been a leader of that family, and she was very keen on International House. She wanted me to take over as chairman. Former President Gerald Ford had been doing it, but he was living in Colorado and couldn't stay involved.

During my tenure as chairman, International House made a successful management change, improved its fundraising staff, and acquired the building next door, permitting us to house one hundred more students. I thought the business-related programming needed boosting in order to increase its long-term value to the students who stayed there and, with my various business contacts, I was able to start a series of lectures by CEOs from large companies. Many of them were friends of mine, such as Roger Smith, the former head of General Motors, and Pete Peterson, the former commerce secretary who is chairman of the Blackstone Group. They talked about internationalism at their company and job opportunities there, and that program was very successful. I was chairman at International House for six years, and then Abby and I passed the baton to Paul Volcker, the former chairman of the Federal Reserve Board.

During my State Department years, I noted with sadness how little Americans knew about Asia compared to what we knew about Europe. This was particularly true of Americans who lived on the East Coast. When we picked a foreign language to learn, it would almost surely be French, German, or Spanish. When we vacationed, it would be to Europe and rarely to Asia. Yet Asia was becoming increasingly important in the world. Its populations were growing fast, its economies were booming. Its political power was rising. It seemed to me that, as a country, we were headed for trouble if Americans didn't have more of an interest in and a better understanding of Asia. Feeling as I did, I quickly agreed to become chairman of the board of directors of The Asia Society when the post was offered to me.

The Asia Society owes much to the Rockefeller family. John D. Rockefeller III, the son of John D. Jr., founded it in 1956 to improve the understanding of Asia. I'd given a speech at The Asia Society when I was in the State Department, and being its chairman was a way to stay in touch with the Asian friends I had made in government. So I suppose I was a natural to succeed Roy Huffington, the Texas oil baron whose fortune came principally from finding and developing the huge natural gas reserves in Indonesia.

When I came on board, The Asia Society had basically turned into an art museum for the display of John D. Rockefeller's marvelous Asian art collection. Impressive as it was, it was only drawing a handful of people every day to its building at 725 Park Avenue, and I didn't think that the society should limit itself to being an art gallery. It seemed clear to me that we should develop more and better programs.

And I found that that was exactly what was happening. The Society was blessed with two exceedingly capable presidents during the years that I was chairman: first Bob Oxnam, a leading American Asia scholar, and then Nick Platt, a former U.S. ambassador to the Philippines and to Pakistan. They developed a variety of cultural programs on Asian music, dance, and theater; several lecture series with leading Asian businessmen and politicians; and a program to grow the membership substantially.

We also opened branches in Los Angeles and Houston, so that The Asia Society wouldn't seem so much like just an East Coast enterprise. But we didn't stop there. We wanted to expand to Asia itself, and Hong Kong seemed like the ideal location for our first Asian branch. We found that Asians were eager to help Americans learn more about Asia, and the Hong Kong branch, which opened in 1995, attracted the interest of a lot of important people there. In fact, it became a significant global forum for ideas in the wake of the Chinese government's 1989 crackdown after the Tiananmen Square protests. The Honk Kong Asia Society proved to be the perfect place for American and Asian leaders to meet to exchange ideas.

In 1996, I made what was perhaps my most important contribution to The Asia Society when I helped persuade Hank Greenberg, the CEO of AIG and maybe America's leading businessman, to succeed me as chairman of the board of directors. The largest insurance company in the world, AIG had started its business in China, and Hank was the perfect man for the job.

24

THE NEW YORK FED

—◦◦◦—

MOST OF THE NONPROFITS I've worked with have had a fairly narrow mission, such as the International Rescue Committee's mission to improve the lot of political refugees. But I have also been involved with a non-profit that plays a broad quasi-governmental role, the Federal Reserve Bank of New York. I served on its board from 1995 to 2000, and for four of those years, I was its chairman. It is not really a nonprofit in the traditional sense of relying on donations to accomplish its goals, but it does operate in the public interest. Any profit it makes goes back to the government, and being on its board is a kind of pro bono activity.

The New York Fed is one of twelve regional Federal Reserve banks that, under the supervision of the Board of Governors based in Washington, D.C., make up the Federal Reserve System. This is the agency that controls the money supply, which is the life blood of the national economy. Tighten the money supply by raising interest rates, and the economy slows; loosen the money supply by lowering interest rates, and the economy speeds up. Because New York is the global money center, the New York Fed is by far the most important of the twelve regional Federal Reserve banks. Many of the actions taken by the Board of Governors in Washington and its chairman, the powerful Alan Greenspan, come only after he has consulted with the Federal Reserve Bank of New York.

As if to demonstrate its world stature, the New York Fed operates out of a massive stone Italian Renaissance-style fortress in the heart of Wall Street. Its fortress quality is not just for show: five flights below ground level, it holds one of the largest collections of gold bullion in the world, some nine thousand tons of gold bars altogether. Much of the gold is owned by foreign governments who have placed it on deposit in the vaults of the Federal Reserve because they consider it safer there than on their own soil.

I was always fascinated by the New York Fed's operations center across the Hudson River in East Rutherford, New Jersey, where they handled all the check-clearing, the sorting of bills, and the scanning for counterfeit money, among other tasks. Several thousand employees were involved in just dealing with the millions of checks that arrived each night at 2 A.M., were processed by huge banks of IBM sorters, and then were ready to be picked up by their destination banks by 6 A.M. A reading-and-sorting machine checked over the currency, and pulled out any worn bills that needed replacing. It also kicked out possible counterfeits for employees to examine by eye. I was particularly impressed with one woman who watched the possible counterfeits stream by her workstation, occasionally plucking one out to scrutinize under a magnifying glass. Most of the bills she selected for inspection were indeed fakes, and the Fed would replace them with fresh, genuine notes.

It was Bill McDonough, the president of the New York Fed, who called me in 1995 to ask me if I'd be interested in joining the board as vice chairman, with an eye toward succeeding AIG's Hank Greenberg as chairman when he completed his term in a few months. It was an immensely flattering offer. After Greenspan himself, Bill was the second most important person in the Federal Reserve System. Before that, he'd been vice chairman of the First National Bank of Chicago. He was a very polished, genial, experienced international banker who was probably the person that Greenspan listened to most when he was setting monetary policy.

It made sense that Bill and his colleagues would think of me. After all my years at Goldman Sachs, I knew a fair amount about finance, particularly international finance, and after my time at the State Department, I knew how Washington worked, too. Still, I had to think about his offer for a few days, since I was, at that point, the chairman of about ten boards of directors already. But in the end, I couldn't say no.

I have been in many impressive places abroad and in the United States, but I found myself in awe at the Federal Reserve Bank of New York the first time I went there as a board member. In a manner that soon became routine, the New York Fed dispatched a standard black government car to pick me up at my office. Once we were on our way, the driver called ahead to the security gate to let them know that I would be coming in. Security was tight, with stout barriers up all around to keep any unauthorized vehicles a safe distance from the bank. But as our car approached, the barriers were lowered and we were waved inside. After I climbed out of the car I was escorted into the building by federal agents.

I had to laugh when I thought back to the only other time I'd ever been inside the Federal Reserve Bank building. It was during the war when I was working as the disbursing officer of the U.S.S. *Thomas Jefferson*. When the ship returned to the United States, I had to replenish the cash supply I needed to purchase food abroad and to pay the sailors in uniform. I couldn't just send for the money. I had to go collect it in person. So after slapping a .45 pistol onto my hip, I gathered an armed guard from my ship and the two of us climbed aboard a jeep and set out for the New York Federal Reserve Bank. That's where the money was. I collected $1,000,000 in small bills from a teller window downstairs, signed a receipt, stuffed the cash into a knapsack, and threw it over my shoulder, and then I and my guard somewhat warily drove back through the streets of New York to the ship in Brooklyn, very grateful not to encounter any resistance on the way.

Now, of course, I was wearing a proper suit, and I was unarmed as I rode the elevator to the tenth floor, and then strode down the long, grand corridor hallway, the walls decorated with oil portraits of some of the great men of American finance, starting with Alexander Hamilton. The board met in the boardroom at the end of the corridor. It is a large room, with walls of paneled mahogany and high ceilings, and a fireplace that is lit year-round. For the meeting, we sat around a walnut table with the Federal Reserve Bank of New York seal emblazoned on it.

Each member of the board had his or her own chair, with a nameplate, and each person represented a different financial interest. Walter Shipley, the chairman and CEO of Chase Manhattan Bank, was there to speak for the large banks; Pete Peterson, the former commerce secretary who headed up the Blackstone Group, an investment banking firm, spoke up for the investment community. There was a member from the medium-sized banks, and one from the small banks, too. Two members represented the broader public interest. Anne Fudge spoke for the point of view of companies in consumer products; she ran Maxwell House, the Kraft Foods coffee company that Sidney Weinberg had been so enamored of.

In fact, we had only a small role to play in setting monetary policy. That is set by the Federal Open Market Committee, made up of the seven members of the Board of Governors in Washington and five of the presidents of the Reserve Banks. Alan Greenspan was the Chairman; Bill McDonough, as President of the New York Fed, was Vice Chairman of the FOMC and a permanent voting member. McDonough's opinions were very influential in helping Greenspan decide about interest rates, and we tended to view him as our emissary to Greenspan. The regional chairmen also met with Greenspan twice a year in Washington.

In the years after 1913, when the creation of the Federal Reserve System was signed into law by President Woodrow Wilson, its moves were followed by only a few large corporations and a handful of wealthy families. But nowadays, almost every family in America is involved in the securities markets in some way through their pensions, IRAs, or their own direct investments. And the decisions by the Federal Reserve to raise or lower interest rates have a profound effect on the stock and bond markets, mortgage rates, and interest rates charged on credit card balances and other consumer loans. Although the stock market is not directly affected by Fed decisions, it is keenly sensitive to statements by the Fed about general economic conditions, and what happens in the stock market in turn has a profound effect on the national economic mood and sense of confidence. So I was always very conscious of the power that the Federal Reserve System had over the economic lives of Americans all across the country.

When I became chairman of the board of the New York Federal Reserve Bank in 1995, it was near the end of Bill Clinton's first term. The economy was well into what Clinton would, with justifiable pride, call the longest peacetime expansion in history. And the stock market was roaring. The Dow had stood at about 1,000 when Reagan assumed the presidency in 1980. By early 1995, it was up to 4,000, and it would reach nearly 11,000 by the time I completed my term in 1999. The Nasdaq, heavy with glamorous high-technology stocks, rose at an even faster rate during the same period.

To me, a stock market expansion of that nature was simply not sustainable, and it could lead only to one result: a terrible crash. I became all the more convinced of this after I assumed the chairmanship and the stock market continued to rise, with the high-tech firms leading the way. The markets were rising far faster than the economy was growing. Stocks were selling at higher multiples of their annual earnings (the price-to-earning ratio grasped by Marcus Goldman) than ever before in history, and at higher prices in relation to their underlying book value than ever before as well. Stock prices had risen so high, in fact, that dividends on NYSE stocks yielded less than 2 percent. All of this was, to me, extremely alarming.

I may have been especially sensitive to this because I'd lived through the Great Depression, which had been so devastating to my father. It had resulted from the only other occasion in our country's history when stocks had risen anywhere near so fast. I remember the fear on my father's face when he lost his job at Western Electric. That was a terrible time and, in some ways, the worst part of it was that it didn't have to happen. The national economy had been reasonably sound in the years before the Crash, and so was ours in the 1990s. There were no other indications that a serious recession was imminent.

In both cases, the dominant problem was the stock market. When I assumed the chairmanship, I introduced a policy that, during each meeting, every member of the board would give a brief report on what they viewed as the most important recent development in the part of the economy they knew best. Was there, for example, an escalation in wages? If so, how long might it last, and what would it mean for the economy? If wages were creeping up it would indicate that inflation might be just around the corner and that the Fed might have to raise interest rates. Nothing like that was happening.

I almost invariably devoted my own report to the dangerously overinflated stock market. I became a Johnny-one-note, I sounded the alarm so often. But

I felt we were in a classic market bubble, and I said so to the board, over and over. I'd report on the gaudy selling price of General Electric, its p/e ratio swelling from its historic norm of about 20 (meaning 20 to 1) all the way up to 50 by the end of the decade. And I couldn't help noticing the astounding prices of all the IPOs of various dot.com companies. They would routinely shoot up by 10, 15, or even 20 percent the very first day—in some cases before they'd turned a single dollar in profit! Everyone kept saying that profits didn't matter anymore. It was all about "buying" market share. To my way of thinking, this was lunacy.

The conventional view at the Fed and on Wall Street generally was that the stock market boom was a gratifying response to a very solid economic performance. It was true that the economy was growing nicely, creating twenty million new jobs over the course of the decade. Corporate earnings were rising steadily, inflation had fallen to the lowest point in twenty years, and consumer confidence reached its highest point since the sixties.

All of that was a remarkable achievement, but to me it still did not justify these astonishing stock valuations. So my fellow board members had to listen to my gloomy pronouncements at practically every one of our meetings. They kidded me about being chairman of the doomsday club, always singing the same sad song, even though I made sure I had new evidence each time. It was never hard to find.

Some board members and acquaintances on Wall Street kept telling me that I didn't understand. This was the "new economy." The high-tech marvels brought about by the computer chip were making all the old ideas about p/e ratios obsolete. Stocks weren't judged on profits any more, but on sales. Or, even more ridiculous in my view, stock prices could be based solely on the company's business plan, rather than on any performance at all. And the fact that stocks kept going up was held up as proof of the wisdom of this strategy.

But I kept thinking of what Sidney Weinberg used to say: "Trees don't grow to the sky." I never thought I was being especially perceptive to think this. All I thought was that just about everyone else was blind.

Still, I had to watch what I said. I certainly did not want to be the one to burst the bubble. No one did. All the same, I thought it imperative to take some of the wind out of this rising market before it rose so high that the economy might be badly damaged by its fall. I was cheered when, in December of 1996, as the Dow passed 6,000 and the Nasdaq neared 1,500, Alan Greenspan finally spoke out about the "irrational exuberance" of the markets. I appreciated Alan's candor, and hoped stocks would fall to more reasonable levels after his remarks. And they did. In the next week or two, stocks declined about 10 percent. That landed Alan in some hot water, and to my dismay he seemed to retreat from his remarks in the days that followed. Whereupon the market rebounded and rose to greater heights than ever.

As the market climbed, I thought the Fed should move more aggressively to tamp down the speculative excesses. Alan Greenspan had a chance to do just that by raising margin requirements, meaning the percentage a brokerage house customer can borrow against his existing stock holdings. For fifteen years, the Fed had set the maximum margin rate at 50 percent. This meant that an investor whose stocks had a market value of $100,000 could borrow up to $50,000 from his broker to buy stock in his "margin account." As prices went up, brokers would call their customers and tell them they could now buy another hundred shares of some high flyer without putting up any more cash. Total borrowings on margin accounts rose alarmingly. To my way of thinking, this contributed very much to the casino atmosphere that I sensed was taking over the stock market. People were playing with the house's money to bid up stocks to previously unimaginable levels.

The charter of the Fed gave it the authority and the responsibility to raise and lower margin requirements in exactly the kind of situation we faced. I thought the Fed should lower the margin rate to 40 percent—meaning that an investor could borrow from his broker only 40 percent of the market value of his portfolio, not 50 percent. Not a great deal, but enough to send the message that the Fed was focusing its attention on market speculators. I made this suggestion repeatedly at our board meetings, and directly to Chairman Greenspan when we met twice a year in Washington, D.C. I was so determined, I occasionally even brought the matter up with him in person between times.

Alan was always deeply conscious of his ability to move markets with anything he said or did, and was famous for his finely calibrated pronouncements about the state of the economy. He had a lot on his shoulders. He was determined to keep the economic expansion going. And he was very careful not to do anything that would compromise it.

But still, I thought it imperative that he raise the margin rates before it was too late, and I kept after him. I was convinced that the higher the stock market went, the more likely it would collapse and bring down with it the very economy that he was working so hard to protect. But Alan didn't see the connection. I'm a great admirer of him, and of the role he has played as the nation's central banker. But as the bull market roared along, I thought it was of paramount importance that he lower the margin requirements. To me, it was the perfect solution, for it made a surgical strike at the speculative element, leaving the rest of the economy alone.

But try as I might to persuade him, Alan told me he simply did not feel comfortable changing the margin rates. He said that he was trained as an economist, not as any sort of market specialist, and he didn't know enough about the effect of margin rates on the stock market to fiddle with them. He also thought the situation was better handled by the Securities and Exchange Commission, which is empowered to oversee the stock market. But I'd looked it up: only the Fed had the power to alter the margin rates. Still, he would not give in.

Alan figured that the stock market wasn't any of his business. The economy was his real concern, and he reckoned the stock market was a separate matter. But to me, the lesson of the Depression was that it wasn't separate. The stock market very much influenced how people felt about their prospects, positively or negatively. If their optimism switches to pessimism, that can produce some seriously negative effects. They stop making those large purchases like a house or a car that can make such a difference to the economy. Employers start cutting back on purchases of new equipment, stop hiring new employees. Eventually, this leads to a recession. And that, of course, is exactly what happened. The bubble burst. The market crashed. A rather serious recession followed. Opportunity lost. I believe the recession could have been avoided by one or two carefully timed increases in margin requirements.

In the meantime, the New York Fed faced other issues. One was the near bankruptcy of John Meriwether's hedge fund, Long-Term Capital Management. Meriwether had been a partner at Salomon Brothers, and was a highly respected player in the financial markets. He'd started an investment company based on the theories of a couple of Nobel Prize winners about the behavior of securities over time. Meriwether had built his company on the idea that bonds that strayed from the trend line were somewhat more likely to return to the mean than to depart further from it. It turned out that, Nobel Prize or no, they were all wrong this time. The bonds they selected did not follow the prediction, and they'd placed too big a bet, mostly with borrowed money, that it would. And so Long-Term Capital faced huge losses that greatly exceeded its capital, and put it on the edge of bankruptcy.

As president of the New York Fed, Bill McDonough could see that this was a dangerous situation. It occurred shortly after the Russians had defaulted on a substantial portion of their international debt, and the world economic situation was already delicate. Lots of major banks and investment houses had made large loans or invested huge sums with Long-Term Capital; if it failed, it would produce some serious collateral damage on Wall Street. As regulators, McDonough and his people had access to all of the banks' financial information, so he could see the full dimensions of the danger in ways that none of the individual banks could. The question was, what to do about it?

The Fed itself had no authority to bail out Long-Term Capital Management. That is not in its charter, and would not have been a good idea anyway. But the Fed could help spread the word on what was happening. It could identify the banks that were the biggest lenders to Long-Term Capital, and therefore had the most to lose. With my support, Bill called the heads of seventeen of them into the Fed's mahogany boardroom. Once everyone was assembled around the table, he said: "I want to tell you what we at the Fed know about the difficulties that Long-Term Capital is facing—and then I'm going to leave the room and let all of you figure out what, if anything, you plan to do about it." Bill's staff then made a presentation that demonstrated to everyone just how urgent the situation was. Long-Term Capital had no more equity. If something wasn't done, it was going under.

Then Bill and his staff left the room. The heads of the firms were all shaken by the news, and they talked nervously among themselves for a while and then they adjourned. Several of them decided not to be involved in any rescue package, saying they could not advocate any further investment in Long-Term Capital, it would be throwing good money after bad.

One of the big financial CEOs called up Bill the next day, and said that they'd all talked among themselves, and they wanted to ask him, "What's the next step?"

"Well, that's up to you," Bill reminded him. "We have done all we can."

After a few more meetings, the group came up with an offer to Meriweather to add sufficient new capital to keep it alive and to take over the ownership. As part of the deal, the group would allow Long-Term's investment group, which had been basically wiped out in the collapse, to keep a 5 percent interest in the new company and to participate in the management. The crisis was avoided. The company was still alive, and only the original investors lost any money.

This was no government bailout. It was the action of a private-sector group that, in their own interests, decided to invest their own money in order to straighten things out. They continued to operate Long-Term Capital and, with a different investment strategy, the company became profitable again. There was never a panic, nor a bankruptcy. I was quite proud that Bill and the Fed could play this limited but catalytic role, as compared to what could have been a more cautious and conservative approach. Some critics at the time carped: "Government shouldn't be bailing out companies!" But the critics tended to relent when they learned how limited the Fed's involvement had been. Everyone was relieved when this troubling situation was resolved.

I completed my chairmanship in December 1999. In March, the markets started to fall, exactly as I had feared they would. Over a miserable two-and-a-half-year period, the Dow tumbled from a high of 10,722 to a low of 7,286, and the NASDAQ's plunge was even more dramatic, from a high of 5,046 to just 1,114 during the same period. Also, as I feared, stunned corporate executives cut back on capital expenditures, frightened consumers put off making large purchases, and a recession set in. The damage to retirement accounts, children's college funds, and life savings was prodigious. And, exactly as I had feared, the market collapse pushed the economy into a recession, costing nearly three million jobs. As in 1929, this recession was caused not by a slowdown resulting from rising costs and rising prices, as often happens, but by a stock market collapse, one that might have been prevented by a simple adjustment in the margin requirements.

Even though I was largely right to be so fearful about the nineties boom, I am certainly not a font of wisdom on the subject of investing. Right now, because of my age, I am probably a more cautious investor than the average person needs to be. I am more concerned about conserving what I have than in increasing it. But it is important for investors to keep their individual circumstances in mind when appraising an investment opportunity.

When I came back from Washington in 1989, I had decided I didn't want to go back to the business world or back on corporate boards. I'd been there, done that. But I did make an exception for one corporate board. Carl Hess, the founder and then chairman of a successful small, private, very prestigious leveraged-buy-out firm called AEA Investors, had been talking to me about succeeding him as chairman of the board of directors. I didn't want to do it on a full-time basis, so we agreed that I would be a part-time chairman, giving the position 25 percent of my time, and that together we would find a full-time president. Vincent Mai filled the bill very nicely. He was a South African who had worked for S. G. Warburg, the London merchant banker, then for Kuhn Loeb in New York, and now was a partner of Lehman Brothers. Together, Vincent and I had a splendid ten years running AEA. Our investing group consisted of about fifty people, almost all CEOs or retired CEOs of Fortune 500 companies. *Fortune* magazine called it an "exclusive little club," but mostly it was old friends from the business world who enjoyed the association with their colleagues and served on the boards of one or more of the companies we acquired. We bought good, solid, established companies and tried to add value over a five-year period. Helped by a steadily rising market, we had a remarkably successful record during the ten years that I was there.

25

HOW TO RUN A NONPROFIT

———

I HAVE SERVED ON OVER TWO DOZEN nonprofit boards by now, and chaired many of them. While I was still at Goldman Sachs, I thought of them as my extracurricular activities, comparable to the Boy Scouting I did in my teens, or the intramural touch football team—we called it Slippery Rock State Teacher's College—I played for in college. Demanding as my Goldman Sachs work was, it did not take up all my time, and I took on out-side endeavors to round out my schedule.

Some of this was just good citizenship. In my home town of Essex Fells, I joined the vestry at St. Paul's Episcopal Church there, and eventually be-came junior warden. I worked up to becoming president of the local Com-munity Chest, the forerunner of today's United Way. I also served on the town council, and joined the Fells Brook Club, the local swimming and tennis club, eventually becoming its president, too. Probably the high point of my administration there was persuading Vic Seixas, a former Wimbledon cham-pion who worked at Goldman Sachs, to play an exhibition match at the club. (Not with me: I played paddle tennis for the B team.)

As the Goldman Sachs years went on, I took on similar activities in New York City and, eventually, elsewhere in the nation. Although I never con-fessed this to my partners, I spent as much as a third of my working day on matters outside the firm while I was co-chairman, most of them involving nonprofits. Why? Principally, I wanted to make a contribution to society. A key criterion for me in deciding which ones to join was whether I could significantly improve their operation. I didn't want to belong to a board just for the glamour of it, although, as a co-chairman of Goldman Sachs, plenty of opportunities along those lines came my way. I was once asked to be on the board of the Metropolitan Opera, a supreme honor in a certain New York circle, and I think I surprised a lot of people by turning it down. But I only wanted to be on a board if I could make a difference, and I didn't see how I could make much of a difference at the Met. It was a thriving organization without significant problems at the time, and I didn't see how I could help.

Nonprofit work involved a lot of hours, all of them unpaid, but it was not without its compensations. It gained me useful perspective, some of it humbling. A woman who worked with me at one nonprofit told me she thought Goldman Sachs was a New York department store. The nonprofit world offered a kind of reality check, too. I think I was more aware of how distorted the stock market had become in the nineties because I wasn't in the financial world all the time. And it didn't hurt professionally to meet and work with leaders of other prominent firms in the course of seeing to nonprofit business.

After Goldman Sachs, I let a lot of the nonprofit work lapse when I joined the State Department. But I returned to it in earnest when I returned to New York in early 1989. I was into my seventies, past normal retirement age, but still blessed with good health and plenty of energy. I didn't want to go back to the private sector, at least not as a principal activity. I'd had a pretty complete private-sector career at Goldman Sachs already. As for other government jobs, the incoming President, George H. W. Bush, decided quite sensibly that he wanted Jim Baker as his secretary of state and not me. So that left the nonprofit sector as my area.

I had been involved in a number of nonprofits over the years since I first got into the field with the International Rescue Committee, but this was the time that I really ramped up my efforts. As soon as word got out that I was available, I was flooded with offers. Almost before I knew it, I found myself not just a member of the board, but chairman of ten different organizations, and I'd pledged 20 percent of my time to each of them. I was married to Nancy by then, and she laughed and said it must be the New Math! The posts ranged from the Harvard Board of Overseers to the Mellon Foundation and included the New York Boy Scouts, Haverford College, Youth for Understanding, the Brookings Institution, the National Gallery (where I was chairman of the Trustees' Council), the International Rescue Committee, the Asia Society, and International House. The work was varied and demanding. But it was a period of my life when I found it impossible to say no.

Happily, it all worked out. I was spread pretty thin over a lot of organizations, but I gained a lot of insight into the workings of such places, largely because I was involved with so many. In my own efforts, I did not concentrate particularly on the actual work—the mission—of the nonprofit. I always figured there were many people in each organization who were far more expert on the substance of their programs than I could ever be. Instead, I focused on their organizational structure, their governance, the definition of their mission and their strategies to accomplish it, and on the monitoring of their performance. I considered myself something of an expert in all of that, and I would like to share some of my observations here.

The nonprofit world is a distinctly American aspect of life. Most of what nonprofits do in this country is done by governments elsewhere, if it is done at all. Almost two hundred years ago, Alexis de Tocqueville marveled at the social spirit demonstrated by America's dedication to the vast array of nonprofit causes, and it still continues: Americans donated almost $250 billion in 2004, the vast majority of it coming from individuals. Such personal generosity is a hallmark of our society. I think it is terrific that the people decide which social programs to fund, not the government.

Thanks to such generosity, the nonprofit sector is very large and growing. I'm often giving speeches that cite the numbers: one out of every ten members of the American labor force now works for a nonprofit; half of all adults do volunteer work for at least one nonprofit. Altogether, there are 1.5 million nonprofit organizations in the United States. The nonprofit sector as a whole accounts for 7 percent of the gross national product.

Legally speaking, a nonprofit is an organization that qualifies under paragraph 501(c)3 of the IRS regulations as a tax-exempt entity. Usually it is governed by a board of directors (or trustees) who have either volunteered their services or are serving for a very small honorarium. They are essential to the smooth running of any nonprofit, and I took my own work on these boards very seriously, and expected others to do the same. I regarded the volunteer spirit as essential for nonprofits, and never took a fee for any of my services. And I always made substantial financial contributions to the causes I served. Over the course of my life, I've given away more than $100 million, and most of these funds have gone to the nonprofits on whose boards I sat. This may account for some of my popularity as a potential trustee.

Nonprofits fall into five categories, and I have served on all types but one. By far the largest is religious organizations—churches, temples, and the like. My only contribution here came with my service at my little Episcopal church in Essex Fells, St. Peter's. But from what I have seen, I think it is fair to say that this religious category is the toughest to run of all nonprofits, largely because the powerful nature of religious feeling can get in the way of efficient management. Just think of the enormous difficulties that the Catholic church has faced over the issue of homosexuality and the priesthood.

Next in size come nonprofit hospitals and health-care organizations, which I have not been part of. Educational institutions—from the likes of Harvard and Haverford, where I have been heavily involved, all the way back to the Happy Time Nursery School, which my children attended—make up the third largest group. The fourth largest consists of the social service and environmental organizations such as the Boy Scouts, the International Rescue Committee, the Nature Conservancy, and others to which I have been devoted. The final segment, comprising cultural or artistic groups like the National Gallery of Art in Washington and the Getty Museum in Los Angeles, has absorbed a good deal of my attention as well.

One quality that runs through all of these organizations, regardless of their size, their geographical location, or their purpose, is that they are all extremely difficult to manage. I often say it is far easier to run a corporation—even a fast-moving global operation like Goldman Sachs—than it is to run just about any nonprofit you could name. Why is that so? There are many reasons, and I have spent a lot of time pondering them.

First, there's the question of mission. With Goldman Sachs, or any other profit-minded enterprise, the mission is very simple: to increase sales and profits. Now, of course, a for-profit corporation has to be concerned with other constituencies besides its stockholders, but if a management and a board increase sales and profits over a period of time, it will be readily accepted that they are doing a good job. But with a not-for-profit organization, there is no equivalent indicator of success. There is no simple numerical "bottom line" with Haverford College, the Mellon Foundation, or International House. More is not always better. It might have been possible to double or even triple the number of students at Haverford, but that would not have meant that we were doing two or three times as well.

How many customers you have and what services you provide to them are important for nonprofits, just as they are for corporations. But the essential issue for a nonprofit is the degree to which it is fulfilling its mission. And so the most important task of any board is to work with the paid staff to identify the mission of the organization and to establish measurements for determining how well the nonprofit is accomplishing it. This can be extremely difficult, for it goes to the heart of the organization, and a lot of people have a stake in the outcome.

An example might help make this clear. One of the jobs I took on after returning from Washington in 1989 was the chairmanship of the Brookings Institution. I had been somewhat reluctant to do it because Brookings was in Washington, and I was now in New York. But I am glad I took it on, and I think I was able to help them address the issue that was central to the difficulties they were experiencing. It had to do with the mission. Brookings had been founded in 1916 as the Institute of Government Research, with the purpose of providing policymakers with the necessary information and insight they would need to make wise choices in their governmental decisions. It was not properly funded, however, and by 1919, it might have faded from the scene if it hadn't been for a St. Louis native named Robert S. Brookings, who despite possessing only a tenth-grade education, made a fortune in the manufacture of rope and cordage. Being generous and patriotic, he wanted to do something to help his country and he decided to rescue the Institute of Government Research. When he succeeded, the institute was renamed the Brookings Institution in his honor.

By 1989, Brookings was by far the oldest think tank in Washington, and probably the most prestigious, but I could see that it had lost a great deal of its impact on Washington policymakers. Other organizations, such as the

Heritage Foundation and the Cato Institute, had started up with a more forceful agenda and, to my mind, a more extreme point of view on the political right. They had gained a lot of influence by turning out a constant stream of journals and briefing papers, and hosting dozens of lectures and gatherings, and then distributing videotapes for even broader effect. They saw their job not just as conducting relevant research, but as marketing their findings to key audiences as well.

Brookings, meanwhile, conducted itself in more of an academic manner. Its scholars, in fact, were often drawn from distinguished universities; they would spend a few years at Brookings to write a book on a topic of interest to them, then return to their universities.

This approach had two problems. First, the subjects that appealed to these visiting professors were not always of significance to politicians. Second, even when Brookings scholars did write about politically relevant issues, they did so at book length. With few and admirable exceptions, politicians don't read erudite books. They simply don't have time.

To me, this was a glaring failure of Brookings to stay true to its original mission, which was as important in 1989 as it was in 1919, namely to reach policymakers with its insights and information. As chair, I did my best to shift the emphasis at Brookings back to that original intention. I tried to shift the output from lengthy books on abstruse subjects to shorter reports on topics germane to the administration and to Congress. And I encouraged the Institution to follow up these publications with seminars and training programs for government officials to increase the reach and impact of Brookings's ideas. Surprisingly, Brookings had never made much use of the media. When it came to TV, it had rarely made its scholars available to reporters and TV producers. I think they regarded all that as somehow beneath them. I did my best to change that, urging Brookings people to come out of their shell and selecting scholars partly on the basis of their ability to advance their views through the popular media.

Or take another example of the kind of issues I would take on as chairman: Haverford College's effort to go co-ed. In the late seventies, when I was chairman of the board, Haverford had become one of the last all-male colleges in the nation. I believed that by holding out in this way, the school was in danger of violating its essential mission, which was to produce a first-rate liberal arts education for students in a small college atmosphere, with an overlay of Quaker principles. I was afraid that by staying all-male, we would not be able to continue to attract the students and faculty necessary to remain first-rate. When both West Point and Annapolis went co-ed, in 1976, I thought we could not hold out any longer. A substantial number of board members disagreed, mostly because of our special relationship with the all-female Bryn Mawr College, which has always been an important asset of Haverford. With the two campuses only a mile apart, students at both colleges could take courses at the other, and they could even reside in the other place. Many extracurricular activities such as the glee club, newspaper, and theater were carried out jointly. The Bryn Mawr board, with no desire to go co-ed itself, was afraid that a co-ed Haverford would no longer need a single-sex Bryn Mawr, which might be compromised by the transformation of its "brother" school. So part of the challenge for us on the Haverford board was to devise a way to go co-ed without damaging Bryn Mawr. If we could do that, the rest was easy.

If this had been Goldman Sachs, I'd simply have said, "We're going to start taking women," snapped my fingers, and it would have happened. That is the beauty of corporate-style decision making. But nonprofits don't work like that and, at Haverford, I needed to bring the rest of the board—and the rest of the college—around to that point of view before I had any chance of seeing it enacted. The college as a whole was mostly in favor of the move, and so was the board. But, as I say, there were significant holdouts, chiefly on the board. Far more than most boards, the Haverford board operated by consensus. We couldn't do anything that we couldn't all agree on. And that meant that when it came to coeducation, we had to start with baby steps that were acceptable to everyone. I proposed that we first admit ten female transfer students in 1976, for their senior year only. That seemed unobjectionable, and after much discussion, the board agreed that yes, that would provide a good test. Happily, that worked out fine, and so, after further discussion, the next year we added ten women transfer students to the junior class, and admitted a handful of freshman women as well. In 1980, we graduated the first four-year women. It took ten years, but Haverford eventually reached full equality in the numbers of men and women among the student body (in 2005, 52 percent of the student body were women). The board achieved consensus every step of the way. And the school remained true to its mission. But it took a very long time. Agreeing on the mission was the key thing. Bryn Mawr has not been damaged, and the close relationship with Haverford continues as before.

Nonprofit organizations can suffer terribly when the mission is interpreted differently at different levels. A prime example is my revered Boy Scouts. I have served for many years on the board of the New York Councils of the Boy Scouts, a regional division of the organization, whose national headquarters are Austin, Texas, where the national board sits. In 1998, that national board made a surprise announcement forbidding openly gay men from being scout leaders. Along with a lot of other people in the Scouts, I was terribly distressed by that. It was grossly discriminatory, and it left the impression that we did not want any gay scouts, either. Some gay scout leaders brought a discrimination suit against the Scouts. It went all the way to the Supreme Court, which declared that, as a private organization, the Scouts were free to restrict membership to heterosexuals if they chose to. Regardless of the legality of the policy, though, my feeling was that it was the wrong position to take and, sure enough, it has been disastrous for the Boy Scouts. Donations have dropped off significantly. Several hundred Eagle Scouts—gay *and* straight—returned their coveted Eagle badges. People asked *not* to be honored at Boy Scout events. Parents were deciding to keep their sons out of the Scouts so they wouldn't be exposed to such bigotry. It has been absolutely terrible to the public image of the Boy Scouts.

A lot of us in the New York Councils have lobbied the national organization to reverse this discriminatory stance, and I'm sorry to report that we haven't had much success yet. It all stems from the fact that the national leadership has not taken the broader interests of the Boy Scouts to heart in interpreting the mission of the organization. I'm proud to say that the New York Council board has taken a different view. We do not discriminate against homosexuals in any way. This has helped to some extent, but we still find the national policy embarrassing.

A second special difficulty in running a nonprofit has to do with the difference between the often largely volunteer workforce of nonprofits and the paid employees at for-profit companies. At Goldman Sachs, employees pretty much expect to take orders from the boss. I certainly did when I was rising up through the ranks, and I expected others to do the same when I became co-chairman. That's the nature of paid jobs: if you don't meet the expectations of your employer, you can be fired. That is a powerful motivation to get with the program.

With volunteers, however, inducements work very differently. Volunteers don't always take kindly to taking orders. And firing them is rarely an option. In the case of the Boy Scouts, I am sure that the national board in Austin was quite irritated by the position that I and so many others took on the gay issue. If I had been the division head of a corporation and I had bucked the system in that way, I probably would have been fired, and deservedly so. But nonprofits can't start firing volunteers who get out of line or they won't have any volunteers.

So how do you motivate—and control—volunteers? A large part of it is by inspiring them with the value of the work the organization is doing. Helping refugees, teaching scouting, bringing art to the public—whatever the work of the organization is. I think it is important, too, to allow volunteers to make use of their talents and energy for the benefit of the nonprofit. That can bring enormous satisfaction and loyalty to the organization. I've always encouraged the idea of having volunteers make a financial donation to the cause, too. Even if it is just a token amount, it greatly increases a sense of investment in the organization. And, at the board level, I've found it a useful incentive to arrange to have the board members see firsthand what the organization is doing. At the International Rescue Committee, I encouraged sending board members on fact-finding trips around the world so that they could see for themselves what the IRC was doing in Somalia, Afghanistan, and other places around the world, many of them in the news. We made sure it wasn't risky, and as comfortable as possible, with decent meals and reasonably pleasant places to stay. Those trips were a great boon, and they frequently paid off in years of service to the organization.

Getting the best out of volunteers is one of the secrets of good nonprofit management. Too often we see in hospitals a capable woman with business training assigned to deliver newspapers to patients when she could be running the gift shop, maybe jointly with a staff member or another volunteer. In the public schools, volunteers can often help start an art or music program or tutor an underachiever. Some nonprofit managers see volunteers as a problem; I view them as an enormous opportunity.

The third and final major difference between nonprofits and for profits lies in the matter of raising money. When a for-profit company like Goldman Sachs needs $100 million to build a new office building, it can go to a bank and, in a few minutes, take out a loan for the full amount. There aren't too many nonprofits that can do that. Instead, they have to go out and fund-raise. At Haverford, that was one of my biggest challenges. Unfortunately, Haverford doesn't have many wealthy graduates to draw on, and its endowment has always been lower than its peers'. Bryn Mawr's endowment, for example, was nearly twice the size of ours. Nonprofits need to have effective professional development officers handling their fund-raising, and this is a heavy cost that nonprofits must bear.

The biggest nonprofits have staffs of hundreds in their development offices, and every college president and every private hospital chief executive spends about half his or her time raising money. For some organizations, fund-raising costs can take up half the proceeds. Donors should be suspicious of such a high percentage, however. It is more customary for the cost of fundraising to run closer to 10 percent. Still, if total giving in this country is around $250 billion a year, that means $25 billion is taken off the top for fund-raising expenses. I've always been distressed about this. There are no banks or investment houses devoted to working with nonprofits, and if I have time and energy left after I have completed my work in lower Manhattan, I hope to help get one started.

I've made my share of these fund-raising calls, and I have received my share, too. It is a very delicate matter, one that has to be handled with just the right touch. A great deal of trust goes into it on both sides, and a lot of ego, too. To show just how complicated it can be, and to demonstrate that I don't always handle everything perfectly, this is probably the place to confess that I was an unwitting victim in one of the biggest scandals in fund-raising history.

It involved an outfit called the New Era Philanthropy Fund, run by a charismatic Philadelphia minister named Jack Bennett. Mr. Bennett came to see me at my office. He made an unusual proposition. He told me he had some generous philanthropists who would match any charitable gift that I made. They knew and respected me, he said, and were willing to match my gift, doubling the amount of the donation I wished to make. As Bennett explained it, his philanthropic backers were extremely wealthy, but very private people. They didn't want any of the publicity that normally comes with large gifts. Despite my adage about investments—that anything that seems too good to be true probably is—I believed him. I wanted what he was saying to be true. I wanted to be able to double my gifts so painlessly. Also, friends of mine like Laurence Rockefeller and the former treasury secretary Bill Simon had gotten involved with Bennett, and they believed in him. They told me he had done everything he'd said. I was still suspicious enough that I decided to try Bennett out with a gift of $100,000 for the Nature Conservancy. He said he'd take my check to his investors and send the Nature Conservancy a check for $200,000 six months later. I figured that wouldn't break me if it turned out to be a fraud. Well, lo and behold, the Nature Conservancy did indeed receive a check for $200,000 six months later, and the leadership there was very grateful. So I gave Bennett $250,000 for Outward Bound, another favorite organization of mine. I used to go on an Outward Bound trip about once a year—I took twenty-two week-long trips in all, and each one was the best week of the year for me. And, sure enough, six months later, Outward Bound received a check from Bennett for $500,000. So it went, through four successful transactions altogether, and I thought, "This is wonderful!"

I decided to pay part of an outstanding pledge to Haverford College via Bennett. I gave him a check for $1 million, but this time, no check for $2 million for Haverford arrived six months later. Concerned, I called up Bennett, and he told me not to worry. In this case, his benefactors wanted to make an even better offer. If I'd be willing to wait another six months, they would double my gift again, and Haverford would get $4 million. Since I had, in fact, made a pledge of $10 million altogether, I said okay, let's do that. True to Bennett's word, Haverford did indeed receive the $4 million he promised six months later.

Unknown to me, however, a Wall Street Journal investigative reporter had been looking into the New Era Philanthropic Fund and two days later, in a

big, front-page story, declared it to be a total fraud. There were no secret philanthropists at all, the story said. The matching gifts Bennett promised were
produced by fresh donations from a new round of donors in a classic Ponzi
scheme. The allegations led to Bennett's being charged with fraud and
money laundering, and in 1997, he was convicted and sentenced to twelve
years in prison.

The bankruptcy court that handled the New Era matter took the position
that the money the foundation had dispensed to different nonprofits was improper, and Haverford, among others, was obliged to return the $3 million
that came from New Era. I felt I had to make that money up to them. Altogether, I ended up being stuck for about $4.5 million to various nonprofits I
had tried to help through New Era.

That was something of an embarrassment to me. But I don't really hold it
against Jack Bennett. He never kept any of the money himself. He truly believed that God would provide and, for a long time, it looked to him like God
did. And now that he is in prison, he continues to do God's work, too. He has
motivated many of his fellow prisoners to lead better lives when they got out,
and has conducted a most useful life in prison. Every prison warden he's ever
encountered has written a wonderful testimonial about him, saying he
should be released early for all his good work. But he has steadfastly refused
to admit to any crime, so no parole board will oblige him. Jack remains in
prison as I write this. I've continued to try to help him, and I send money to
his wife and two children every year. Even though I probably should feel ag-
grieved, I feel sorry for him.

To summarize, then, those are the three biggest reasons that nonprofits are
so much harder to manage than for-profit businesses: the mission, the volunteers, and the fund-raising. Yet when I got more deeply into the nonprofit
world, I realized that business schools were not doing very much to address
any of these difficulties. For the most part, they were turning out corporate
managers only. So in the early nineties, I gave $10 million to the Harvard
Business School to help set up the Social Enterprise Program, to educate students in the management of nonprofits. Started in 1993, it gives every student
of the Business School some training in nonprofit matters, and for those who
are interested in a career in nonprofits, it provides an opportunity to special-

ize in the subject. I am pleased that almost all the other business schools in the country have since come up with similar programs.

I have also set up my own family foundation, the Whitehead Foundation, which I mention in hopes that it might be an inspiration to others to do something similar. Anne and Greg serve with me on its board, and they will run it after I am gone. I started it back in the 1970s, when I realized that my income had far exceeded any personal needs I had for the money, and it was more than I could give away intelligently. So I thought of the foundation as a place to stockpile the money while my children and I decided what to do with it. It's been a great pleasure to work with Anne and Greg on this. Most of the gifts I have made have passed through the foundation. Most of those gifts were my idea. But some of the programs we fund have been my children's ideas, and it has been a pleasure to me to see them develop an interest in philanthropy. Both of them have been very generous to their universities— Haverford College, in Greg's case as in mine, and Stanford for Anne. At their behest we have supported all of these institutions although, of course, I've been inclined to be very generous to Haverford myself. Because of Greg's particular interest in environmental issues, he has supported a number of environmental organizations on Nantucket, where he used to live, and in Lenox, Massachusetts, where he is now.

But both children have gotten me into things that I never would have thought of, and some of them have led to fascinating adventures. For instance, Anne persuaded us to back an archaeological excavation of an underground cave in Israel where John the Baptist may have hidden from Roman soldiers during the time of Christ. I've actually been there myself, crawled through the mouth of the cave on my hands and knees. That has been an education, and I find it yet another example of the marvelous way that philanthropic gifts can pay for themselves over and over again—in the value of the work they fund, and in the great pleasure they offer to people who choose to get involved.

26

IMPRESSIONISTS AND DEVILS

———

JUST AS SERENDIPITY STARTED my philanthropic career, it also sparked my interest in collecting art. And in both instances, the key events occurred when I was on vacation.

In the case of my art collection, it began with a trip to London that Sandy and I took in the summer of 1978. We were casting about for something to do one evening. None of the plays listed in the newspaper appealed to us, but I noticed a big article in the arts section of *The Times* about an art auction to be held that evening. Sotheby's was selling the collection of Robert von Hirsch, a noted German collector of Impressionist art who lived in Switzerland. I knew nothing about him, nor about his collection, but it seemed that this was going to be a great social event as well as an artistic one, and I thought it might be fun for us to attend. A colleague of mine from Goldman Sachs had gone to work at Sotheby's in London, and I called him up and asked how we would go about getting seats. Could we just show up, or did we have to get tickets in advance? My friend chuckled at my naïveté, and said we'd need tickets. Officially the auction was sold out, but Sotheby's always kept a few tickets on hand, and he'd be happy to give us a couple of them. That sounded terrific, and he sent them over to our hotel.

The seats ended up being right in the front row, practically under the nose of the auctioneer, which was slightly unnerving, since we knew nothing about how art auctions worked. Still, I was fascinated to be there. The whole scene was exciting, and the prices seemed astronomical, with most of the pieces going for more than $100,000 and a few for $1 million or even more. The auctioneer handled the bidding crisply. Since the catalogue contained all the information a bidder needed to know, the auctioneer would simply say something like, "And now we come to number six, a very fine Degas. Do I hear an opening bid?" And then they were off. Sixty pieces might be auctioned off in the course of an hour. That's one every minute.

All of this was very rich for my blood, but I was intrigued. As the auction proceeded, I looked ahead in the catalogue to see what was coming up. For each item, an expected price range was listed, and I noticed that the least expensive item, a Modigliani drawing, would be offered for sale near the end of the auction. It was expected to go for about £12,000, or $22,000. I'd noticed that the bidding usually started at about half the estimate, so I expected that the Modigliani would begin at about £6,000.

The Modigliani drawing was actually more of a sketch, done very faintly, of a young woman named Beatrice Hastings. I didn't exactly love it. But when the auctioneer started the bidding, I tentatively raised my hand. He saw me, and said, "I have six thousand pounds." I'd meant five, but I wasn't about to argue. He looked around the room. "Are there any other bids?" he asked. No other hands went up. "Going, going, gone, sold to the gentleman in the front row for six thousand pounds. Congratulations, sir."

And, just like that, I had bought my first serious piece of art, for $10,500. Before that, I had bought paintings here and there, but never for more than a few thousand dollars, and usually because they went with a particular sofa or matched the rug at our house in Essex Fells. This was an entirely different matter, and Sandy couldn't quite believe what I had done, it was so out of character. Still, I was pleased with myself. And I was even more pleased when a gentleman came up to me afterward, and congratulated me on my purchase. "That was the best bargain in the show," he told me.

We were going home the next day, and in the morning, I returned to Sotheby's to pick up my purchase and pay for it. I tucked the picture under my arm and carried it onto the plane with me.

After we returned to New York, I went to the library to get a book out on Amedeo Modigliani. I learned that my drawing had been done during a period in his life in Paris when he had befriended the sculptor Brancusi. The simplicity of Brancusi sculpture had encouraged Modigliani to simplify the lines of his drawing. I was fascinated, and started to read more about Modigliani and other artists of the French Impressionist and Post-Impressionist period. With its light and color, Impressionism also definitely attracted me, although I wished the prices weren't so high.

I started attending other auctions, and bought a few Impressionist paintings. I became a bit more sophisticated. I would read the catalogue in advance and carefully look over the paintings ahead of time, trying to decide whether I liked them. This sort of appraisal was entirely new to me, nothing like anything that I'd had to do at Goldman Sachs or in any other aspect of my life. It drew something different out of me. But I remained enough of a financier that I took an interest in the prices, and I tried to predict what price an individual piece would go for at auction, going on what I knew about the artist and how much I liked the piece myself.

I didn't start to become any sort of serious collector, though, until a few years later in the summer of 1981, when Sandy and I were in London again. We were walking through the city one afternoon when we got caught in a sudden downpour, and we darted into the nearest shop to get out of the rain. It proved to be an art gallery owned by a Swiss national named Achim Moeller. He introduced himself, and very kindly offered us a pair of umbrellas to keep us dry, but I was sure the showers would stop in a few minutes, and told him we'd rather look around his gallery instead.

He had a lot of French Impressionists, and when I expressed an interest, he told me about the paintings, and I told him I'd developed a fondness for the period. We didn't stay very long that afternoon, but Achim and I stayed in touch after I returned to New York, and in short order, he became a good friend and my principal art dealer. He would read the catalogues of upcoming auctions, and point out some of the things he thought I should take a serious look at. A professional, he knew much more about the paintings than I ever could as an amateur. His guidance has been invaluable. He has saved me more than once from making a bad mistake, and he's brought a number of opportunities to my attention that I would not have known of otherwise. Best of all, he's been absolutely honest with his opinions, and has never pushed me into a purchase I didn't want to make.

My collection has grown substantially in the years since. I have over a hundred pieces of art now, most of them paintings and drawings, but a few pieces of sculpture, too. Virtually all of it is either French Impressionist or Post-Impressionist. I've tried to collect at least one piece from each significant artist of those periods. With some of the major artists, like van Gogh, I have been able to afford just a drawing or a watercolor. The larger paintings I own have come mostly from the lesser-known artists of the period, although I still find them to be wonderful works of art. While I have bought pieces to fill holes on my collection here and there, I have never bought anything that I didn't love, that I didn't feel I'd enjoy looking at for the rest of my life. There is always a temptation to buy things because someone thinks you "ought" to have them or because they seem to be bargains, but I've tried to resist that. Nevertheless, I'm constantly amazed at how my tastes have changed and developed over the years, I hope for the better. Pieces that I thought I loved some years ago, I don't love quite so much now, and there have been a few things that I can't believe I ever could have loved. Most of the art is in my town house at Sutton Square, but a few works are in my office on Fifty-fifth Street. One of my problems as a collector is that I'm running out of wall space.

Each piece of art moves me in a different way, but I feel something for all of them. I have a lady's fan that Gauguin decorated with a scene from a Tahitian marketplace; I find it particularly beautiful, even though it is quite simple. He painted it as a kind of tourist trinket to sell for a few francs when he needed money. It's worth many hundred thousand dollars today, and several times what I paid for it. I also own a Caillebotte still life of some chrysanthemums. He set his easel up beside Monet's in a garden at Petit Gennevilliers, and they both painted the flowers. Monet's view is completely different, but his was well out of my price range. And I have a Rodin sculpture in marble of a girl tormented by a pair of evil spirits. I find the delicacy and softness of the nude figures astounding. And for them to be carved out of marble, with such intricacy. I could go on and on. Every work has its story.

The one piece I enjoy above all the others is a pastel sketch that Renoir did of his son Pierre when the boy was about five years old. If I had to spend the rest of my life on a desert island and could take only one of the pictures from my collection with me, I would take this one. It is a simple portrait, done in pastel, and not very large. But I find it completely beautiful. There is such an innocence to the boy. Is that my inner self? A happy memory of when my own children were young? I don't know.

I never intended my art collection to be anything more than a pleasure, but it has also turned out to be a remarkably good investment. Most of the pieces I own have doubled or tripled in value over the decade or two that I have owned them. At this point, my art holdings form the largest single portion of my net worth. Achim has taken to calling it the "Whitehead Collection," but it is really not that. It is just an accumulation of things I have acquired here and there over a period of time. The word "collection" connotes a central purpose, a common theme, and my things never had that. And I find it presumptuous to consider my pieces comparable to the great private collections of French Impressionist and Post-impressionist works that have been assembled by people like Walter Annenberg, Chester Dale, the Havemeyers, and the Garbishes. My own holdings cannot possibly compare in scope and quality. Besides, my collection is still incomplete.

Nevertheless, it has given me great pleasure over the years. My first two wives were fairly supportive of my collecting, but Nancy actually got quite involved with it. Several of the pieces we picked out together, and several of them I bought for her. I suppose that, when I think of the collection now, I think largely of the fun that she and I had with it. I am always eager to see what will be in the next spring's auction.

It was by a similar fluke that I ended up being an owner of a piece of the New Jersey Devils hockey team. I would never have thought of it. But one day in 1982, my friend Governor Tom Kean of New Jersey called to say he had a problem. He had built a sports arena in the Meadowlands—a marshy, mostly underdeveloped area of northeast New Jersey. The arena proposal had attracted an NBA basketball team, the New Jersey Nets, which had agreed to play its home games there. But the arena needed a hockey team as well or it would not be able to generate sufficient revenue to survive. I was a banker: Could I find him a hockey team?

I knew little about hockey teams, or about hockey for that matter. I'd had weak ankles as a kid and never learned to skate, although I had been a pretty avid fan of the New York Rangers. Still, I felt obliged to do what I could to help the governor.

I couldn't think of anyone at Goldman Sachs who knew anything about sports franchises, but my old Boy Scout friend, John McMullen, the one who had allowed me to share his tent at Boy Scout Camp, had become very successful first as a naval architect and then as an investor in the shipping business, and had then taken a financial interest in professional sports. A decade before, I had helped him purchase the Houston Astros baseball team. I'd read in the papers that he had recently sold it, and I thought he might now be interested in Governor Kean's need for a hockey team.

I called up McMullen, and yes, he was interested. He looked into the matter and discovered that the National Hockey League did not want to award any new franchises now. That meant we needed to try to buy an existing one and move it to the Meadowlands. Further investigation revealed that there were three for sale. Of them, the Colorado Rockies (not to be confused with the later baseball team) would be the least expensive, since it was near bankruptcy. He reported the news back to me, and then asked if I might be interested in going into a deal with him as a partner. He assured me he would do all the work; I would be a "silent" partner, and we settled on a 75-25 arrangement. We had a study done of the New Jersey hockey market, which was extremely encouraging: Its authors claimed that virtually everyone in the state would be clamoring to buy season hockey tickets. On the strength of this study, we went ahead and became the proud owners of the Colorado Rockies. The National Hockey League charged us heavily to move the franchise to New Jersey, even though the relocation to a larger market was obviously in the league's interest. And the other regional teams, the New York Rangers, New York Islanders and even the Philadelphia Flyers, all exacted high payments for sharing their exclusive television rights. Yet the banks, impressed by our market study, were very generous, and we were launched in 1980 to great acclaim with a capitalization of $1 million equity and $29 million bank borrowings—hardly a ratio that Goldman Sachs would have approved of.

We renamed the team the New Jersey Devils, after looking at the results of a thirty-day public poll of possible team names. Bishop Boland, the Catholic bishop of the Newark diocese, strongly opposed the new name, but when

John McMullen, a devout Catholic, explained to the bishop that we didn't mean his kind of devil but the devil invoked in "devil-may-care," he came around, even appearing on opening night to bless the new devil-may-care Devils.

At Goldman Sachs, the partnership agreement required each partner to offer any investment opportunity to the firm before investing in it himself. As I recall, the response was either a curt "No, thank you" or "You must be crazy!"

We were on some thin ice ourselves. That first year, we sold 8,000 season tickets, a far cry from the 19,042 sell-out that our study had predicted. And the fans who did come did not have much to root for. Desperate for cash, the previous owner had sold off what few good players the team had. Four years in a row, the Devils finished dead last, with the worst record in the entire league. Meanwhile, the Islanders won the Stanley Cup, hockey's championship trophy, four times. The franchise was often on the brink of financial collapse, and occasionally McMullen and I had to personally guarantee some of the bank loans. But, to our credit, we were patient and we hung in. We invested in some of the best scouting staff in the league, and they used the prime draft choices that are the spoils for a losing team to extremely good effect. We worked closely with our principal farm team to develop young talent and, most important of all, we hired the hockey genius Lou Lamoriello, then the athletic director at Providence College, to be our general manager. He quickly became generally recognized as the best in the league.

Under his guidance, the Devils scouts concentrated heavily on European players, and this paid off nicely, especially as the Cold War wound down. In 1986, we drafted Slava Fetisov and Igor Larionov, two of the best players for the Soviets' famous Red Army team—but that only provoked laughter from the hockey establishment when the Soviets wouldn't let them out. I tried to get the Soviet ambassador to the United States, Anatoly Dobrynin, to let them play here as a goodwill gesture, but he was unable to win permission in Moscow. But after the Cold War ended in 1990, we were able to add both of them to our roster. They were past their prime but still excellent players, and they helped turn around the Devils from one of the league's worst teams to one of the best. In 1995 and 2000 the team won the Stanley Cup.

In the year 2000, just before we won our second Stanley Cup, a group of investors headed by Ray Chambers, a successful investor who had the dream of building an arena in Newark, made McMullen and me an offer for the team that was simply too good to refuse. Chambers had already acquired the Nets and, like Tom Kean almost twenty years earlier, needed the Devils to make an arena in Newark practical.

My time with the Devils was a nice break from the tensions of investment banking and, later, of international diplomacy. I enjoyed being around the players and the coaches, and became good friends with Lou, and with Yogi and Carmen Berra, who were regulars in our owners' box. The partnership with John McMullen was great. He ran the show, but he always kept me posted. He had terrific business instincts, and he was certainly right about the Devils. That partnership turned out to be the best single investment I ever made, at Goldman Sachs or anywhere else. So, I guess it pays to help out a governor.

27

A VISION FOR GROUND ZERO

———

WHEN I ACCEPTED GOVERNOR PATAKI'S OFFER of the job of chairman of the Lower Manhattan Development Corporation, and was introduced at that press conference in November of 2001, I had no staff, no office space, and no money. Of these, the most urgent need was for money. I'd been around government long enough to know that an unfunded agency is an orphaned child. It was not easy to know how much we'd need to rebuild Lower Manhattan, nor where the money would come from, but President Bush soon determined that this disaster was not confined to New York City, nor to New York State, but was a catastrophe for the nation, and that a few dollars from every taxpayer's taxes should go to the recovery. He pledged a minimum of $20 billion in federal funds for the effort. We would not have accomplished anything without that. The governor and mayor, both Republicans, went to work to be sure congressional Republicans followed through with the necessary legislation. The same message of urgency needed to be carried to the Democrats. Fortunately, New York's two senators, Charles Schumer and Hillary Clinton, were already hard at work to secure from Congress the money that President Bush had promised us.

Even though they are both Democrats, I knew them both. I'd first met Hillary in the receiving line at a White House function during her husband's first term. She wasn't particularly interested in me, but she was positively thrilled to meet Nancy. She lit right up. "You're not the Nancy Dickerson who used to cover the White House on TV, are you?" she asked when she heard Nancy's name. When Nancy said she was indeed that Nancy Dickerson, Hillary just glowed. "I grew up watching you on the evening news on TV every night! You were such an inspiration to me. You showed me how much a woman could do if she just put her mind to it."

She went on like this for quite a little while in the receiving line. Afterwards, she made sure that Nancy and I were invited to a lot of White House events, far more than most Republicans attended. We became friends with her and her husband. Hillary and I still have breakfast occasionally to talk about things we're doing, and how the work is going at Lower Manhattan.

And I knew Chuck Schumer from the time he was first elected to Congress from Brooklyn in the early seventies. Half of his new constituents worked on Wall Street, but he was a lawyer, and he knew little about finance. I was chairman of the securities industry trade association then, so he came to see me and I set up a kind of training program for him. I had him spend a couple of days at the New York Stock Exchange, a couple of days with the Federal Reserve, and so on. He was a quick study, and we got along very well.

These relationships put me in good stead with Congress. Since Mayor-elect Bloomberg and Governor Pataki were both Republicans like me, the Democrats needed some assurance that I wouldn't treat the LMDC as a partisan body, and Schumer and Clinton were able to vouch for me with their fellow Democrats. Also, ever since that famous headline from the Ford Administration days, "Ford to City: Drop Dead," there has been a fair amount of anti-New York bias in Washington, a feeling that a big, brash city like New York doesn't need—or deserve—the federal government's help. It took some effort to counter that, as well.

Schumer and Clinton did their work well. And I think that my particular brand of moderate Republicanism helped, too. A few days after my appointment, Congress voted to appropriate $2 billion of the $20 billion to the LMDC. We were in business.

But we still needed office space. Here, my friendship with John Zuccotti, the co-chairman of Brookfield Properties, proved useful. I had been a director of a previous company of his, and we'd stayed in touch. He had space for us in a Brookfield building at One Liberty Plaza, on the edge of Ground Zero. It had been damaged in 9/11: all the windows on the World Trade Center side had been shattered, but everything had been repaired by then. He offered it to us for free. I appreciated the gesture, but I didn't think that looked right, so we paid market rates for an office there on the twentieth floor, which was perfect for us.

Now for a staff. I'd been considering four or five other people to be the LMDC's president, who would be responsible for its day-to-day operation while I concentrated on the big picture as the chairman. But I'd found it a difficult choice to make, since I was so unfamiliar with the worlds of architectural planning and urban development in which I was now operating. Governor Pataki spoke highly of Lou Tomson, an energetic and often humorous member of his staff, for the post, and I accepted his suggestion, thinking it would be helpful to have someone close to the governor, and it was. Lou quickly developed a good working relationship with the Port Authority of New York and New Jersey, which owned the Ground Zero site, and could have made life very difficult for us if it chose to. Half the board of the Port Authority is appointed by the New York governor, and the other half by the New Jersey governor, which is, to say the least, a very complicated political arrangement.

Lou continued to live in Albany and was only in the city four days a week, which somewhat compromised his effectiveness. But he got us up and running and, under his direction, we quickly built a very competent staff. When Lou left after a year or so, Kevin Rampe succeeded him as president and has done an outstanding job. He had worked previously as an attorney at Sherman & Sterling and was also favorably known to the governor. Stefan Pryor, originally my deputy and now our chief operating officer, has been another outstanding staffer.

The federal pledge of $2 billion helped establish our credibility. Nothing wins respect like money. It also helped that Governor Pataki granted us his powers of eminent domain. That meant that we could seize property if we thought it in the best interests of the public. It's significant clout, but it works much better as a threat than as something you actually use. Like all power, once you use it, you use it up. So we husbanded it very carefully. Three years into the work, we've taken only two small properties by eminent domain.

Still, the LMDC was the new kid on the block, and there was a fair amount of understandable resentment from other, more established city agencies. The zoning board of New York City, for instance, was bothered that we were the ones deciding where new buildings would go in Lower Manhattan. And the city planning board sometimes felt encroached upon for the same reason. And that's just the city; there were competing state organizations, too. There was the Empire State Development Corporation, a state agency headed by Charlie Gargano which, not unreasonably, thought development in Lower Manhattan should be *its* business. And it had a staff of 2,000 people! So there were a lot of people around who would have been delighted if we didn't exist, and some of them tried by various schemes to make that happen. It made life difficult at times.

There were important government officials to look out for, too. Remembering my experience with Senator Jesse Helms, I took the precaution of contacting Sheldon Silver, the speaker of the New York State Assembly, whose district was Lower Manhattan. I told him I was new at this, and would like some advice on how we might proceed. He had me come right down. As I sat with him in his office at 120 Broadway, I asked him what he thought Lower Manhattan should look like in five or ten years, so that we could properly take his views into account.

He looked at me with a sweet little smile. "I can tell you are new at this," Silver said.

I guess I was, because I had no idea what he meant.

"Look, that isn't how it works," he said. "The way it works is like this. You decide what you want to do, and you have a press conference and announce it. Once it's printed in the newspapers, I'll walk around the neighborhoods, talk to people on the phone, see how it's all going down, find out if people basically like what you're saying. Then, once I size it all up, I'll have a press conference and say what I think of your idea. And you'll read it in the newspapers. That's the way it works. That's the way it's always worked."

Then he laughed and said I seemed like a good guy, and it was nice of me to come down to his office. So, just for the fun of it, he would tell me what he wanted Lower Manhattan to look like in five or ten years. And Silver launched into a ten-minute speech, and I agreed with almost all of what he said, and I told him so. And for the most part we've gotten along fine ever since. I make sure to invite him to all of our public events if we're going to be announcing anything, and I always thank him publicly for his support. He's a good man and he's worth listening to.

I've enjoyed pretty good relations with the press through the years, both at Goldman Sachs and at the State Department. So I wasn't quite prepared for how savage the coverage could be. Two weeks after my appointment, the *New York Post* ran an editorial wondering whether I was the man for the job. They complained that I had been at work for *two entire weeks*, and what had I done? I thought that was a little premature, to say the least.

The *Post* later ran a big story that irked me even more. It ran under a front-page banner headline "Play for Pay," and the "story" related to my having been chosen as the honored guest at the annual fund-raising dinner for the New York State Republican Party dinner. The paper claimed that builders had to buy a ticket to the dinner if they wanted to get contracts from the LMDC. That made me very angry because it was, of course, completely untrue.

I called Governor Pataki and asked him what I should do. "Well, John," he said, "the *Post* has been writing those kinds of stories about me ever since I was first elected. It's just the way it is."

"But it's not true," I told him, unable to hold back my annoyance. "I want to set the record straight."

"I know that," he said. "But you won't get anywhere with that. It will only prolong the story. If I were you, I'd just withdraw from the dinner. Tell the people putting it on that you can't make it after all. That will kill the story."

So that's what I did, and the *Post* ran a little item saying I would not be attending the dinner, and that was the end of it. I suppose it was ridiculous that anyone could think I could be bought off in that way. But I didn't find it at all funny at the time. It was very distressing to me, but it's the sort of thing that politicians have to put up with every day. It's a tough business, and the press makes it tougher. There seems to be no penalty for writing stories that are completely untrue.

The big question, of course, was how the LMDC was going to rebuild the World Trade Center site. I didn't come to the job with any clear ideas about that. I didn't think the answers should come from the board, either. Actually,

I thought the best way for us to proceed was to do . . . nothing. So my first official act was to impose a two-month moratorium on all significant decision
making. I was afraid that if we made any big decisions too soon, we'd make
serious mistakes, and pay a heavy penalty trying to fix them later on.

Instead of charging forth on our own, I thought we should spend those first
two months listening to what *other* people thought we should do. So we set
up advisory boards to meet with each of eight different constituencies: the
families of the victims, commuters, residents, representatives of the companies in that part of Manhattan, and so on.

We also had hearings for the general public, so they could come in and
have their say, too. As I write this, we've had over seventy-five public hearings
for various groups on different subjects. I attended over half of them myself,
which made for a lot of late evenings.

One of the first things we discovered was that a large number of people
who lived there were leaving. Some were upset about all the dust and ashes,
which they considered unhealthy. Others were leaving because so many an-
cillary businesses in the area—grocery stores, restaurants, newsstands—had
closed down, reducing the quality of life down there. A lot of them said they
were not coming back, either, which was the most worrisome part.

So we developed financial inducements to encourage people to stay. If
people in the area signed a two-year lease they received a rent subsidy of up
to $6,000 a year, depending on how close they lived to Ground Zero. We of-
fered companies a similar deal. If they signed a seven-year lease, we provided
up to $5,000 for every employee they retained at that site. These were two of
our most successful programs. They cost almost $300 million each, but they
helped stabilize the area, and gradually led to what is now a housing boom
in Lower Manhattan.

After listening to commuters, we worked hard to restore the dozen or so
subway stops that had been knocked out in the attack. The heavily damaged
World Trade Center Port Authority (PATH) tunnel through which 70,000
people had traveled daily to get from New Jersey to New York, was going to
be down for at least a year, so we looked for alternative modes of transporta-
tion for railway commuters. We ended up borrowing ferries from up and
down the East Coast, assembling the biggest assortment of ferries you ever

saw to ply the waters around Manhattan, and they have proved very popular. Even though the trains are now back in service, almost half of the original train commuters have stuck with the ferries.

But the greater public remained focused on what we were going to put up where the Twin Towers and the other buildings had been at Ground Zero. For that we employed the standard procedure of most urban planning boards for new development: We put out a request for proposals, or RFP. This was an unusual RFP, though. We were seeking a plan for the entire sixteen-acre site—not just the buildings, but the memorial that we viewed as the center-piece of it, and the street plan, too. We got back proposals from four hundred and twenty architects from around the world. Several of the candidates were well known. Many more, of course, were not. We sifted through all of them, and ended up selecting a prestigious New York firm, Beyer Blinder Belle, to produce what amounted to six variations on their ideas for the site that we thought were worthy of public consideration.

We put a lot of work into it, and with some fanfare, we put the six on dis-play at the Javits Center on July 20, 2002. It was a Saturday, an extremely hot day, but to our amazement, 4,000 people showed up to look over the various proposals and hear a presentation about them. I thought that was a wonder-ful turnout. We wanted the public involved. This project was for them, their children, and grandchildren. We arranged to assign everyone to a table where they wouldn't be just with their friends, but with a mix of people that represented something of the mélange of the city. Commuters and residents, rich and poor. All of them sat together. We'd given out a little gadget that al-lowed each person to record their response to each proposal by pushing a button.

But this was New York, and New Yorkers are not known to be shy about ex-pressing an opinion, especially a negative one. The votes were tabulated each time and presented on a big screen in the room, and you heard a fair amount of Bronx cheers in the room each time a new idea went up, only to get clob-bered in these instant polls. The public voted down each plan quite decisively.

Some people think we actually planned it that way, to show that the pub-lic's views were being respected. We certainly did want people to know that they were heard. But it was painful to all of us to have worked so hard and get such a negative reaction from so many people. That was a very low moment for all of us at the LMDC.

For better or for worse, the Javits Center presentations were democracy in action. Even though the people who attended the showing did not go for any of the proposals, they demonstrated that they were intensely interested in the project. At each table, people who didn't know each other started talking to each other about the design of the city's public spaces and they didn't stop. The event formally concluded at four P.M. But practically no one left! It wasn't until five that anyone got up, and a lot of people were still there at six, when I finally had to leave. It was fascinating, and reassuring, to see how intensely people were captivated by the whole discussion.

So we went back to the drawing board. We realized that we'd made a mistake in relying so much on just one architectural firm to draw up so many of the plans, even though we thought they'd done good work. We needed to devote more attention to selecting a wide variety of architects if we wanted to have a good range of architectural ideas for the site. So we put out another call for architects, and we were gratified that again, over 400 architectural teams from around the world responded.

This time, with the encouragement of the LMDC's head of planning, Alexander Garvin, I relied more heavily on a couple of our board members with a particular interest in public architecture: Roland Betts, who'd built the Chelsea Piers sports complex in Manhattan, and a wonderful young New York architect named Billie Tsien to winnow down the 400 applicants. They in turn assembled a panel of outside advisers, including Terence Riley, the head of the department of architecture at the Museum of Modern Art, and Toshiko Mori, the chairman of the Department of Architecture at Harvard, among several others. That group went through all the proposals, and eventually settled on seven designers.

Interestingly, one of them—the winning one, as everyone now knows— was by Daniel Liebeskind, who'd been born in Poland but raised in Brooklyn before moving to Berlin, where he'd become known for the Holocaust Museum he designed. He was originally supposed to be on the advisory committee, but he had a schedule conflict, so he ended up contributing a proposal instead.

We arranged for a new presentation to take place at the Winter Palace in the World Financial Center. Unlike the six proposals put on display at the Javits Center, the nine designs (nine because one of the seven design teams contributed three) caught a lot of people's imaginations, and that lifted our spirits considerably. Finally, we were doing something right in the public's mind. Many of the ideas were astonishingly bold. One plan, by the architect Richard Meier, consisted of a massive grid, with five 1,111-foot-tall towers linked by horizontal sections. Another by an English peer named Norman Foster called for the world's tallest building, actually a pair of buildings, each 1,700 feet high, that sort of wrapped around each other as they rose. "Two towers which kiss and touch and become one," he said very poetically when he introduced his proposal to the public. The *New York Post* devoted its entire front page to a color photograph of it the next morning.

This time, we didn't give out the little polling gadgets that we'd used before. CNN and some of the newspapers ran their own polls, and they found considerable enthusiasm for almost all of the plans. Although there was no one clear winner, it was gratifying to sense all the public enthusiasm.

It was also important to us that the plans be workable. To evaluate that, we had our planning director, Alexander Garvin, and Stanton Eckstut, the Port Authority's urban-design consultant, go through the various plans and rate them on such mundane but essential matters as how well they handled the traffic flow and whether the projected costs involved were feasible. The visual statement that these various plans made was important, but the practical details were given serious consideration as well. When the plans were all rated on this basis, two plans, one by Liebeskind and one by a team known as THINK, headed by an innovative Argentinean architect named Rafael Vinoly, came out ahead.

Now that opinions had started to settle out, there did seem to be common agreement, both at the LMDC and among the public, that these were the two best, all things considered. They were very different, though. The Liebeskind plan was a bold, slashing design that, to me, evoked the heroism of our country with its slim tower, which rose exactly 1,776 feet from the ground. The THINK design was softer and more romantic, with an airy, ghostly latticework that gently evoked the memory of the fallen towers. I preferred it slightly, although I could happily live with either.

To decide between the two, we assembled a small group of just seven people. I represented the LMDC board along with Roland Betts and our new president, Kevin Rampe. We also had two people from the Port Authority, which, as the owner of the site, needed substantial representation. One of the two Port Authority representatives was Charlie Kushner, a New Jersey real estate man (he later had to drop out after he was sued by his brother for abusing the assets of a company they owned together by making illegal contributions to the campaign of Governor McGreevey). Governor Pataki and Mayor Bloomberg each appointed representatives from their staffs.

When we took an early informal vote of this group, there seemed to be a slight preference for the THINK plan, just four to three, but several people, including me, could have gone either way. Being so split, we thought it all the more important that Governor Pataki and Mayor Bloomberg, as the two major stakeholders in the government, have a chance to weigh in personally on the competing designs. We set up displays in the office, and had the architects come in and explain their proposals to the two political figures separately. They each spent a couple of hours looking at the models and discussing them.

Bloomberg was torn between the two proposals, just as most of us were.

But Pataki took me aside after he'd seen the two and he said, "You know, I simply can't stand the THINK plan."

Surprised by his reaction, I asked him why he felt so strongly.

"It just looks to me as though those two towers are the burned-out skeletons of the two World Trade Center towers, as if that is all that is left of them." Pataki shook his head. "No, I find that very disturbing, and I just can't be in favor of that one."

That changed my mind, and it changed the minds of a couple of others on the board when I passed it on. We certainly didn't want what might look to some like a burned-out skeleton of a building as the symbol of everything we were trying to accomplish. When it came time to take a vote, the sentiment of the group had shifted in favor of Liebeskind. And that was our choice.

In hiring him, we weren't selecting an architect for a new tower, but for the plan for the entire sixteen-acre site. His proposal settled a lot of big issues, such as where the streets would go. I was glad that we would be reopening the whole length of Greenwich Street, which had been blocked off by the original World Trade Center towers, much to the detriment of the traffic flow in the area. That would release a lot of the pressure on Broadway as the major route linking Lower Manhattan and uptown. By deciding where the surface roads would go, Liebeskind also established the locations and contours of the five other buildings besides the tower, so we could start our long-delayed work planning them.

And it freed us to focus to the most important element of the site, the memorial. When the RFP for the memorial itself went out, we were deluged by even more entries—5,201, to be exact. Again, they came in from all over the world, from professionals and amateurs alike. The only requirement was that the designer had to be over eighteen. Otherwise, the competition was open to everyone.

I didn't think the group of seven that we had assembled to evaluate the site plans had the expertise to decide on the memorial, which was more of an aesthetic judgment. So we appointed a new group of twelve judges, of whom probably the two most well-known were the Vietnam Memorial designer, Maya Lin, and a former Brown University president, Vartan Gregorian. I asked David Rockefeller to be an honorary judge, in recognition of his years of service in Lower Manhattan as chairman of Chase Manhattan Bank. If he hadn't committed Chase to expanding down there when other banks were leaving the area in the seventies, I doubt there would have been much of a lower Manhattan before 9/11 that would be worth rebuilding afterwards.

The twelve voting judges were drawn from various parts of the architecture world. I called up each one personally, and not a single one turned me down. We assured them that it would take only a couple of weeks in August or early September. But we hadn't expected to get nearly as many entries, so it took much longer to evaluate them all. Still, everyone served for free.

We set up a viewing area for all 5,201 entries in a secret location. I remember hearing speculation that it was out in the far regions of Queens, or maybe

Staten Island, but I can now say that it was at 120 Broadway, not far from our office downtown. The entries took up an entire, vast floor of a loft, with all the plans spread out on racks that the jurors could appraise.

The jurors took weeks, then months, going through all the entries. We were almost two years into the project now, and I was getting impatient. I kept telling Vartan Gregorian, "Look, you've got to get this settled. Can't you move a little faster?" But the jurors wanted to be very thorough, and I can now see that it was a terrific act of civic responsibility on their part to devote so much time to the project. As they went along, they came to some important conclusions about the memorial—that it needed to include water, and several points of entry to minimize congestion. Along with the aesthetic considerations, these requirements helped them narrow the entries down to two hundred, to one hundred, to fifty, to twenty and finally to just eight. Up to that point, the judging had been completely blind, without any awareness of who the designers were. Presumably some famous architects' work was passed over, for the eight finalists proved to be almost complete unknowns, although most of them were practicing architects.

We provided funds for the eight to make three-dimensional models from their drawings. They were also free at that point to modify their design if they liked.

The eight models were all put on display in the Winter Garden, in the World Financial Center overlooking the World Trade Center site. The jury had decided ahead of time that its final judgment did not need to be unanimous. Nine votes out of the twelve would be enough to win. On the first ballot, though, no entry received anything close to nine. The top two entries tied with three each, and a third plan, that of Michael Arad, a young Israeli architect, got two for his plan that featured a pair of recessed squares, partly filled with water, congruent with the original footprints of the fallen towers, amid a stand of deciduous trees. Four others received one. The judges talked over the results, and then tried to win more votes for one entry or another. But as they progressed through more rounds of voting, neither of the leading entries increased their total. Instead, the jurors gradually shifted their votes to the third choice, Arad, and eventually he received the required nine. I didn't have a vote, but I agreed with the process and with the decision. It will be a wonderful memorial.

It turned out that Arad's father had been Israel's ambassador to the United States when I was deputy secretary of state. I'd known him well. The day after Michael's selection was announced, his parents flew over from Israel to participate in all of the excitement, and we had a nice reunion. My office was turned into a temporary nursery for Michael's wife and very new baby. It was fun to see such a young man have such a large success.

Choosing the architects for the site and for the memorial took place very much in the public eye. Behind the scenes, we did many things that no one ever heard much about. We either built or reconstructed nine parks. We built a new 500-student high school, the Millennium High School, on three floors of a former office building on Broad Street—right next door to Goldman Sachs, as a matter of fact. All high school students in Lower Manhattan used to have to take a subway ride to go to high school because there wasn't a school for them in the area, but no longer. We encouraged the creation of a private secondary school, the Claremont School, to open a few doors up from Millennium High, on Broad Street, at number 47. It's in the former New York headquarters of Bank of America.

Fortunately, most of the anchor tenants have remained in the area: the New York Stock Exchange, the Federal Reserve Bank, the American Stock Exchange, NASDAQ, the Commodity Exchange, Goldman Sachs, Merrill Lynch, American Express, AIG, Bank of New York, and many others. Citi-Group and J. P. Morgan–Chase have moved some of their facilities uptown, but are beginning to trickle back. I have spoken personally to the heads of many of the Lower Manhattan firms to persuade them to renew their leases once they expire, and I have had a fair amount of success with them. The trends are very positive. The percentage of unoccupied office space in Lower Manhattan is now not much higher than in the city as a whole.

We have also hired architects and designers to develop plans for three streets that run east-west in Lower Manhattan: Fulton, Vesey, and Liberty streets. There are sites for a library branch, an elementary school, churches, retail stores, and offices. And we are planning a performing arts center and a museum, both adjacent to the memorial. So, slowly, the area is coming back to life.

The new Lower Manhattan will not operate just at the hours of the Stock Exchange, but around the clock, seven days a week. It will be thriving and vibrant, just like the rest of this city I love.

The fear of another terrorist attack on the area is receding, and I think rightly so. It was a remarkably audacious plan to fly airplanes into those two skyscrapers, and it depended on a degree of disbelief on our part that anyone would attempt such a thing. That is all gone now, obviously, so I doubt terrorists will try again. They are more interested in "soft targets," those that are easier to attack. Because of everything that has happened, the World Trade Center site is a very hard target now.

My work on the LMDC has been a captivating experience for me personally. Because of the diversity of elements involved, the time pressure, the relentless publicity, and the sheer scale of the project, this has been by far the most challenging work I have ever done. I feel we are over the hump now. After a lot of work from a lot of people, the plan for rebuilding Ground Zero is now pretty much in place. A grievous wound to our city, and to our country, is being healed.

For me, it has been an exhausting effort. Many nights I have fallen asleep over a large stack of LMDC paperwork. Still, I don't regret any of it—with the possible exception of that *Post* headline. I've made a lot of wonderful new friends in the Port Authority, on the staffs of the governor and mayor, among other local politicians, and in the community of architects and urban planners; these had all been foreign worlds for me. It has not always been fun, but it has been interesting and challenging and worthwhile. I'm glad I answered yes when the governor made that phone call three years ago.

28

QUIET LEADERSHIP

——ᔊᔊ——

I WOULD LIKE TO CONCLUDE MY BOOK with a few ideas about leadership that I have found useful, and then a comment or two on our foreign policy and the general state of the nation.

As I look back on my life, I'm struck by how often I have ended up in leadership positions, ranging from heading up a group of small boats to storm Normandy Beach on D-Day or, sixty years later, leading the effort to rebuild Lower Manhattan after 9/11. And I have headed up more than a dozen other groups, large and small, in the many years in between.

I never set out to do any of that. At D-Day, I was just as frightened as anyone else, and I would have been happy to be left out of the landing itself, as it looked for a time that I would be. But once it became clear that I was going to be involved as a first-wave leader, I was determined to do the very best job I could. To me, this meant staying calm, maintaining our formation, and taking it upon myself to make whatever decisions were required: for example, to stop in the face of those menacing Element C barriers rather than crash straight on to the beach, as my orders stated.

Although I have always had a fairly deep-seated confidence in my ability to get things done, I don't have a huge ego, and have never felt a powerful need to be in charge. So why have I ended up running so many operations? I think that the answer is that I have simply sensed, possibly earlier and more strongly than others, the need for direction in every organization, and I have responded to that need by trying to provide it. I suppose the classic example was at Goldman Sachs in the fifties, when I alone started to worry about what would happen to the firm after Sidney was gone. None of the other partners gave it a thought, just as many leaders of organizations often don't give much consideration to the large issues that are evident on the horizon but do not require immediate action. At Goldman Sachs, I simply couldn't help myself; I had to act on my concern for the firm. True, some of my response stemmed from self-interest: if the firm went down, I would go with it. But I could see that my interests *were* the firm's interests, and vice versa. The firm and I would succeed or fail together. I think that is the difference: My sense of my own interests is wider than usual, and includes those of the entire group. That is an essential element of my definition of a leader.

The classic image of an American leader is someone like Teddy Roosevelt, leading his men up San Juan Hill in a hail of bullets. General Douglas MacArthur, Lee Iacocca, Bear Bryant, and Bobby Knight are all in that mold—brash, charismatic, compelling, and seemingly fearless. That has never been my style, though. I've always believed in the virtue of what I call quiet leadership. My models are people like President Dwight Eisenhower, General George Marshall, David Rockefeller, Kofi Annan, and Mother Teresa. They are not the swashbuckling heroes of the Hollywood variety. Instead, they are quiet, patient, thoughtful people who rarely let their passions rule them. Their inspiration is calmer, almost spiritual in nature, as they are guided by high ideals. They are not thundering orators, nor dashing figures, but they can be remarkably persuasive all the same by appealing to the better side of a person. I think society can use more people like that; such people usually accomplish more than the loud, flamboyant types.

If I had one suggestion to a young person reading this book, it would be to think of yourself, whatever your personal style and whatever your chosen career, as a leader. The world cries out for leadership. Why not you? Just to think of yourself as someone others should look to for guidance is often the beginning of a discovery of your own leadership potential. If you want to bring positive change to the world and to make a difference in your life, you need to be a leader. Followers are important, but leaders are essential.

Another quality: The best leaders do a lot of listening. As I counseled my new-business men at Goldman Sachs, you can't learn anything when you're talking. You are just repeating what you already know. To learn, you need to listen. My encounter with President Craxi of Italy on my first presidential assignment when I was at the State Department is a case in point. Only by letting him speak freely did I learn what was troubling him; and the simple act of listening to him helped resolve the diplomatic crisis. I didn't have to talk at all. Now, when I am presented with a difficult problem, I call together the relevant experts and seek their advice. Afterwards, even if they disagree with the conclusion I reach, they at least have the satisfaction of knowing that I valued their views enough to solicit them. I find there is much to gain, and little to lose, by listening to a wide range of advice.

A good leader also has to have a feel for the prevailing mood of the organization, and to counterbalance it. I call it leaning against the wind. That means that in good times, when business is streaming in and everything is rosy, the sensible leader thinks ahead to what will happen when the good times turn bad, as they inevitably will. By the same token, in bad times, when business has fallen off and everyone is glum, the good leader is reassuring and reminds everyone that things will turn around eventually. That way, the organization is always prepared for what lies ahead. It remains stable and steady, and more likely to survive from one cycle to the next.

Another key part of successful leadership is a willingness to delegate tasks to others, rather than insisting on doing too much yourself. This is a lesson, in fact, that I was slow to learn in my own career. I wish I had delegated more at Goldman Sachs. The small, highly competent personal staff I had at the State Department greatly increased my effectiveness. I could do far more by letting others contribute. They might not do things exactly as I would have, but they had extraordinary talents of their own that I benefited greatly from utilizing.

Finally, I believe good, effective leadership has to have an ethical dimension. I am a big believer in codes of ethics, be it the Golden Rule, the Boy Scout Oath, or the Ten Commandments. They may sound simplistic, but these codes bear time-honored truths. I am very proud of the code of ethical conduct I set down at Goldman Sachs, and am flattered that it is still relied on.

I am convinced that a social conscience is sound business practice. No one wants to work for, or do business with, an organization that is in any way sleazy or irresponsible. Wise leaders set a high standard. Service businesses such as investment banking should pay even more strict attention to ethical practices than many other types of organizations. The most upstanding organizations are the most likely to attract the most desirable employees and to win the most valuable customers—infinitely more than companies that are considered crass, ruthless, or in some way unsavory.

Sidney Weinberg convinced me of this by his example. It was typical that it utterly galled him that Donald Coster, a.k.a. Philip Musica, could have conned that pharmaceutical company of which he, Sidney, was a corporate director. He had zero tolerance for dishonesty. And it said a lot about Gus Levy that he spent so many hours at Mount Sinai Hospital and the other nonprofits he made time for. Such attitudes made Goldman Sachs a more attractive firm to both prospective employees and clients. And I am convinced that a reputation for ethical behavior is rewarded by stockholders, too. I am sure that it has dimmed the luster of General Electric stock, for example, that the company was charged with having polluted the Hudson River. By contrast, when Johnson & Johnson's CEO, Jim Burke, moved decisively to restore public confidence in Tylenol after the tampering scare by taking Tylenol off every drugstore shelf, he improved the public perception of his company and its stock price by quickly demonstrating the company's responsibility to the public interest, regardless of how much it cost. Good ethics is good business.

Leadership is not confined to individuals. Organizations can demonstrate leadership, and so can countries, and I would like to address some of my final comments to the issue of the leadership that I believe our country is now failing to provide. I've always tried to keep reasonably well informed on what's going on in the world, as any good citizen should, to have opinions on public issues of the day and to be willing to express those opinions whenever appropriate. So I can't resist the opportunity now.

I'm a Republican, but a moderate one, not an ideologue. I voted for Roosevelt in 1944 when I was in the Navy, and our country was still at war. But I've supported the Republican candidate for president ever since. If ever there was a time when I might have voted for a Democrat, the 2004 election was it. Yet the Democratic candidate did not seem to have a plan that held much promise, and I voted again, somewhat reluctantly, for President Bush.

I was not so much concerned with who was to blame for Iraq. Looking back and finding fault have never seemed to me to be constructive. What has happened is water over the dam. But I was worried about our eagerness to take unilateral action without regard for the attitudes of other nations. I worried about our contempt for the United Nations and the fact that we have become so disliked, even hated, all over the world. I must admit disappointment with many of the policies of the current administration, both foreign and domestic. I think our government often has acted in ways that are painfully short-sighted. Still, I remain hopeful that things can improve.

Now that the United States has emerged as the world's sole superpower—not just in military terms, but in economic and technological terms, and in countless other ways, too—we can pretty much do whatever we like around the world. We have every right to be proud of our accomplishments as a nation, and a relatively young one at that, but we also have every need to be cautious about how we exercise our enormous power. Having run a global investment bank and helped direct the State Department, I know from experience that power is not inexhaustible. If we flaunt our global power too much, we will begin to lose it. We will arouse our enemies, and create more of them, forcing us to expend our power to control them. History does not treat even the most vaunted empires kindly. They rise only to fall, often because they develop illusions about their strength. Nations can hold on to their power by conserving it. If we use our power infrequently, reluctantly, and benevolently—in the interests of other nations as well as of our own—it will last for a far longer time. Shouldn't we begin to think not only of what's good for the United States, but of what's good for the world as a whole? Shouldn't we act more in the mode of quiet leadership—with less arrogance, with less of the conviction that we alone have the right answers, with less talking, and with more listening?

I've always felt that one of our greatest achievements as a nation came during the anxious period after the close of World War II, when two powerful military forces, the United States and the Soviet Union, faced each other from diametrically opposing points of view in a Cold War that lasted forty-five years. The points of disagreement were many, the dangers were great, and yet the tensions never broke out into a hot war, and were eventually resolved peacefully. It was a triumph of diplomacy for both sides, but especially for the United States, which displayed tremendous patience and determination in keeping the Cold War cold—and ultimately in winning it. Unfortunately, we tend to be prouder of the wars we've won by using our military power than of the wars we avoided through patient diplomacy. I wish it were the other way around. To me, the diplomacy that led to winning the Cold War is no less worthy of our national pride.

The last several years have had their unhappy moments for those of us who believe that diplomacy, given time and patience, can almost always prevail; and that it's better to seek international support—from the United Nations and other international bodies, as well as from other individual nations—for our initiatives, rather than to undertake them by ourselves, unilaterally. This is the privilege of being the world's only superpower, but it is also the burden. We go it alone because we can. But, to me, our power should allow us to take a risk on diplomacy that a weaker nation might not be in a position to try. Because we are so dominant in the world, we can—and should—pursue diplomacy with all the greater determination. I wish we would reconsider the full implications of our superpower status so that we might use it more effectively to achieve a more peaceful and a more stable world for all nations, including our own.

Countries, too, need friends. America cannot go it alone or we will find ourselves isolated in the global community. From my days at Goldman Sachs and in the State Department, I know full well the necessity of maintaining good relations around the world. Every country needs to be a good neighbor, if only to encourage other countries to be good neighbors in return. It grieves me to see how low America's reputation has sunk around the world since the Iraq War began. As I remember from my days in London after 9/11, practically everyone in the entire world felt for America then. Very few foreigners do now. What a terrible tragedy!

A breakdown in foreign relations, and in the public image of America abroad, is dangerous in itself. But it has serious repercussions for American business as well. Geopolitics and economics are inextricably linked in these days of international trade. Eventually, citizens of other countries who dislike American foreign policy will start to dislike American products, as well.

One of our greatest strengths is that our U.S. economy has for many years been recognized as the strongest economy in the world and the dollar as the strongest currency. Indeed, our huge trade deficits can only be tolerated if other countries are willing to invest their favorable trade balances in U.S. government bonds. If they lose confidence in the U.S. economy and are unwilling to continue to do that, we will face very dire consequences indeed. When we move from budget surpluses to huge government deficits, can we retain their confidence? When we ignore the huge future financial costs of Social Security and Medicare, can we retain their confidence? When both political parties seem to vie with each other to see who can spend the most, can we retain their confidence? When we continue to decrease our income by reducing taxes and increasing our expenditures with a never-ending array of new spending programs, are we not tempting real economic disaster? I fear that the Republican party, which has always been the party of prudence and fiscal responsibility and of less government, has lost its bearings and no longer provides a healthy balance to the Democratic party. Already, in the last three years, the dollar has dropped some 30 percent or more against the world's other currencies. Isn't that a warning signal?

I should not conclude this book on a gloomy note. Looking back, I can't help thinking how extraordinarily lucky I have been. Mine has been a good life, filled with lots of fun, interesting experiences, drama, and an engagement with serious issues at the highest levels. Growing up in Montclair, I never would have imagined how much was in store for me. I was blessed with parents who had good values, and I had the drive to act on them. I have lived in a time when there has been a lot to be done, from fighting the Nazis to battling terrorists. I like to think I have risen to many of these challenges in my own quiet fashion, and I am confident that the next generation of leaders will meet them in their turn. I have been glad to do my part in all of these great endeavors. More than glad. From first to last, I have been thrilled to be in on the action.